# MOONWALKER

# Charlie& DottyDuke

# *MOONWALKER*

OLIVER
NELSON

A Division of Thomas Nelson Publishers
*Nashville*

Published in Nashville, Tennessee, by Thomas Nelson, Inc.

Printed in the United States of America.


### Library of Congress Cataloging-in-Publication Data

Duke, Charlie, 1935–
    Moonwalker / Charlie & Dotty Duke.
       p.    cm.
    ISBN 0-8407-9106-2
    1. Duke, Charlie, 1935–    2. Astronauts—United States-
-Biography.  I. Duke, Dotty. 1935–    II. Title.
TL789.85.D84A3  1990
629.4'0092—dc20
[B]  89–71105
                         CIP

5 6 7 LSC 24 23 22

**To the Lord God Almighty
whose love and grace has given us
abundant life**

*"Yours, O LORD, is the greatness,
The power and the glory,
The victory and the majesty;
For all that is in heaven and in earth is Yours;
Yours is the kingdom, O LORD,
And You are exalted as head over all."*

1 Chronicles 29:11

# ACKNOWLEDGMENTS

We would like to acknowledge our appreciation to three good friends, Suzanne House, Nancy Johnson, and Kathy Bock, for the many hours of typing and prayer they have given in support of this work.

Then with much gratefulness, we would like to thank our children, Charles and Tom, who have been so much a part of our story in every way and especially for their love and encouragement to us in writing this book.

# CONTENTS

Introduction ............................................. ix

1. Blast-Off ................................................ 11
2. Heroes .................................................. 22
3. Midshipman ............................................. 28
4. Grim-Jawed, Steely Eyed Fighter Pilot ...................... 34
5. Fantastic ................................................ 46
6. Snake Bit ............................................... 56
7. '64 Charlie .............................................. 66
8. Moon-Bound ............................................ 78
9. Original Nineteen......................................... 89
10. Overcoming Problems ..................................... 101
11. "One Giant Leap" ........................................ 111
12. "Sweet Sixteen Has Arrived!" .............................. 118
13. 16 Training Begins ....................................... 126
14. Dress Rehearsal .......................................... 132
15. Countdown .............................................. 143
16. "No CIRC" .............................................. 152
17. "Old Orion Is Finally Here!" .............................. 158
18. Moonwalker ............................................. 168
19. Survival ................................................ 183
20. Moonwalk II ............................................. 189
21. Moonwalk III ............................................ 199
22. Good-Bye, Moon! ........................................ 209
23. The Return .............................................. 219
24. How Do You Top a Flight to the Moon? ...................... 229
25. Dotty's Story ............................................ 240
26. To Make My Million ...................................... 253
27. The Love and Power of God ............................... 266
28. The Crowning Glory ...................................... 275

Acronyms and Jargon ...................................... 282

A year or so after I got back from the moon, my wife, Dotty, and I were invited to a party at the home of Dr. and Mrs. Bob Gilruth. Dr. Gilruth had been director of the Manned Spacecraft Center, Houston, during the 1960s and had led the NASA team in the Mercury, Gemini, and Apollo programs. The success of those programs, culminating with landing a man on the moon and bringing him safely back, was now being called "the greatest achievement man has ever accomplished."

We were enjoying being at the Gilruths'. Dr. Gilruth is a fine man, and I have very high admiration and respect for him. Since I love to tell stories, I proceeded during the evening to relate some personal anecdotes from my flight.

As Dotty and I got ready to leave, I was surprised when Dr. Gilruth said, "Charlie, you should write a book about *Apollo 16*. Ruth and I were fascinated by your tales; you have a great way of communicating to the ordinary person what it was like to fly to the moon. We think you should write a book about Apollo from a human and personal standpoint—in a way no one else could. Why don't you think about it?"

I laughed and said, "Yes, we could title it *Gee Whiz, What's It Like on the Moon*." Such an idea seemed very remote, and Dotty and I left, not giving it any more thought.

But "Gee Whiz, What's It Like on the Moon?" became a favorite speech of mine over the next ten years, as I traveled all over the world giving lectures to people of all ages and persuasions. I enjoyed sharing my experience with others. I had had a ball, and many times during the mission I had put aside the fighter pilot jargon and acted like a little kid at Christmas in a roomful of toys.

Everyone wants to know, from first graders to the most sophisticated astronaut buffs—"Gee whiz, what's it like sitting on top of six million pounds of fuel and being blasted off into space? What's it like being propelled twenty-five thousand miles per hour, floating in zero gravity, and heading for the moon? What's it like taking that first step? Gee whiz, what's it like on the moon?"

Much has been written about the science and technology we learned from Apollo and the importance of that investment in the future of the United States. I believe we should continue being a leader in spaceflight. But what about a book for the layperson—an astronaut's personal story? Wouldn't it be great to write a book relating all the emotions, the feelings, the things that the average person would like to know? *Moonwalker* is my personal story of this great adventure.

I didn't become an astronaut for fame or fortune, and I don't think that there was one guy in the program for that reason. I got there as a captain in the Air Force with one desire—to fly into space, anytime and anyplace, just for the thrill of having such a flight. It turned out that we were explorers too, as we traversed across the moon, but the original motivation was strictly to get up there, see what it's like, and feel what it's like, on that strange vehicle called a rocket.

The reason I'm writing my book now, seventeen years later, is because I have two stories to tell. A number of years after my moonwalk, I began another walk—a walk with God. This experience is even more exciting than my first trip. My walk with God has taken me to some high places— praying with prime ministers and presidents, rightist dictators, and Communist juntas. It has exposed me to the supernatural and mighty power of God. But most exciting of all, it has led me from a life of continual striving and restlessness to one of peace and fulfillment.

I hope that through the pages of this book you will feel with me the thrill and excitement as we fly to the moon, and I pray that if you haven't already, you will join with me in the greatest experience of all—both in and out of this world—a walk with the Son.

# 1

# BLAST-OFF

*April 15, 1972—Launch Pad 39A, Kennedy Space Center.*

"*Fantastic,* Stu baby! That's the most gorgeous sight I believe I have ever seen, and *tomorrow* that beauty belongs to me."

"Right on Charlie boy! What a ride! *What a ride!* It's better than a friendly forty-eight pack on Saturday night. You just don't know, Charlie; I'd give anything to be going again. Too bad it's not going to be the old dynamic duo."

Stu Roosa and I were talking it up as we sat at the base of the gigantic Saturn V launch vehicle. Being best friends since test pilot days, we had always hoped to fly in space together. But it was not to be. Stu had already flown the year before on *Apollo 14,* and now *Apollo 16* was to be mine.

I just couldn't wait to get on board. I was really on an emotional high, because this was the rocket that was to launch me, John Young, and Ken Mattingly into space and propel us to the moon!

The stars twinkled brightly overhead; it was a beautiful evening. The service structure had been pulled back, and powerful spotlights were illuminating the vehicle. The Saturn looked almost otherworldly as it sat there bathed in this bright light. People were scurrying around the launchpad in the final stages of preparation. They were beginning to fuel the propellant tanks.

We continued sitting there, admiring the beauty of this scene. Stu reminisced a little bit about how exciting it was to fly—the feelings he had going up the launch tower, climbing aboard, and getting strapped in.

After a while we drove back to the crew quarters, but being so wound up, I had a tough time getting to sleep. Finally I drifted off for about five hours.

At 6 A.M. the flight surgeon knocked on our doors. "Okay, guys. Time to go." I was instantly up and out of bed. The big day had finally come!

We went down to the medical office that had been set up for our last preflight physical and got a short thirty-minute checkup: say "ah," check ears, check eyes, check temperature. It was a very brief exam, just to make sure everything was go. The docs had been a little concerned, because three months earlier I had been admitted to the hospital with a severe case of double pneumonia and was hospitalized for a week. The pneumonia had really sapped my energy, but fortunately I was in good shape now, having recovered completely.

Well, everybody passed the physical with flying colors, and we urinated into the jars one final time. I knew I was okay, but it was a relief to hear the doc pronounce me fit. Then we went in to breakfast for our celebrated last meal before lift-off.

This meal had come to be a special time for all the crews. Lou, the cook, would give us anything we wanted, within the limits of our low residue diet, and we chose the traditional steak and eggs. The backup crew were there along with Deke Slayton, Director of Flight Crew Operations; also the heads of many of our support teams joined us. It was a light-hearted time; everybody was joking.

The Sunday edition of the Cocoa Beach *Today* newspaper had arrived. There was a big front-page article about *Apollo 16* and a couple of pictures of us. That made everybody feel good, our making the front pages. It was sort of getting old hat with some people, being the fifth landing on the moon, but around the Kennedy Space Center and Cocoa Beach it was still a big deal.

After our meal, in walked one of our suit technicians. "It's time to go get suited up."

Reality hit and I thought, *Hot dog! We're getting close! This is the day— no drill—ready or not here we go! I sure hope the suit checks okay.* I didn't want anything to collapse and cause an abort. I really wanted *16* to get off the ground.

Our suit room was a special, environmentally controlled, clean room with filtered air. We were good friends with all the suit techs. They had gone through training with us and were like mother hens with our space-suits, treating them like their babies. Everybody was jovial and relaxed.

First on were our medical leads or sensors, so the ground could keep track of our heartbeat and respiration during flight. Then we began suiting up: a diaper, in case we had to defecate at an inopportune time, long underwear, and a UCD (urine collection device). Then we donned our space-suits and the technicians zipped us up. Gloves were checked out and the last thing—the helmets—were locked on. It's a good feeling to have that helmet snapped on and the cool oxygen flowing in; you knew you were one step closer.

I lay back in my special recliner while they did a final suit check. *Boy, I thought, I sure hope this suit is fitted right.* It was going to be my life support, and I didn't want anything wrong with it.

We were to breathe pure oxygen for three hours before lift-off—due to the fact that the spacecraft had a cabin pressure of 5.5 pounds per square inch, instead of the normal 14.7 pounds. Breathing pure oxygen would remove the nitrogen from our bodies, so we wouldn't suffer from the

*12*

bends due to the reduced pressure. This phenomenon is the same a scuba diver experiences if he surfaces too quickly from a deep dive.

A few hours before lift-off, we took the elevator down from the suit room to head out to the launchpad. We were able to continue breathing the pure oxygen by means of portable ventilators, which we carried around like small briefcases.

As we exited the operations building, we were met by a couple hundred well-wishers cheering us on. They seemed almost as excited as we were, and were screaming and shouting and jumping up and down. It was like a pep rally complete with signs and American flags. ALL THE WAY APOLLO 16! ATTA BOY, JOHN, CHARLIE, AND KEN!

I felt a great sense of pride and appreciation for these people who had taken their day off to come out and send us off. Many of them we knew and had worked with. We waved back and climbed in the van for the ride out to the launchpad, which was about ten miles away.

When we arrived at the pad and climbed out of the van, I turned around and there it was—this *magnificent flying machine* towering above us. It was enormous—360 feet tall, 33 feet in diameter, and weighing 6.5 million pounds. It seemed to be reaching into the very heavens itself.

Not only impressive was its sheer beauty and size, but also its feeling of power. Liquid hydrogen and oxygen were boiling off from the rocket's three stages to relieve the pressure in the fully fueled tanks. It looked alive.

I could see ice beginning to form on the vehicle because of the chilldown effect of the liquid propellants. It was an awesome sight with the sun's rays glistening on the frost. And emblazoned in large black letters on its shining white surface was proudly written—USA! Anticipation was intense, and I was eager to get strapped in and on our way.

My only thought as we rode the elevator up the launch tower was, *Let's go. Don't mess up now. Don't let anything happen that will keep this beauty from lifting off.*

Too much risk was involved with a delay. A delay usually resulted in at least a one month's postponement, and during that month, anything could happen. You might get sick—just a cold would do it or an ankle sprain— anything and you would be removed from the flight crew and replaced by your backup. A million things could happen to you, and you wouldn't get to go at all.

I had firsthand knowledge of this because as a backup crewman on the *Apollo 13* mission two years before, this very thing had happened. In fact it had been my fault.

A week before *13* was due to launch, I became very ill. The diagnosis was German measles, which it seemed I had caught from a little three-year-old friend, Paul House. Unfortunately, before any symptoms had appeared, I had exposed all the prime and backup crew. The NASA (National Aeronautics and Space Aministration) docs were caught short. We had the finest medical care, but this childhood disease had sneaked through and could result in a serious problem.

The rest of the crew were given tests, and it was determined that of the prime crew Lovell and Haise were immune, but Mattingly was not. The docs recommended Ken be removed.

NASA had a big decision to make. This was a major glitch—nothing like this had ever occurred so close to flight. Should the mission be delayed or should backup Jack Swigert step in with only four days to go? Jack was trained, and the whole philosophy of the backup crew said he could do it. The decision was made to substitute and press on. The new crew had an intensive two days of training to fine-tune their coordination as a team.

I had felt terrible about it, but Ken was a good sport and never blamed me for missing that flight. He took it stoically, even though I knew he was very disappointed. Ken was then placed with John Young and me on our crew and had two more years of training with us. So now, two years later, he was flying as our command module pilot on *Apollo 16*.

What a devastating thing to have happen to you, and I certainly didn't want it to happen to me! There would be no other opportunity to fly if I was removed from this crew, for NASA had scheduled only one more Apollo moon launch after ours, and their prime crew was already in training and had been for over a year. So I urged, "Let this beauty go!"

The elevator took us up to the spacecraft level of the launch tower, four hundred feet above the ground. Then we walked across the swing-arm to the white room, a small cabin that covered the open hatch of the spacecraft, which is similar to the jetway that comes up against the airliner when you embark.

A group of technicians were there to strap us in. Guenter Wendt, who was the head of this group of men, was a favorite of ours and had been with us through all our testing. If there was ever any tension, Guenter always knew how to break the ice.

He had noticed that John had short arms and had a difficult time reaching some of the switches when strapped to the couch in the cockpit. Therefore Guenter presented John with a little arm extension he had created specially for the occasion. It was in the shape of a little hand on the end of a stick, so that John could grab hold of things from a distance.

"Okay, John, if you have any trouble, here's what I want you to use!"

Guenter announced as he revealed this little gadget. Even though we weren't permitted to take it with us, we all had a big laugh and it eased the tension.

The backup crew, too, had prepared some surprises for us. As I climbed into the spacecraft, I noticed a little sign on my seat, TYPHOID MARY'S SEAT—a "gotcha" from the backup crew to remind me of *Apollo 13* and the measles. That was the first of many gotchas that we came across during the flight.

I climbed in after John, and Ken followed me. John was seated in the left couch, Ken in the middle, and I was to the right. The couches were like little wheelchairs without wheels. They had a head support, a backrest, a seat, and a leg and foot support. The seats were tilted backward so that our backs would be parallel to the floor. This reclined attitude provided increased G (gravity) tolerance on ascent; in this position the G forces pushed us back into the seat, instead of draining the blood from our brain.

The technicians closed and locked the hatch, did a pressure check, and then left the pad. No one could be around when those F-1 engines sprang to life. Now we were all alone on the launchpad. John, Ken, and I each got busy performing various checks, as directed by Launch Control.

"*GO* at T [time] minus 90 minutes and counting."

My thoughts keyed into the countdown. After every systems check the launch director would give us a "*GO* at T minus" so many minutes. With every "*GO*" we came one step closer to lift-off.

No fear, no reluctance, no second thoughts entered my mind. I was consumed with the thought, *Let's GO, keep counting, no abort, let's launch this beauty.* I had the feeling this was my one chance.

All I wanted to hear were the words, "Lift-off! We have a lift-off!" I knew at that point there was no turning back, no chance for NASA to say, "Hey, wait a minute. Come back; we decided to cancel." At lift-off we had our chance. Come explosions, failures, or whatever, we were on our way and could handle whatever happened.

I quickly reviewed the emergency egress procedures in my head. The thought flashed by that the procedures we would use, I had helped develop as part of the Emergency Egress Working Group. Did we do a good job?

After the tragic *Apollo 1* fire on the launchpad that had killed White, Grissom, and Chaffee in January 1967, a team had been formed to work out escape procedures for Apollo. If the main rocket engine tanks sprang a leak, or if a problem started in the electrical system that resulted in a fire, or if a multitude of other problems occurred, then we had to make an emergency egress out of the spacecraft and leave the launchpad. Stu Roosa and I were assigned to be the astronauts on the team, and after months of work we had developed two escape routes in case of an emergency on the pad.

One way that was developed was to get out of the spacecraft as fast as possible and to run back across the swing arm to the elevator. The elevator, being a high-speed free fall, would take you quickly to the bottom of the pad. Then you'd rush through an automatic sprinkler to wet down your spacesuits, jump into a slide tube, and go down the tube to the blast room. This room was about a hundred feet underneath the pad and was mounted on springs. In this room, the whole vehicle could explode right on top of the pad and you wouldn't be hurt at all. It was like being inside a bank vault. We had enough food there to last thirty days, because it might take that long for you to be dug out.

The other escape route was easier and faster. It involved a slide wire or cable that went from the top of the launch tower to a point on the ground about a quarter of a mile away. After leaving the spacecraft and running across the swing arm to the launch tower, you'd jump into a little basket that was attached to the slide wire. You'd then slide down the wire in the basket. At the bottom some netting supposedly would stop the basket and you'd jump out and dive into a special bunker or foxhole-type affair that was outside the radius of the fireball. The bunker would give plenty of protection if the vehicle blew up.

Stu and I asked them to let us test-ride the system, thinking it would be one spectacular ride. Unfortunately, we were never given permission, because they thought it involved too much risk. Now at T minus 60 minutes, I didn't want the opportunity!

Also, if a problem occurred late in the countdown, we had the capability of the spacecraft itself being jettisoned off the Saturn with a device called the launch escape tower. If such a catastrophic failure happened, John would twist an abort handle that ignited the launch escape tower rocket engines and separated the spacecraft from the Saturn. The escape tower engines would carry us a safe distance away from the exploding vehicle. Parachutes would automatically open, and we'd descend for splashdown in the Atlantic, just off the beach. The launch escape tower was designed to be used on the pad and also during the first three minutes of the flight.

But everything was looking okay as the count moved toward launch.

*"GO at T minus 60 minutes and counting."*

Only three miles from the launchpad were Dotty and the boys. They were watching the lift-off from the astronaut viewing area, a special private area set aside for the astronauts and families, away from the press and crowds.

All of my relatives had come for the lift-off, plus it seemed at least half of South Carolina had made the trip to watch one of their own. My home-town newspaper, *The Lancaster News,* had been carrying articles all month, and the town was really excited and proud. They had chartered I don't know how many buses to come to the launch.

John and Ken had teased me about all the bus- and car-loads of South Carolinians. "Every other car has a South Carolina license plate on it, Charlie. Who'd you invite? The whole state?"

This morning's *Today* newspaper had said almost a million people were expected for the launch. They had been thronging into town from all around and were all lined up bumper to bumper along every highway and road wherever they could find a spot. Others were in boats, watching the lift-off from the Banana River. People were scattered all over the Cape area, waiting for our rocket to blast off.

*How are the boys doing?* I wondered. *How is Charles doing?* Charles, our seven-year-old, had been having the hardest time with the upcoming flight and had told his mom a few days ago that he wasn't going to look at the rocket when it started. He didn't want to see the fire coming out of the big engines when they ignited.

He had seen the *Apollo 15* launch last summer when I had taken them all down for a dry run, hoping to prepare them for this day. *Maybe that's when he began to get so scared.* Tom, who was nearly five, had seemed okay. *I guess he's so young, he doesn't really know what's going on. . . .*

The voice on the radio jolted me and brought my thoughts back to the countdown.

*"GO at T minus 30 minutes and counting."* My heart began to beat faster and faster.

I knew that ignition was to start at eight seconds before lift-off. The sequence was to ignite all five of the huge F-1 engines, while keeping the spaceship strapped tight to the pad. This would allow the Launch Control computer to check out each engine and make sure all were at full power and nominal performance before committing to lift-off. It amazed me how those arms could hold down this 6.5-million-pound vehicle while the en-gines were reaching lift-off thrust of 7.5 million pounds. If all checked out, the computer command would release the strong clamps or hold-down arms that kept this 360-foot monster on the ground, and we would be on our way.

I quickly shot glances at John and Ken. John had made three previous flights and seemed cool as a cucumber. He was the perennial Mr. Cool-stone. We'd been training together for three years, and I had really devel-oped a love for him. I could tell what he was thinking and knew how he

*17*

worked. I was so familiar with him, with his personality, and his response to situations, that I knew almost innately what to expect.

John had been in the astronaut program since 1962 and now at this time was the most experienced astronaut in the office. As commander of the crew, he was the one who would make all the final decisions in emergencies. His couch was in front of the flight instruments and flight controls.

Ken was the command module pilot and during lift-off was responsible for the computer and making sure it was cycling through its programs. We had been selected as astronauts together in 1966. In fact we had both come to the space program from the test pilot school at Edwards AFB (Air Force Base). Ken and I had known each other since 1965, and he was a good friend. He wasn't saying much now, but was as keyed up as I and was intently watching the instrument panel in front of him. He was thoroughly competent and knew the spacecraft inside out.

After months of training together, the three of us had been molded into an efficient team that we believed could handle any emergency in the spacecraft short of a catastrophic explosion. We had a great deal of trust in each other.

At various stages in the flight, you realized that the other person's mistakes could kill you. So we had developed an explicit childlike faith that each of us was going to do exactly what he was supposed to at the right time. We had trained so much together, that I had this confidence. And confidence not only in the crew, but also in the Mission Control team.

*"GO at T minus 10 minutes and counting."*

*Keep counting, baby!* I studied the instruments in front of me on the right side of the spacecraft, the systems for which I was responsible—communication, electrical, and environmental—nominal. My anticipation mounted as the countdown moved into the last minute.

*"T minus 60 seconds."* The closer we got to lift-off, the faster my heart beat.

*"T minus 30 seconds."* My heart was really pounding now and my palms were sweating, like the big game was about to start.

*"T minus 20 seconds. . . . T minus ten seconds."* We were really going to go!

Thump! The spacecraft shook as the huge thirty-inch valves opened to feed fuel into each of the five main engines.

*"T minus 8 seconds . . . IGNITION!* We have ignition!" radioed the launch director.

We heard a muffled roar from the huge engines below as they gulped down fuel at about 4,500 gallons per second. As the engines built up thrust for lift-off, I felt a tremendous vibration, and the spacecraft began to shake!

I was startled. *Why is it shaking so hard?* I wondered anxiously. *What in the world is happening? There's something wrong with this thing.* I didn't recall any briefing to expect this—this violent vibration as we sat on the launchpad.

John was saying, "We're go." The Cape was saying, "We're go." Everything is saying go, and I'm just sitting there shaking like crazy thinking, *This thing can't fly. It's going to shake to pieces.* If anyone ever wonders what an astronaut is doing at lift-off, this astronaut was *holding on!*

*"4 . . . 3 . . . 2 . . . 1 . . . LIFT-OFF!"*

The Launch Control computer sent the signal to release the hydraulic pressure from the hold-down arms, and we slowly started moving off the pad, like a big elevator.

*Fantastic!* We are on our way! I got my chance! No turning back now! It's too late, Houston. We are on our way! No changing your mind! No canceling the mission or saying, "Hey, wait a minute. Come back—you forgot your sandwiches!"

I was bursting with excitement. Later I discovered my heartbeat was 140 per minute at lift-off. Coolstone John's was at 70. We almost had to wake him up—he was so cool.

We were on our way, and the only thing that could stop us now was a catastrophic failure. I forgot about my nervousness and became glued to the instruments and my job at hand. At lift-off I had started two stopwatches to time us through the launch sequence.

"Yaw program," John acknowledged, as the auto pilot maneuvered the Saturn V. The vehicle was directed to move sideways, away from the launch tower, to reduce the chance of tower collision.

"Tower cleared!" radioed Launch Control.

Now communication shifted from Kennedy Space Center Launch Control to Mission Control in Houston and I heard the CapCom's (capsule communicator's) voice saying, "You are *GO, Apollo 16.*"

"Roll program!" announced John. The vehicle started to turn around its long axis so that we would be head down during ascent.

"Pitch program!" The spacecraft started to pitch over to begin accelerating downrange.

We were still shaking like crazy, and now I could feel this pitch sensation! John was hollering *"GO,"* and the CapCom was hollering *"GO,"* and I felt like, *Yeah, we're going to* GO, *we're gonna* GO *right into the Atlantic Ocean!* It felt like we were pitching over onto our heads and diving back toward the Atlantic. But the instruments showed we were right on track.

Everybody was dead serious. We were each concentrating on our tasks and whatever we had to do to get this beauty into orbit.

*Fantastic, feel this baby move out.* I could feel the slow buildup in G forces and knew we were beginning to move. The acceleration was slow at first, but now as the engines consumed the fuel in the first stage, we began to accelerate faster and faster and faster.

At one minute into flight, we broke the sound barrier. At this point we were also at maximum dynamic pressure, which put great stress on the vehicle, but we sailed on through with no problem.

At two minutes after lift-off, we were accelerating at 4½ Gs—which is 4½ times your weight on earth. CapCom gave a *GO* for center engine shutdown. The G level dropped to 4 as shutdown occurred, then built again to 4½ Gs. It was like being on a runaway freight train.

I glanced over at Ken, in the center couch. I could see his intense concentration. He was the ultimate grim-jawed, steely eyed fighter pilot. I couldn't see John, but I knew he was the same.

Two minutes, twenty-nine seconds into the flight. "*Sixteen,* you are *GO* for staging," announced Capcom.

"Staging!" The first-stage shutdown.

"Wong!" Train wreck! The remaining four engines shut down simultaneously and instantly. The spacecraft rattled as we suddenly went from 4½ Gs to 0 Gs. It was like traveling at 5,000 miles per hour and hitting a wall.

I had known what to expect and had reached out with my right hand to brace myself against the instrument panel. It seemed like we had stopped, but of course we hadn't; it's just that we were no longer accelerating.

The engines had now burned up 4½ million pounds of fuel. We were traveling about 5,000 miles per hour and were at 35 miles altitude.

I turned around and took my first look out the hatch window, which was over my left shoulder. I could see all of the debris, as the first stage was separated and blown away from the spacecraft. This was the only window that we could see through. The other four windows were still shaded by a protective cover so that they would not be scarred by atmospheric particles while we accelerated into orbit.

Two seconds later the second stage ignited. It was not a violent ignition—it was as smooth as glass. All of the vibration had stopped when the first stage shut down. From that point on, it was like skating on ice.

Three minutes, twenty seconds into the flight. "Tower jettison," John reported, as he flipped the jettison switch.

The launch escape tower separated with a roar and with it the protective covering over the rest of the windows. I looked up out my overhead window.

"Man, we're really up here!"

We were already at 65 miles altitude and traveling about 10,000 feet per second (6,818 miles per hour). Our heads were pointed down toward the Atlantic Ocean, and as far as the eye could see was this crystal blue ocean beneath us. There wasn't much sensation of movement, because the ocean looked all the same and effectively drowned out the sensation of speed.

As I glanced away from the ocean toward the horizon, the deep crystal blue of the ocean turned into the paler blue of the atmosphere. Then the pale blue faded into the whitish color of the upper atmosphere and eventually disappeared into the blackness of space.

*Fantastic! Look at that sight.* The beauty was absolutely overwhelming. We began to jabber over the intercom. "Hey, Gordy. You ought to see that horizon; just gorgeous!" I exclaimed over the radio to CapCom Gordy Fullerton.

I was experiencing a great feeling of exhilaration and also a sense of relief. We had passed through the first critical phases of the flight—lift-off and staging—and were on our way. The real thing had seemed like a piece of cake compared with our simulations. By this time in sims, we were holding the thing together with gray tape because everything was broken.

But now things were great. The vehicle was flying flawlessly. "We got it made! We got it made! We are going to make orbit!"

Back at Kennedy—when the excitement of a successful lift-off was over and the spacecraft was too far away for anyone to see—Dotty and the boys were taken to the press viewing area for their first news conference. It was to be the first of many for them. The families were considered fair game by the press corps, who covered their daily activities and reactions to the flight. Dotty saw it as part of her job to be available to them, but being aware of Charles's and Tom's shyness around strangers and their anxiety over all the activity, she hoped that the reporters would not ask the boys any questions.

I heard later that the first question asked was directed to our older son, Charles. They wanted to know how he felt about his daddy being in space. He was so petrified, he couldn't speak a word. To be singled out frightened him so much, that he would not appear before the press again during our entire flight. Tom, too, was scared; nevertheless he would go out of the house with Dotty for the interviews. Probably his fear of letting her out of his sight was greater than his fear of the press.

But thoughts of my family were far from my mind at this time. I was totally absorbed in the thrill of a lifetime.

What a *view*! What a *lift-off*! What a *day*!

I had looked forward to this day for six years, ever since I was selected to be an astronaut back in 1966. I couldn't help feeling that I had finally made it. I had finally achieved the ultimate, my dream, *my crowning glory!*

# 2

# *HEROES*

Going to the moon had not been a childhood ambition. When I was a kid, there wasn't any space program; nobody even dreamed of flying in space, not for real anyway. There wasn't even the word astronaut, except maybe in science fiction—but I wasn't interested in science fiction. When I was a youngster, I had other dreams, other heroes.

I remember as an eight-year-old going to the Saturday afternoon movies to watch Hopalong Cassidy, Johnny Mack Brown, and the Durango Kid. They were my heroes—the cowboys of the Wild West. I'd also watch war movies, like *Flying Tigers,* and so the pilots became my heroes, too. They were he-men, always into a lot of action and always on the winning side. They were the good guys who wore the white hats, and I wanted to be like them.

I was born in 1935 in Charlotte, North Carolina. Before that my mom and dad had been living in New York City, trying to earn a living during the Great Depression of the 1930s. Both South Carolinians, they were part of a large contingent of southerners who had traveled north during the hard times of the depression.

Mom's father had been a fairly well-to-do South Carolina landowner and businessman, but during the depression he basically lost it all. Mom had been in college and had to quit school and get a job. There were no jobs available in South Carolina, and when she heard that the only place for work was in New York City, she and a friend got on a boat in Charleston, South Carolina, and sailed to New York. They arrived with no jobs, but with hope for the future.

The same thing had happened to my dad. He was in college when his father, who was an insurance salesman in Pageland, South Carolina, lost much of his business, and so Dad too went to New York City. It was like a familiar voice in a land of strange voices when they met. They started going together and were married a year later at the Little Church Around the Corner in downtown New York City.

It was hard times, but they were able to find work—my mom as a buyer at Best & Company and my dad with two jobs. During the day he worked in an office of an insurance company, then at night he waited tables at one of the Schraft's restaurants.

They enjoyed their time there, but when Mama discovered she was pregnant, they decided to come back to South Carolina to live with my dad's parents, so the baby would be born in the South. She planned on using a midwife, which was common at that time, then she found out that she was going to have twins. Knowing she'd need medical help for the delivery, she selected a doctor at the hospital in Charlotte, North Carolina, thirty-five miles away.

Sure enough, there were two of us! On October 3, 1935, I was born first, and six minutes later emerged my identical twin brother, Bill. My mother had her hands full raising two rambunctious boys. She claims we never gave her a minute's worth of trouble, but it was fourteen years before she had another child.

I was six years old when on December 7, 1941, the Japanese attacked our American base at Pearl Harbor. I can remember listening to the radio as President Roosevelt spoke to the nation, announcing that the United States had declared war on Japan. The war had a major impact on our home, as with every other American family. My dad, at thirty-three years old, volunteered for the Navy and was sent to North Island Naval Station in Coronado, California. One of my first remembrances is boarding a train in North Carolina to ride all the way to San Diego, California, to join Dad. What a long train ride. For a while it seemed like every time we'd wake up, we'd still be in Texas.

We lived in California for about a year, and then Dad was sent to the South Pacific. Mom decided to take us back home to stay with her mother in Johnston, South Carolina, while Dad was overseas.

For an eight-year-old, Johnston was a great place to live. It was a small farming town, about a thousand people, in the western part of South Carolina. We lived in my grandmother's two-story antebellum house on the edge of town. My uncle's farm was close by, so we were a big extended family with lots of aunts, uncles, and cousins. Bill and I had a first cousin, Bobo, that was our age, and the three of us were constantly getting into a little mischief.

We were always playing war or cowboys and Indians. One day the three of us imagined ourselves as Indians. We built a tepee out of burlap sacks and then decided that we were going to have a fire in our tepee, and so we built ourselves a little fire. Unfortunately, the fire got out of hand and caught one of the burlap sacks, and the whole thing started up in flames.

Panic set in. "*Quick!* Put it out!" I said, but all we had was a small sand pail, and the only water was around in the front yard. Bobo ran out there and filled up the bucket and ran back so fast he barely hit the ground twice. By the time he got back to the burning tepee, there were about two drops left in the bucket—in minutes the tepee was in ashes. Three little Indian bottoms got paddled that day.

One Christmas Bill and I got a toy Lionel train. We took it up to the porch on the second floor of my grandmother's house and instead of building the track in a circle, we built it straight out to the edge of the porch. We put the train on the track, started it full speed, and watched excitedly as it went roaring off the side of the house, smashing into smithereens! To us it was just like in the war movies—when the Americans would blow up the bridge as the German train was crossing over, sending it crashing into the gorge below with a tremendous explosion. Unfortunately it was paddle time again.

We also used to build little model airplanes of the P41s and the P38s and pretend they were Japanese zeros. We'd stuff them with little Black-cat firecrackers, light them, and thrown them off the second-floor porch. They'd sail around, and eventually the fire would get to the firecrackers and they'd explode! In my mind I was fighter ace Duke of the Flying Tigers.

About this time I began to notice that Bill was not able to keep up with me physically, in play and sports. The doctors discovered he had a congenital heart defect—a hole between one of the chambers in the heart causing it to pump blood inefficiently. This made him tire easily and prevented him from playing strenuous sports, like football and baseball. Later on after the war, we found golf was a sport we could enjoy together. So we began to spend many hours on the local golf course.

As we grew older, Bill became more cautious and reserved and was a good restraining influence to our rambunctiousness. I trusted him implicitly. His judgment was good, and he always seemed to make the right decisions. He was also inquisitive and sought to understand his heart problem. He became more and more interested in medicine, and so in his early teens decided to become a doctor. Today he is a successful internist in gastroenterology in Lancaster, South Carolina.

At the same time, circumstances and events were working in my life to lead me to a military career. Patriotism for the United States was very high during World War II. And the more war movies I saw and the more I heard of my dad's experiences serving overseas in the Navy, the prouder I became of America defending freedom worldwide. I even had my own small part in the war effort, collecting aluminum foil and other little things like that. I felt proud when I finally collected enough foil to turn in as my contribution.

In the summer of 1944, my dad came back from the Pacific and was sent to the Navy station at Daytona Beach, Florida, so we moved down there to be with him. Being exposed to military life with my dad over the next two years, and these early experiences of World War II, began to instill in me a desire to serve my country.

After the war was over, in 1946, we moved back to South Carolina and settled in Lancaster. We had a lot of relatives there, and it was just twenty miles from Grandmother Duke in Pageland. Mom opened an exclusive ladies' dress shop, and Dad began an insurance company.

Dad was well liked in town and knew just about everybody on Main Street. He was well known for his love of animals and would feed every stray cat in town that would come by his insurance office. He always kept a large sack of cat food, and every day dozens of strays would come in and out of his office to be fed.

He loved animals so much he wouldn't even kill an ant; if he found one in the house, he'd pick it up on a piece of paper and shake it off outside. And he always had a dog. The last one, a big black Labrador, went with him everywhere and was allowed to sleep wherever he wanted, even on the sofas and chairs.

Dad loved to cheer on the South Carolina Gamecocks and the New York Yankees. He was a big fan, and whether or not they'd win or lose, he was a faithful supporter. He hardly ever missed a Gamecock game and each year would swear, "This is the year," even though they lost with astonishing regularity. And whenever the Yankees played in the World Series, Dad would travel to New York City to root them on to victory.

All this love and affection that Dad showed to animals and to others, he could never show to his own family. It's always been a mystery to me why this was so. I think it was because he grew up in a strict Victorian atmosphere. But whatever the reason, I don't ever remember my dad telling me he loved me. I knew he did, and I knew he was really proud of me and all of my accomplishments and all that my brother and sister had achieved, but he could never break down and give me a hug and say I love you. In spite of that, he was a good dad.

Mom tried to make up for Dad's lack of affection. She was very loving. She was also very proper and dignified, concerned about proper manners and what we said. "Never say or do anything that will cause embarrassment" was her rule. Dad, on the other hand, was more the good old boy type of southerner and said what he thought whether it embarrassed anyone or not.

Mom was rooted in family and her aristocratic upbringing. Her family name was Waters, and her ancestors had been traced back nine generations when Philemon Berry Waters came to America from England. His descendants had fought in the Revolutionary War. She was very proud of that and always instilled in us a sense of pride in our heritage and our family.

She'd tell us, "Now when you go out, remember who you are." You might not have a penny in your pocket, but to Mama you were somebody because your family had been somebody and you should act that way. She was a good mom and wanted us to have material things; therefore she and Dad sacrificed a lot so we would never be in need.

Mama always made sure we went to Sunday school and church. Dad didn't go with us very often, so usually just the three of us would get ready on Sundays and go to the Baptist church in town. Dad felt some of the people in church were hypocrites, because of their unethical business dealings. He said, "I don't need to go and sit in a place with people who profess to be godly, yet in actual practice are not." Therefore he would rarely attend church.

Bill and I were baptized when we were twelve years old, and Mom continued to take us regularly every Sunday. I really enjoyed church and liked the pastors and Sunday school teachers. They encouraged us to be good, and I wanted to please them. In fact I wanted to please everybody— my parents, my teachers at school—I wanted people to like me and be proud of me.

When Bill and I were fourteen, our sister, Betsy, was born. It was really an experience having a baby in the house. Mom taught us how to baby-sit, change diapers, and feed her. It was fun having a younger sister; she was like an angel. With such an age difference, it was as if we had two families. Betsy was a blessing to my parents and became the apple of my dad's eye.

My patriotism grew during my school years. Every day in class I proudly affirmed the pledge of allegiance. Then one day as a teenager, I saw a movie called *The Long Gray Line*; it was about West Point. I was really impressed with how sharp everybody looked and how proud they seemed. In fact it looked so much fun to me that, in the tenth grade, I made the decision that I would like to go to a military academy and serve my country as a military officer. Because of my dad's experience in the Navy, I decided I wanted to attend the Naval Academy at Annapolis, Maryland.

We saw our local congressman, James P. Richards, Sr., who was also from Lancaster. He was thrilled because I was the first one from Lancaster to apply for a service academy in many years. Without any hesitation he gave me the appointment from our district. It was recommended that I attend a military prep school for my junior and senior years to help prepare me for the Naval Academy entrance exam. It would have been difficult to pass the exam, if I stayed at home, since Lancaster High School wasn't accredited at that time.

After looking at a number of schools, my parents and I chose Admiral Farragut Academy in St. Petersburg, Florida. And so at sixteen years of age, I left home to spend my next two years at a naval prep school. Although I was homesick at first, I knew I had to be there in order to get into the Naval Academy, so I stuck it out and after a while was having a ball.

Admiral Farragut is a small twelve-year prep school for about two hundred boys, located on the edge of Boca Ciega Bay. Palm trees and bougainvillea encircle the several buildings that make up the academy. The main structure is a large Spanish-style beige stucco building with a red tile roof, which houses the administration offices, the dormitory, and cafeteria. Then there are a few smaller buildings for classrooms, an old gym, and a combination football field and parade ground.

I liked the military environment at Farragut—the uniforms, the parades, and the discipline. This confirmed in me all the more my decision to attend the Naval Academy. I worked hard and tried not to get any demerits, in order to have a good report and make a favorable impression on all the people who knew me. I was a people-pleaser. It made me feel important when people were complimenting me for being a good boy.

But I'd swing with the crowd. If there were some folks that were talking dirty, I'd fit in with them. The next day I might be in church and would conform there. I would pattern my life so I would be accepted by everybody, and they would think I was part of their group.

Living away from home with a bunch of guys was an eye-opening experience. One of the first things I received at Admiral Farragut was a dormitory course in sex education. I was real naive because of my home environment, so when the boys got together and bragged about sleeping with this girl and that and using words I hadn't even heard before, I sat there and was all ears.

In the middle of my senior year, the time came to take the entrance exam for the Naval Academy. I was more than a little nervous. I was weak in English and needed to pass tests in both English and math to be accepted. I can't say I passed with flying colors, but I *passed*. Not long after that, I received a letter from the academy saying I was accepted to enter with the class of 1957. School would begin in June of 1953.

Well, I was *ecstatic*. I called my parents and they were elated! Their large financial investment in me at Farragut had paid off. On the front page of *The Lancaster News* was an article and picture of me in my Farragut uniform announcing my acceptance. Everyone was proud, and I was the proudest of all.

I aced the program at Farragut, graduating valedictorian and president of the senior class. Then in June my parents drove me to the Naval Academy. Jim Partlow, my Farragut roommate, was also accepted, and we planned on rooming together this plebe year. Things looked great for me. I had accomplished my goal and was ready to set new objectives.

# 3

# *MIDSHIPMAN*

The Naval Academy, often called Annapolis, is much larger and more impressive than Admiral Farragut. The over one thousand acres of grounds are situated on the banks of the Severn River, which empties into nearby Chesapeake Bay. Large Victorian gray stone buildings with green tile roofs surround a plush green yard of huge, hundred-year-old elms, oaks, and magnolia trees.

On one side of what everyone calls The Yard are the chapel and superintendent's house. They look out toward the Severn River. To the left of the chapel are classroom buildings and on the right is Bancroft Hall, dormitory for the more than four thousand midshipmen.

Bancroft Hall is an imposing structure. Stone steps lead up to a big foyer in which huge paintings depicting important events in Naval history are displayed. Off the foyer are smaller reception rooms where the midshipmen can meet their families and dates. In front of Bancroft is a large stone statue of Tecumseh—a famous Indian leader and warrior from Revolutionary War days.

Well, my parents dropped me off and immediately I was sent to have my head shaved, get my uniform and gear, and be assigned to my dormitory room. Late that afternoon, we had a big ceremony in front of Bancroft, where we were sworn in as midshipmen fourth class. I began to have an almost overwhelming fear that I was getting into something that was going to be tough. We were able to see our folks for a few last minutes, and then we were marched off to our evening meal. From then on it was rugged for two months.

I got homesick and at times so discouraged that I thought about quitting—a lot did. We started out with about twelve hundred in our plebe class, and four years later slightly over eight hundred graduated. Most of those four hundred dropped out during that summer and first year. As these guys were leaving, the only thing that kept me going was my pride. It would have been humiliating if I quit, since I was the only boy there from my hometown.

So I stuck it out and learned how to drill, and march, and sail, and everything else you do over plebe summer: polishing shoes, making beds, keeping our room spotless. All our time was structured; we were wakened early in the morning and kept going until late at night.

We learned how to navigate sailboats in the Severn River and command a forty-foot powerboat. I didn't particularly like sailing. It was boring and a lot of work. I never could get the sailboat to go where I wanted, and it just didn't go fast enough for me. But I did enjoy the powerboat. It was like driving a Porsche instead of a Greyhound bus—and it had to have been sturdy, because all of us crashed into the pier while attempting to dock.

Regular academics weren't to start until the fall, but we did have to memorize a book called the *Reef Points* and be prepared to answer questions at any time from the upperclassmen and recent graduates, who were there to help out in our summer training. It was no picnic. And when all the upperclassmen returned at the end of summer, things got even tougher.

Mealtimes were the hardest. Twelve of us would sit at a table—two first classmen on one end, two second classmen at the other, and third and fourth classmen scattered around the remaining eight places. As plebes, we had to sit on the edge of our chairs with a straight back, looking directly ahead, and eat what was called a *square meal*.

In a square meal, we couldn't bring our forks directly to our mouths. We had to put the food on our forks and bring them straight up in front of us to eye level and then make a square corner to our mouths. If we fouled up, they made us *shove out*. That meant we pushed our chairs out from under us and sat there in that half-squat position, legs burning and trembling, until they said, "Okay, as you were," or until we fell flat on our behinds.

At the same time during the meal, the upperclassmen would be firing questions at us. "What are the movies in town?" "What are the headlines in the paper today?" "Who's the chief of Naval operations?" We had to stay current on what was going on in the world and all the time eating a square meal. Since we were last to get served and had all these questions, I learned to gulp down my food and to this day am a speed eater.

There was a way out of all this misery. We were given two ways to be excused from eating a square meal and answering all the questions. One was Navy winning a football game—all the plebes were at ease, or what was called *fallout,* for the rest of the weekend. The other way was eating all twelve desserts at the table, after eating your regular meal. These weren't just any twelve desserts, but what we called *cannonballs.*

Cannonballs were huge baked apples with an extremely heavy crust and covered with whipped cream. It was a monumental task to eat one, much less twelve, and to my knowledge only one guy in our class made it. He earned fallout for the rest of the year! I tried, but only made it through three and thought I was going to throw up.

The regimen was strict and structured. We were assigned sections for marching to meals, classes, and everywhere. Up early at 6:30 A.M., we marched to breakfast at 7:00. Dismissed from breakfast, we marched back to our rooms to straighten them up for inspection, and then it was time for classes.

In those days everyone took the same courses. The only option we had was in foreign language, so we'd form up and march to morning classes. After classes, we'd march to lunch. Then after a short break, we'd form up again and march to afternoon classes.

After classes, off we'd go to various physical training activities for the rest of the afternoon. Evening meal formation was about 6:30 P.M., and then after dinner we'd march back to our rooms for a couple of hours of study hall. Lights went out at 10:30 P.M.—the end of another day.

That first year as a plebe, we couldn't date at all until the last week of school, but with each passing year we got more and more freedom. Since we couldn't leave Annapolis, the girls would come in from Mary Washington, Mary Baldwin, or others girls' schools around the Washington area and stay at *drag houses.* These were local rooming houses.

We'd usually take our drags to a sporting event or a dance. Then we'd have about an hour before we'd have to get back to the dorm. To have some courting we would all rush to the basement parlor of the drag house, trying to be the first there to get the darkest corner. You couldn't see a thing—it was pitch black down there, and we would stumble over people as we tried to find a place to settle in and neck for half an hour. You could hear all the "ooh's" and "aah's" and a lot of heavy breathing.

Then when time was about up, we'd make a mad dash back to the academy, because the officer of the day was standing on the steps of Bancroft Hall with pad in hand, waiting to get you. If you weren't on the steps by the time the chapel clock chimed the end of liberty, you'd had it! I'll bet many a track record was shattered by us midshipmen, running back from the basements of the drag houses to Bancroft Hall.

One of my roommates at the academy was Bud Coyle, from Rochester, New York. He was a great guy, with a good sense of humor and easygoing. On Sundays Bud and I would to go to a local Baptist church to visit the Annapolis girls. There weren't any girls at the Naval Academy then, so we'd jump at any opportunity to have some female companionship.

Neither Bud nor I were real stars in athletics, but since everyone was required to do something, we chose the minimum you could get by with, which was intramural cross country. It really wasn't cross country at all, but a four-hundred-yard jog down the road, a couple of times a week. Our real interest wasn't getting in shape but a big ice cream sundae at the Gedunk, the soda fountain in Bancroft Hall.

That was fall and winter. In the spring I played on the academy golf team. I was never quite good enough to earn a letter, but I was manager of the team my senior year.

Another good friend was Jim Partlow. "Prep" had been my roomie at Farragut, and miraculously we were placed together for our first three years at the academy. Jim was a whiz in Spanish and helped me immensely.

There were some fantastic military officers at the academy who were tremendous inspirations for me. One was our company officer, a Marine captain named Charlie Mize. He was a man of integrity and compassion and was a great help to me, especially that plebe year when I was having a difficult time.

Another officer was a captain in the Army, on an exchange program with the Navy. His name was George Patton, Jr. His father was the famous World War II General Patton. We nicknamed him Tank-Tracks, as he was a very stern and demanding officer, tough as a tank.

During the summer after my first year, we went on a two-month cruise to Portugal, Spain, and France. My ship—the *Ciboney*—was an old cargo ship, which had been converted into an aircraft carrier. Well, it wallowed and rocked and rolled and pitched and heaved across the Atlantic! And I got very seasick! Others were so bad they were running at both ends.

I thought, *Boy, if this is going to be my career for the next twenty years, I am really going to be in trouble!*

We went on another cruise the next summer and I felt miserable again. Then the third summer on our first-class cruise, I still got squeamish, especially when we were on the North Sea, where it was very rough. I never got my sea legs. Navy life wasn't looking too promising. The academy was great but sea duty was a drag. Then an experience halfway through the academy determined the direction my military career would take.

Across the Severn River the Navy had some airplanes called the N3N Yellow Perils. These were open cockpit, biwing seaplanes, painted bright yellow. Midshipmen were given an occasional familiarization ride. It was tandem seating—the student sat in front, the instructor in the rear.

One day it was my turn. I remember strapping in and watching as two seamen started the engine with a great big hand crank. Engine sputtering, the plane then slid down a ramp into the water and, for what seemed like an eternity, we roared across the river until airborne. We then climbed to about five hundred feet over the Chesapeake Bay, and with my scarf flying in the breeze I felt like Eddie Rickenbacker chasing the Red Baron. Compared with sea duty this was really living! So I began to think about flying as a career, but what branch of service?

There was Naval aviation . . . or flying with the U.S. Air Force. I knew that a certain number of Naval Academy graduates could volunteer for the Air Force. The Air Force Academy had just been established, and their first graduating class was not until 1959, so they were accepting volunteers from Annapolis and West Point. In fact 25 percent of our class could leave the Navy and go Air Force. Daydreaming about the thrill of flight, the high-performance planes in the Air Force, and thinking about my seasickness, I began to consider that option.

My final year came. I was doing well academically, passing with distinction. I was also doing well militarily, but something happened that put an abrupt stop to any more promotions within the midshipmen ranks. At the time I was a lieutenant commander, one of the top ranks.

On this particular day I had come back to my room from Saturday classes when I noticed my pair of rubber overshoes on my desk. Next to the shoes was a note that said, "The owner of these overshoes report to the Officer of the Day."

I was in trouble! I had gotten caught stuffing an old pair of unpolished, cracked shoes inside my overshoes. I knew this was against regs. Cracked shoes was about ten demerits, and leaving shoes in overshoes was even more demerits, but everybody did it.

I got suited up in my midshipman commander's uniform and went to see the officer of the day who happened to be a Marine captain. "Midshipman Lieutenant Commander Charles Duke reporting as directed, sir."

"Why are you here?" he asked.

"I came back to my room, and there were these overshoes on my desk and a note that said for the owner to come report," I answered. "So here I am, sir."

"Oh, yes," he said. "I remember that. Do you own those shoes?" "Yes, sir," I replied. "I sure do."

"Don't you know what you did is against the rules?" he asked. "Yes, sir," I said.

"Then," he asked sternly, "what do you have to say for yourself?" "Well," I answered, "I think it's a stupid regulation!"

With that he almost dropped his teeth and literally jumped over his desk! We were nose to nose and toe to toe. He proceeded to give me the worst tongue lashing I had ever received—no profanity and he didn't touch me at all, but it was a withering blast of words to put me in my place. He bellowed that I was not to question authority, that it was not up to me to decide whether rules were good or bad. My responsibility was just to carry them out.

You know I really agreed with him. That was why I was at the Naval Academy—to learn to obey orders. I responded with a meek, "Yes, sir," and was dismissed. I was humiliated, and that started my slide in military deportment. I wasn't going to move up in rank anymore at the Naval Academy.

More and more I thought of flying for the Air Force and when decision time came, I volunteered along with over half of my classmates. There were so many of us, we had to draw names out of a hat. Luckily my name came out, and I was assured a place in the Air Force.

Elated at the possibility of flying, I went along for my commissioning physical. I was shocked when it was discovered that I had a minor astigmatism in my right eye and failed the Navy physical. Thankfully the Air Force said they would take me and that cinched my decision to take my commission in the USAF (United States Air Force).

So came the end of my four years at the Naval Academy. June week, or graduation week, was full of excitement. Parties—parades—girlfriends—diploma—and a car! The only time you could have a car at the academy, back in those days, was the last week of school—so I scraped together all the money I had (I think it was about $2,200) and bought a brand new '57 Chevy. Was I proud!

Later I realized I had made a dumb move. My dad had wanted me to use the money to buy a beachfront lot at a place called Hilton Head Island. I thought he was crazy and bought the Chevy. A few years later the '57 Chevy went to the junkyard, but today a beach lot at Hilton Head, South Carolina, is valued at $400,000 plus. Win some, lose some.

The graduation ceremony was inspiring. After the speaker finished, we each filed up and individually received our diplomas; then we sang "Navy Blue and Gold," our alma mater. With that the superintendent of the academy declared, "The class of 1957, *dismissed!*" At that point we threw our hats into the air, and it looked like white rain falling down in the gym. The hats were left to be collected by the younger brothers and sisters, who streamed out of the stands. We weren't going to need those hats anymore.

When I got back to Lancaster, there was a front-page article about me in the paper. Everyone gave their congratulations; being a small town, it seemed like everybody knew. I went by to thank Congressman Richards, who had appointed me to the academy, and he was very happy with my performance.

Another goal had been achieved. I was pleased with my accomplishments. I had worked hard and was now a Naval Academy graduate and a lieutenant in the U. S. Air Force. My sights were now set on becoming the best pilot in the USAF. I wanted to be a fighter jock, and I was prepared to work hard to reach that goal.

*4*

# GRIM-JAWED, STEELY EYED FIGHTER PILOT

Good-bye Navy, hello Air Force! Although I had loved the Naval Academy, I was really excited about going to the Air Force—it had a macho image, and I liked everything about it.

About the middle of July, all the West Pointers and Annapolis graduates who had come into the Air Force, about four hundred of us, reported to Maxwell Air Force Base in Montgomery, Alabama, for two weeks of orientation on Air Force customs and traditions. It was an easy two weeks; time for golf and partying at night. At the end of this orientation, we all split up like a covey of quail to the various training bases. I went to Spence Air Base in Moultrie, Georgia, for primary flight school.

Spence Air Base was a civilian facility, under contract to the Air Force. It was a small complex made up of old World War II buildings. Since it was a civilian contract base, all the flying instructors were civilians. Though we had military supervisors, we didn't have the strict discipline and spit and polish of the Naval Academy. The uniform of the day was flight suits, and only once in a while did we suit up in our service uniform.

Bob Dundervill, a friend from the Naval Academy, went to Spence with me. My roommate was an ROTC (Reserve Officers' Training Corps) graduate from California named Don Lyon, a real great guy. (He was later killed in Vietnam.) We were all eager to learn to fly.

The first three months was to be ground school and flying the T-34, and the second three months was to be in the T-28, both propeller aircraft. Jets would come later. My flight instructor was Lee Bradbury, a slow-talking southerner. He had a wealth of flying experience, flying more by the seat of his pants than out of the textbook.

Like everyone else, I wanted to be the first one to solo. I wasn't the first, but I was in the top three. One day Bradbury and I had been working on landings when he said, "Well, let's go back for a full stop."

As we landed and taxied off the runway, he drawled in his south Georgia accent, "Don't botha to shut down. I'm just gonna to climb out, and you can take it up and get a couple of landings and then bring it back in." Well, I was just elated as I watched him climb out of the rear cockpit.

It was September, hot as blue blazes, so the canopy was open. I taxied out, did my checks, and called the mobile control for permission to take off. Mobile responded, "You're cleared for takeoff."

I added power and began to roll down the runway. The T-34 is not the best performing airplane, but I could feel the acceleration as I reached 50 knots. I applied back pressure on the stick and at 60 knots was airborne! It wasn't exactly Mach 2 but I was solo at last!

Then the thought hit me, *I've got to get this plane back on the ground.* After two passable touch-and-go landings, the knot in the pit of my stomach was gone, and I was home free. I made a final full-stop landing and the flight was over. I was popping my buttons I was so proud. I knew flying was going to be the greatest. I had found my love!

Flying came naturally to me, and it wasn't long before I thought I was the world's greatest. Of course everybody else thought he was the greatest pilot, too, and so the competition at every phase was intense.

We were graded not only in ground school, but on all phases of every flight—on preflight, taxi, takeoff, air work, aerobatics, and landing. Whatever part of the flight you were in, your instructor would mark down one of five grades (from below average to outstanding), total it up, and that would be your grade for the flight. These individual flight scores were important, but more important were the periodic check rides. All were used to determine who would be the top graduates. Everyone worked their rear ends off trying to come out the best.

*Man, I can do it all.* The thought of failure never entered my mind. I knew I could do it because, *I was the best.* I had no fear of killing myself. I thought, *It might happen to the other guy, but it's not going to happen to me, and even if I do have an emergency, I'm good enough to handle it.*

It wasn't long before I had my first close call. It happened as a result of a flight surgeon's report following a routine physical. He told me, "Your depth perception is marginal. You've got to watch out. Don't fly that thing into the runway."

Well, the next day fear was in my heart as I started my flight. When I made my landing approach, all that was in my mind was, *Don't fly this thing into the runway.* As you can imagine, I overcorrected and flared out for landing about twenty feet off the ground. Consequently the airplane just stopped flying ten feet off the runway, and I stalled it in, hitting the runway like a ton of bricks.

It didn't take a genius to realize I was in trouble. I added power just before I hit and when the plane bounced, the engine roared to life. The left wing dipped and I veered left off the runway. The nose was so high I couldn't see forward, so I tried to look around the side; it was barely flying. I had a heart-stopping stab of panic and wondered whether I had bought the farm.

The mobile control officer was screaming, "Go around! Go around! Get your nose down!" As instinct took over, I held what I had. The engine was at full power by now and slowly it started to fly, fortunately heading in a direction where there were no towers or buildings. When I landed, I made up my mind that I wasn't going to listen to any flight surgeon.

A story like that races around the squadron, so I was the butt of the jokes at happy hour.

Another experience shattered my ego even more. I had been assigned to get a check ride from a military pilot. A check ride was always a big deal, like a midterm exam in college, and this captain had the reputation of being a hard-nose—a strict grader and a stickler for procedures. I'd prepared late into the night reviewing procedures.

My anxiety level was off-scale high, and I had butterflies in my stomach as we strapped in. Start . . . taxi . . . take off climb out . . . acro (acrobatics) . . . all went great! We were about 4,000 feet up, when all of a sudden he yanked the throttle back and hollered, "Engine failure! Forced landing!"

I got excited and started looking around for someplace to land. The routine was to make an approach down to 50 feet altitude, then add power, and climb out. Only in a real emergency would you actually land. I selected a field over to the right and started my approach with a big, lazy 360-degree turn. My technique was good but judgment was lousy. I realized I was high, and there was no way I was going to make the field even by sideslipping.

I thought, *Rats! I've really messed this up.* But I didn't say anything and just kept my turn, frantically looking for another field.

There was one farther in front of us, so I headed for it. As we flew over the field, I looked out and there were dead trees and big logs and stumps everywhere. We would've crashed had we landed there. I was sure I had flunked the flight.

To my amazement, I heard this voice from the backseat say, "Good pattern, Duke. Your procedures were great, airplane configuration was perfect, but I'm going to have to grade you down on that field. It was the lousiest field I've ever seen anyone select."

All I said was, "Yes, sir." I wasn't about to tell him that the field I'd picked was a half mile behind us.

These experiences matured me as a pilot, and I began to see that I wasn't invincible. I started to realize that there were many things I didn't know, and so experience became my teacher.

Moultrie was a small, south Georgia town with not much to do on the weekends and since my girlfriend, Mary Ann Medford, attended college in South Carolina, I'd get in my car and drive three hundred miles to see her most every weekend. Other weekends, I'd go with some of the guys to Jacksonville, Florida, to the dog races, where we'd lose a few bucks. The only one who ever won was the rabbit.

In March 1958, our six months' training was completed, and I was assigned to Webb AFB in Big Spring, Texas, for six more months of flight school. Our grades were sent to our new assignments, for it would be at the end of the year's course of primary and basic training that we would get our wings and be ranked in our class. So the race for the top continued.

I packed my car with all my belongings and headed off to west Texas. I was full of excitement. Webb was a real air force base with lots of transient aircraft, the latest fighters that I couldn't wait to see. But most of all my next phase of training would be in a jet—the T-33 made by Lockheed—the first line trainer of the day!

Old lead-foot made it to Webb in record time. When I got there, the base was super, but west Texas was another matter. It looked like the end of the world. You could see for a million miles. The biggest tree was about fifteen feet tall, and there were more oil wells than trees. Cattle and cactus outnumbered the people who were geared up in cowboy hats and boots.

Big Spring itself was a sleepy truckers' stop and a farming, cattle, and oil community. This was a strange new environment for me, but one I grew to love. The air was clean, and the people were friendly, and I liked being able to see forever.

On arrival at Webb, the first thing I did after checking in was to go down to the flight line to look at the T-33's, nicknamed the Shooting Star. My first impression was, *Man, that is an enormous airplane. Look at the size of that thing.* It dwarfed the T-34 and T-28 I had been flying at Spence.

I was really eager to check out and get my first flight. I pictured myself streaking across the west Texas terrain at 500 knots in air-to-air combat like the aces of old. After a few weeks of ground school, the time came for my first ride.

My heart was pounding as I released the brakes, engine at full power, and we accelerated rapidly down the runway. At 115 knots, a little pressure on the stick and instantly we were off the ground. As we began our climb, I realized that already I was going faster than I had ever gone before, and we had barely cleared the runway. "What a ride! What a ride!" I exclaimed. It was a thrill that I would have many times in the future.

One funny incident happened during our first solo flights. I was sitting about the number three position for takeoff when a friend of mine took the runway, ran the power up, and began to check out his instruments. His radio was on because he needed to transmit his instrument readings to the mobile control unit, so they could clear him for take off. All I could hear was this very, very heavy breathing; I could tell he was on the verge of panic.

Then an almost desperate voice came over the radio, as he continued his deep heavy breathing. "Uhhh . . . huhhh . . . *oil* pressure in the green . . . Uhhh . . . huhhh . . . *exhaust gas* temperature in the green . . . Uhhh . . . huhhh . . . *hydraulic* pressure in the green . . . Uhhh . . . huhhh . . . I think I need another *dual ride!*" Immediately the canopy opened and he taxied back in.

I was roaring with laughter by this time and could see the guys in mobile control doubled up in hysterics. Naturally he caught it at happy hour that night. Though it was humiliating for him, I really respected the guy. He was honest and knew he wasn't ready for his first solo flight. He got another couple of rides with his instructor and after that was okay.

All wasn't funny though. A few weeks later we had our first fatality as John Stanley crashed on a solo flight. He was the first of many friends I lost over the next thirty years. It was a serious business.

Living fifteen hundred miles from South Carolina, my romance with Mary Ann waned. She still had a year of college, and absence didn't make the heart grow fonder. Marriage wasn't in my plans. My life was flying, golfing, and partying.

The competition got more intense as graduation day approached. The better you did, the better choices you got on assignment. When you got your wings, what airplane you would fly from that point on—whether it be fighters, bombers, transports, or whatever—was determined on where you graduated in the class. The number one guy got first pick. If there was only one fighter assignment he usually took it, because most everybody wanted to go out and fly the F-86s or F-100s—the hottest planes there were.

Fortunately for me, I was near the top and got the best assignment I believed offered to our class—the F-86L, the interceptor version of the F-86. At graduation I marched onto the stage and received my wings, plus a certificate saying I was a distinguished graduate, one of the top students in the class. You can imagine the pride I felt in front of all my peers, as I patted myself on the back.

Most of the class got sent to bombers and transports. I was elated that I was to be a fighter pilot. *It's the best job in the Air Force,* I thought. The F-86 had been the stalwart in the Korean war, and many a pilot had become an ace in that machine. One of the things that excited me the most was that I was going to be flying a single-seat airplane; nobody in a backseat to bug me.

Training for the F-86L was at Moody Air Force Base in Valdosta, Georgia, about forty miles from Spence, where I had begun flight school. This was to be six months of advanced training—learning how to be a fighter-interceptor pilot, flying radar, plus a lot of instrument work. Back in those days the fighter interceptor pilot was the first line of defense for our country, so we took our training seriously.

Like our previous training, we first spent weeks in ground school learning the aircraft systems, plus normal and emergency procedures. Our skills and knowledge needed to be tested in the simulator before actual flight. Then what a great feeling when I strapped on the F-86 for the first time.

As I throttled up to max power, I got a definite *kick* in the tail when the afterburner lit off. The sabre jet almost leaped off the ground. It was light on the controls, and I felt one with the machine. From the instant of breaking ground, I knew this was for me. I'd found my home, and that feeling has never left.

A typical mission started with a formation takeoff and climb to altitude. Then under control of a ground-based radar, we would split up and practice intercepts. The GCI (ground control intercept) officer would give us steering instructions, and we would commence our mock attack. After the intercept we would rejoin and, fuel permitting, sneak in a dogfight or two. This was against regulations but what grim-jawed, steely eyed fighter pilot would let a challenge go by. Then we'd return for a practice instrument approach and landing. That night at the Officers' Club, the lies would be thick and heavy as the battles were retold.

One morning I remember taking off around 8 A.M. to do some intercepts, when I noticed a fog layer over the swamp. The Okefenokee Swamp was just a few miles south of our field. I reported it to the tower and continued on out to my training area.

After a few minutes I suddenly heard an emergency transmission from Moody tower saying, "Weather recall. Weather recall. All aircraft return to the field and land immediately. Weather recall."

By the time they cleared me to land, I looked down and I could see that the fog had already reached the far end of the runway. *Not much time,* I thought.

I began my pattern, and as I started around the final turn for landing I noticed that in less than a minute a low cloud deck had obscured the runway. Now I really started sweating it out and my heart began pounding.

At 700 feet I entered the clouds. *Man, suppose I don't break out and the fog's right to the ground. I'm not on an instrument approach. This is crazy. I better go around.* All these thoughts were wildly racing through my mind. I was getting very nervous. The pucker factor was in full operation.

Just as I began to throttle up to go around, I broke out of the clouds and right in front of me was about 1,000 feet of beautiful runway. *I've got it made. There it is.* With a great sigh of relief, I touched down, but then the runway disappeared into a wall of fog so thick that you couldn't even see the sides. In fact you could just barely see the white line down the center.

I carefully steered my bird down to the end of the runway and found ten other airplanes sitting there; it was impossible to taxi. After I touched down, they closed the field. I was the last plane to land.

For the rest still airborne, it was every man for himself. Some were scattered to other airports around Valdosta, one landed on a highway, and one pilot had to eject. That day became known as Black Thursday.

With the training at Moody completed, a list of assignments came down. Again I was one of the distinguished graduates and so was able to get my first choice. I chose to fly the F-86D with the 526th Fighter-Interceptor Squadron at Ramstein Air Base in Germany. I chose Germany because it was really the front line; we would be intercepting airplanes coming out of Communist Europe. I wanted to be in the thick of things. I'd been trained for combat, and I was ready to fly and fight if called upon.

It was now May of 1959, and the first group of astronauts was announced. I had been reading about the U.S. space efforts; the program seemed exciting, but I knew I didn't have a chance to be selected, so didn't think about becoming an astronaut. I was happy—for a fighter pilot, Ramstein Air Base was like I'd died and gone to heaven. I was thrilled with my assignment.

Germany to me was hard driving, fast living, and great flying. The 526th was a tremendous squadron. Our squadron commander was Lieutenant Colonel John Pedigo. Pedigo was a bachelor and was always ready for a party. He reminded me of Steve Canyon of comic strip fame—square jaw, blond hair, and blue eyes. He was a great pilot, plus a great golfer—which I liked because every time I didn't fly, we were on the golf course.

There were eight bachelor lieutenants in the 526th, and we all lived in the BOQ (bachelor officers' quarters). The BOQ was just about a half mile from the flight line and right across the street from the Officers' Club annex. The annex was the fighter pilots' hangout—a great place for a beer and hamburger. If we drank too much we didn't have to worry about driving home; we could just walk. And if anyone was too drunk to walk, he could crawl.

I spent a lot of time there. We didn't have to get all dressed up in a coat and tie or in our uniform; we could just wear our old scroungy flying suit. Our waiters were Franz, who reminded me of a sneaky German soldier of World War II movies, and Louisa, like Rosa Kleeb in the James Bond movies—very stern with a heavy German accent. We had a great time kidding them.

Our squadron nickname was the Black Knights, so the eight of us bachelors got together and rented an extra room in the BOQ, converting it into the Black Knight Bar. We stocked it with everybody's favorite whiskey and beer and invited the girls over so we could have private parties. Another squadron, the Fifty-third, named theirs Heeb's Moon Bar.

Some really wild parties took place in the Black Knight Bar and Heeb's Moon Bar. I remember one night a guy got really tanked up and as the hour got late, he decided he was going to fly home. We asked him how he was going to do that. He said, "Well, I'm just going to jump out the window and fly home."

Some guy said, "Roger, cleared for takeoff." And so he *jumped* out the third floor window, hit the ground, and fractured both ankles! He was grounded for three or four months while his ankles recovered.

We had a lot of great guys in our squadron. There was J. Bird, Gayland Kirkland, and then there was Freddy Smith. Freddy was a West Pointer who loved to party with the girls, as most of us did. Freddy's dad was a four-star general and commander-in-chief of the U.S. Air Force in Europe. He was always in need of young bachelors to come to diplomatic functions, which he hosted in Wiesbaden or Bonn. We were ready volunteers and had some great times rubbing shoulders and hobnobbing with the aristocrats.

Jim Hildebrand, or Hildy, was probably the biggest party guy of the bunch, and Dick Huie was the quietest and most reserved. Unfortunately about a year after we were there, Dick flipped over his little MG sports car and had a severe head injury, which took him permanently off flight status.

You would imagine an accident like Huie had or another automobile accident where four of the pilots in another squadron were killed would make us slow down, but I can't say it slowed us down at all. The autobahns were too tempting. I wanted to be in the fast lane so bought a baby-blue Porsche 1600. She wasn't the fastest thing over there, only about ninety miles per hour, but I loved her.

We had a lot of fun. One night during Oktoberfest, a group of us were having a good time—drinking beer and wine—and decided to write postcards.

Jim Dunn, who was a helicopter pilot flying search and rescue, was with us so we wrote one to his mom. Jim was from a tiny Arkansas town named Hampton. "We're having a great time in Germany. Wish you were here." And we addressed it, "Jim's Mom, Hampton, Arkansas." A couple of weeks later Jim got a letter back from his mom saying, "Thanks for the postcard." She had gotten it with that simple address, so you can imagine the size of Hampton, Arkansas.

Our job as a fighter-interceptor squadron was to sit on alert and be prepared to get airborne within five minutes to intercept any unidentified aircraft that came out of Communist Eastern Europe. Pilots were placed into flights composed of six or seven guys. Each flight was on duty twenty-four hours, and within that flight two pilots were always on alert.

There was a facility called the alert barn that held four airplanes. When the bell sounded Bong! Bong! Bong! we'd jump into our airplanes, make a quick start, and off we would go.

The ground control intercept officers would then direct us to the potentially hostile target. We would lock our radars on the target so that we could come close enough to identify it, but even if hostile, we weren't allowed to shoot unless fired upon. Although I never did fire any missiles while on alert, I did have some exciting intercepts with some strange objects.

One time I intercepted a glider that had wandered across the Czechoslovakian border. I got a radar contact and then a visual sighting on him. As I got in close in order to identify him, the glider pilot suddenly saw me in this big jet right on his wing. He almost lost control! His eyes got big as saucers and his mouth hung wide open—as I waved to him and drifted on by.

A couple of times we intercepted Russian airliners that had wandered off course or that were late on their scheduled flights to Paris, but I never saw any Russian military aircraft. I believe the airliners were used by the military and were off course on purpose, because their track across the ground always took them over one of our military bases.

The closest I ever came to a midair collision occurred while I was at Ramstein. I was scrambled to intercept two airplanes which were flying out of East Germany across the border into West Germany. I got a radar lock about one mile range. The indications were that the targets were above me, so I pulled back on the stick and started to climb. Unbeknownst to me, they were descending.

In just a few seconds I looked up and *immediately* above me were these two planes in close formation in the clouds. I passed within *fifteen feet* of them—whizzing by to the right. I know they were as shaken as I was! They were two West German planes that had wandered off course into East Germany and were flying back.

Things were in a high state of alert on the part of the forces in both East and West. The Berlin wall was built while I was in Germany, which created a lot of tension. Everybody was very edgy. Our forces wanted to see how quickly the East could scramble their airplanes and intercept. To test their response, we'd start flying toward Czechoslovakia at supersonic speed, and right before we'd get to the border, we'd make a hard turn and head back. They did the same thing to us, so we were always getting scrambled.

We didn't have a live firing range in Germany and for that training we went down to Tripoli, Libya, to Wheelus Air Base. This was before the days of Khadafy. There we could fly out over the Mediterranean and safely fire missiles and rockets. The rag, or target, was towed on a long cable by another airplane. Actually it looked like the banners you see pulled along the beach, EAT AT JOE'S.

Wheelus was extremely hot, and we'd almost expire on the flight line. One of our guys we nicknamed Pig Pen because he never washed his flight suit. After flying, he could take his sweat-encrusted suit and stand it up in the corner.

Also at Ramstein I came the closest I have ever been to having a serious accident. I had been on a routine mission with some Danish pilots when a yellow warning light in front of me flashed on, indicating a main fuel control failure. I immediately switched to the emergency system and headed back to Ramstein. The procedure was to set up a simulated flame-out pattern over the field. This pattern was a lazy 360-degree descending spiral, which would enable me to land anywhere within that turn if the engine stopped completely.

I called Ramstein control tower and informed them that I was setting up my simulated flame-out pattern and was now over the field at 8,000 feet. "Well, we don't have you in sight," the tower answered. By now I was 180 degrees through the 360-degree turn, traveling downwind.

*Those dummies!* I thought. *I don't understand. There's the runway, and I'm right here. The visibility is bad, but it's not that bad. Surely they can see me!*

"We still don't have you," reported the tower, "but we have the fire trucks waiting and you are cleared to land." I turned into my final approach, about 800 feet above the ground and called the tower again. "Final approach," I announced.

"Well, we still don't have you, but cleared to land." At that moment I glanced toward the ramp and control tower. Suddenly the thought hit me, *Ramstein doesn't have a yellow tower!* I realized that I was at the wrong field! I was at Sembach Air Base, fifteen miles away! The runways were parallel, but fifteen miles apart.

*I'm the dummy,* I muttered to myself. In anger I fire-walled the throttle, turned away from the airport, and with disgust said, "Ramstein, you don't have me. I'll be there in a few minutes." I didn't want to tell them where I was.

But as I turned away from the runway, I realized, *This thing ain't flying very good. It's about to stall!* My anger quickly turned to fear. I was down to 105 knots, and the engine wasn't producing any power due to the fuel control problem, compounded by my poor throttle technique.

I tried hard to keep it flying. But I was slowly settling in on a German village, and right in front of me . . . a church. I was bore-sighted on a *church steeple!*

I knew I was in deep trouble, but I had presence of mind to pull the power back and then gradually bring the power back up. It seemed like the wrong thing to do but it was right, because the engine slowly came to full power, and I just missed the steeple. As I went flying by, I looked down—below me were startled faces and big eyes, and a few villagers running for cover.

The fear now turned to humiliation and embarrassment. I knew when I got back to Ramstein, I was really going to catch it from my friends in the squadron. There wasn't anything we liked more than ridiculing and putting down someone when he'd blown it on a flight.

At the club that night, they were lying in wait for me. First off, I had to buy a drink for everybody at the bar. And then it came. "Well, Charlie. Time for your airport identification quiz." And they produced crude posters depicting the two bases. Everybody had a big laugh on me, and it turned into a great party.

My three years in Germany were about to come to an end. I couldn't believe the time had gone so quickly. I thought about extending my stay; I loved the flying and we were now in the F-102s, which were the hottest airplanes around. But the Air Force was recommending that young officers get as much education as possible, and so I decided for the benefit of my career to go to graduate school.

I volunteered for a master's degree in aeronautical engineering at North Carolina State. State wasn't available, but I was accepted at MIT (Massachusetts Institute of Technology) to study for a master's degree in astronautics and aeronautics. I didn't even know there was a degree like aero and astro, but since it was the only one offered I said, "Sure, I'll take it."

It was a difficult decision to leave the cockpit and go back to school. I really loved to fly and knew that at MIT I would be a full-time student and basically out of flying. If lucky, I'd be able to get a couple of rides a month in a T-33 out of Hanscom Field, but that would be it.

I also didn't know what assignment I would get when I completed my degree—whether I'd ever get back in the cockpit or not. But my love for flying was overcome by my desire to get ahead in my career. Even though I was enrolling for a degree in astronautics, I didn't give a thought to the possibility of becoming an astronaut.

The previous year on May 5, 1961, Alan Shepard had made the first manned U.S. space flight. Then on May 25, President Kennedy had announced the beginning of the Apollo program. "I believe this nation should commit itself to achieving the goal, before this decade is out, of landing a man on the moon and returning him safely to earth."

The reaction to Kennedy's speech by my squadron in Germany was one of incredulous unbelief. Looking at the Mercury spacecraft and seeing all the problems that the space program had in just launching small satellites, none of us honestly believed that the United States would ever be able to land a man on the moon by 1970. So when I left Germany for MIT in June 1962, there was no dream or desire on my part to be one of those astronauts who would be sent to the moon.

# 5

## *FANTASTIC*

"*Apollo 16,* Houston. You're GO for orbit. Predicted cutoff, 11 plus 49."

"Roger; 11:49."

We were ten minutes into the flight and getting ready to enter earth orbit. Our eyes were glued to the displays in front of us. All systems were being controlled by a computer in the instrument unit on the Saturn S-IVB.

We monitored the engine for a nominal shutdown at the proper velocity. We were prepared to engage a manual shutdown if we saw any overburn.

Thump! Shutdown. "Right on!"

The third-stage engine shut down automatically to insert us into orbit at 95 by 90 nautical miles altitude and 17,453 miles per hour.

"*Sixteen,* Houston. The orbit is GO." CapCom confirmed that we were in perfect orbit. Mission Control was tracking the flight through the MSFN (Manned Space Flight Network), which consisted of a series of radars scattered around the world.

"Roger. Boy, it's just beautiful up here, looking out the window," exclaimed John. "It's just really fantastic. And the thing worked like a gem."

I looked out my window and could see the west coast of Africa approaching. There was a giant storm system way off to the north. Minutes later we hurtled into darkness, and I could see brilliant displays of lightning in numerous thunderstorms penetrating the blackness. It was incredibly beautiful—these storms lighting up the clouds ninety-five miles below us.

"Well, we're just starting to come into darkness now, and the sunset is just as beautiful as always in this space business," John said over the radio to CapCom. He had seen these sunsets before in Gemini and Apollo.

We settled in to configure the spacecraft and check that everything was functioning normally, at the same time taking off our helmets and gloves while keeping on the rest of the spacesuit. We were now in zero gravity, and I could sense the uniqueness of weightlessness.

We unstrapped from our couches for the first time and began to float around the cockpit to get acclimated to this new environment. John and Ken were having no difficulty whatsoever adjusting to zero gravity; they were having a wonderful time bouncing around, but not so with me. I was about to barf. I knew if I moved very quickly, I was going to get sick.

There are two possible responses to zero gravity. You are either going to say, "This is the greatest," or you are going to say, "Don't get close to me, I'm about to get sick." Well, I started feeling seasick and wasn't sure I was going to like this weightlessness.

"I hope this doesn't last very long," I complained.

Fortunately it didn't, and within an hour I was bouncing around like the others. "Yahoo—this is super!" I shouted, as I floated from one side of the spacecraft to another.

NASA continued to track us through MSFN. We passed over stations in Africa, Australia, Hawaii, California, and other locations around the earth. Each station had large antennae that could communicate with the spacecraft and determine our speed, altitude, and flight path—thus verifying our onboard computer data.

In an hour we were back over the United States.

"Hey, Charlie, look at this," John said excitedly.

I rolled over, and right out the window was the city of Houston. We could see Galveston Island and Galveston Bay, the freeways leading into Houston, the Johnson Space Center, and even the runway at Ellington Air Force Base. Of course we had to look quickly because at 17,453 miles per hour, it didn't take long to travel over Houston. From California to Florida took only twenty minutes.

Back over the Atlantic we had more work to do. My final peek at Houston was all the sightseeing I had time for before we left earth orbit and headed for the moon. We had to stow the helmets and gloves, break out some checklists, unstow a camera, configure the TV camera for the undocking and lunar module join-up, and complete various other tasks. My job was to monitor the radio and electrical and environmental systems and to copy pages and pages of data from Houston.

"This is Apollo Control, Houston," reported the official voice of NASA communicating our status for the news releases going all over the world. "One hour, 54 minutes ground-elapsed time. We're at a little over a minute away now from LOS [loss of signal] with the *Apollo 16* spacecraft. We'll stand by and continue to monitor. This is Apollo Control, Houston."

Apollo 16 was now over the Indian Ocean and again in darkness. We were approaching the continent of Australia and about forty minutes from the TLI [trans lunar injection] burn. Our abort information had been received. An abort would be necessary if TLI was not exactly according to schedule, or if we had some emergency in the spacecraft either during or immediately after the burn out of orbit.

"*Sixteen,* Houston. About 30 seconds to LOS," reported CapCom. We were to be out of radio contact with the earth for about 30 minutes.

We strapped into our couches in preparation for this major maneuver.

When the third stage of the Saturn with its J-2 engine ignited, it would produce 100,000 pounds of thrust. We had the times written down for the start of ignition, how long it would last, and in what attitude the spacecraft was to be. All these things we were monitoring.

"*Apollo 16,* this is Houston through ARIA (Apollo range instrumentation aircraft). Over."

We were contacted by Houston through the ARIA. ARIA was airborne over the South Pacific to help with communications in case of an emergency. Usually this comm link was lousy, but today it was super.

"By gosh, loud and clear there," responded John. "Everything looks good here. We're 10 minutes and 30 seconds to the burn."

Shortly before the burn, we felt the maneuvering jets fire on the third stage. The vehicle began to maneuver to its proper attitude for the ignition sequence.

Thump, thump! Every time the jets fired, we heard a muffled thump and then felt a shake in the entire spacecraft. The spacecraft shook itself into correct position for the burn. We were getting very tense while we waited for this major phase of the mission. The spacecraft had performed beautifully up to this point. We had had no problems, and so as we watched the clock count down, we were anticipating a smooth ride out of earth orbit.

"*Sixteen,* Houston. You're GO for TLI."

Right on schedule the J-2 ignited, and that 100,000 pounds of thrust began to accelerate us toward the moon. We needed to gain 7,073-miles-per-hour velocity, in order to escape the earth's gravitational pull.

This burn produced a very high frequency vibration in the spacecraft, which was an unusual feeling. I questioned if we had a problem, but John had been up before, and he said everything was looking good. At five minutes after ignition, the S-IVB shut down. We had achieved a velocity of over 36,000 feet per second, or 24,545 miles per hour, and were out of earth orbit.

*Apollo 16* was on its way to the moon!

We had been out of communication with Houston for a brief time, but as the J-2 shut down we picked up communications again through Hawaii. A rapid calculation in Mission Control confirmed our computer solutions. We were right on course, rapidly leaving earth behind us and bound for our rendezvous with the moon. As we climbed away from the earth, we were still in darkness but swiftly approaching sunrise.

"Houston, this is the most spectacular view in the—, that you can possibly imagine." John just realized that he couldn't say "in the world" anymore, from our vantage point in space—and what a view!

Sunrises in space are always spectacular, especially in earth orbit. It doesn't remind you of a regular sunrise as there are no clouds for the rays of the sun to illuminate. First the horizon begins to light up. There are blues and reds and hues of white all along the horizon as the sun's rays are diffused throughout the earth's atmosphere.

Even though the atmosphere is about twelve miles deep, it appears as a thin strip from our perspective. Above that slim strip is the blackness of space, and right below is the earth in darkness. For a few seconds the sun's rays appear to diffuse more and more, and then instantly you have sunrise. There is the sun, so bright you can't look at it.

I never tired of viewing this fantastic drama. But we couldn't take much time looking at the sunrise now, because we had so much to do.

Our next task was to separate from the launch vehicle. The S-IVB had done its work, but before final separation, it was necessary to dock with the LM (lunar module) and retrieve it from its stowed position atop the third stage.

The plan was to separate and make a 180 degree pitch maneuver so that we in the command module would be facing nose to nose with the S-IVB. At that point we would then be able to see the lunar module, which had been riding along beneath us for this almost three hours of flight time.

The onboard computer set in motion a sequence that would bring about this separation. We could again feel a thump each time the small altitude control engines fired to maneuver us into the proper altitude.

Once in our new altitude, Houston gave us clearance to separate from the launch vehicle, and Ken fired the explosive bolts, releasing us from the S-IVB. We were now free from the third stage and began to move a safe distance away so we could start the pitch maneuver. At about fifty or sixty feet, we stopped and began pitchover.

"Look at this," Ken exclaimed excitedly as he looked out of the left side of the spacecraft from our new attitude. John and I quickly floated over to the left window to see what he was talking about.

What I saw was the most awe-inspiring, breathtaking sight I had ever seen in my life. There out the window, about eighteen thousand miles away, was the *whole circle* of the earth! It appeared we were directly over Baja California.

To the top and tilted a little left was the north pole region—there was a big storm system over Alaska, and Canada was mostly under clouds. And then there was the United States—from East Coast to West Coast and north to south, almost free of clouds. It was a spectacular sight.

"Gordy, I can't get over the view of that earth," enthused Ken. "None of the pictures do it justice! Absolutely beautiful!"

"We kind of get the idea that you're impressed," said CapCom Gordy Fullerton.

"Man, the thing about it, Gordy," burst in John, "is that the whole southern United States, Mexico, and Cuba and the Virgin Islands—they're all clear of clouds. It's just *fantastic!*" Fantastic had instantly become our favorite word.

"Did you take some good pictures?" asked Gordy.

"Got some," answered John.

"The way we're going," added Ken, "we may have to get a reload before we get to the moon."

"As a matter of fact," said John, "you can see as far north as Lake Michigan and Lake Superior."

"And," I continued, "all the way down past the Yucatán and into Central America."

We were so excited we were all talking at once, trying to describe this fantastic sight out the window.

I was impressed as I looked at this circle of the earth. We could see only three colors—the brown of the land, the pure white of the snow and the clouds, and the crystal blue of the oceans. This jewel of earth was just hung up in the blackness of space. It was as if someone had taken a brilliant diamond and placed it on a black velvet pillow, and then shone a light as bright as the sun on that little diamond.

The colors were so vivid that it looked like a Christmas tree ornament hung out in the blackness of space. And space was so black that I felt like I could reach out and touch it. The sun was off to our left, too bright to look at. It shone on the spacecraft and on the earth, but everything else around us was pitch black. Due to the reflection of the sun in the spacecraft, it blotted out the stars.

We could clearly see the Rocky Mountains and the major features of the continental land masses, but surprisingly from eighteen thousand miles away, you couldn't see any evidence of civilization. There was no evidence of man. I couldn't see cities or highway systems. None of the things that we take for granted here on earth could I see from that distance.

I was glued to the window but there were things to be done, so John called us back to work to keep us from falling behind the time line for our docking and extraction maneuver of the lunar module. We returned to our couches.

Looking out my front window I could see the lunar module. "What is that?" I exclaimed. We had just set up the TV camera, and I placed it in the window to let Houston take a look at what we were seeing. "Gordo, we must have a zillion particles along with us."

What appeared to be droplets of fluid were escaping from the upper part of the LM and were floating away into space. As they came out of the shadow of the spacecraft, they hit the sunlight and sparkled like little diamonds.

*We've had a leak from one of the propellant tanks on the LM,* I thought to myself. *That means* abort*! We're not going to be able to land on the moon!*

It looked like the mission was in deep trouble, because the particles were coming from the area of the ascent-stage fuel tank; if that was leaking, then there was no possibility we would make a landing on the moon.

Houston was watching on the tube, but since the resolution of the TV wasn't that sharp, they couldn't tell exactly what it was or where it was coming from any better than we could. They advised us to dock, extract the lunar module from its stowage position, and then they would make a decision.

Ken deftly maneuvered the spacecraft into the docking attitude and we moved toward the lunar module.

"About a foot out now, Houston."

"Roger."

"Okay, we're captured there, Houston."

We made contact with the lunar module at about one-foot-per-second velocity, which doesn't seem like much but it was quite a jolt. The impact was about the same as driving your car into a brick wall at two miles per hour.

The docking arrangement utilized a probe and drogue, a male-female joining system. The probe was on the command module, and the drogue was on the lunar module. A series of latches were cocked open on the drogue, and when the two sections made contact these latches automatically closed, locking us together.

The twelve latches around the docking mechanism clicked into place, and we had the LM secured. But before we could extract the lunar module, we had to hook up the electrical connectors and do some other preliminary work in the docking tunnel. This tunnel, thirty inches in diameter, was our passageway into the LM once the docking mechanism was removed.

Ken was trained for this, and while he was working, I floated over to look at the earth as it was receding. Almost visibly you could see it getting smaller and smaller and smaller.

"We got another spectacular view of the earth down here. The polar ice cap. We can see the whole sphere, and the United States is absolutely spectacular," said Ken.

"And out the other side, we've got a crescent moon!" exclaimed John. Our first view of the moon from space!

Well, Ken made the necessary connections, and now it was time to remove the lunar module. John fired the explosive bolts that held the LM to the S-IVB as Ken pulsed the maneuvering jets on the service module, and the two spacecraft slowly began to move away from the third stage. This maneuver was like pulling a vehicle out of the garage. Firing the jets was similar to stepping on the accelerator while in reverse gear.

"Houston, Orion is out of his bag," reported John to CapCom.

"Okay, we copy a GO for the S-IVB maneuver."

As we drifted away from the third stage, Mission Control sent a command that initiated an S-IVB maneuver to give us ample separation. The plan was for both vehicles to continue traveling toward the moon on slightly divergent paths, and then three days later our ship would enter lunar orbit, while the S-IVB would crash into the front side of the moon. Knowing the energy of this impact, the scientists could use it to calibrate the seismic instruments and help understand the moon's interior.

During the docking sequence and extraction, we continued watching these mysterious particles; more and more were escaping from the lunar module. Now we could see an area on the side of the LM that was tattered and shredded, and which was continually spitting particles off into space. The surface looked like shredded wheat. We tried to figure out what was the problem.

"*Sixteen,* Houston," reported CapCom. "On this panel that you were looking at that the particles are coming off of—that's just a thermal protection covering over the top of the RCS A (reaction control system A) systems tanks. What we're concerned about is that one of those tanks may be leaking and affecting the thermal protection on top."

My heart sank at the possibility of an aborted mission. Were we jinxed, too? John and I had worked as backup on the ill-fated *Apollo 13* flight. A major explosion in the oxygen tanks had aborted their mission. *Apollo 13* didn't get to land on the moon, and now it looked like we weren't going to land either.

"I see something coming off of the lunar module now that I just noticed. It looks like it's coming out of a vent. This is definitely coming out in a stream, not very many particles, but they're just being propelled away from the lunar module at some velocity." John's voice was very concerned.

"Let's get in there and take a look at it," Ken suggested for the three of us.

We were scheduled for a rest period at this point, but Houston agreed that we should open the hatches and float over into the lunar module to determine the nature of the problem. We were all pretty certain that it was a fuel leak.

We unstowed the proper checklist for the activation and checkout of the lunar module, then removed the hatches and the docking mechanisms. John and I floated into the lunar module, quickly taking our stations, and began to power up the LM.

Within a few minutes we were able to determine that it was not an ascent- or descent-stage propellant leak. In fact none of the liquids we had on board were indicating any leakage problem. So now we had something that was leaving the lunar module which was apparently of no consequence, but we didn't know what it was. We reported this back to Mission Control.

"Well, you are GO," said Houston. "Continue on with the mission."

We shut down all LM systems, *greatly relieved* that it wasn't a fuel leak. Had it been, we would have aborted the landing and the mission would have been a total failure. Our main objective on *Apollo 16* was to land in the central highlands of the moon, collect rocks, and emplace and perform experiments. Our spirits soared again when we discovered it wasn't a serious problem!

The mystery wasn't solved until four days later when we landed on the moon. As I walked around the side of the lunar module, I looked up and noticed that some of the paint had been peeling off. What we had been seeing were little flecks of paint floating off into space, and when the sun hit them it gave the impression of ice crystals.

After power-down we reinstalled the hatches and mechanisms and floated back to our couches. As we settled down for our three-day journey to the moon, the first thing we did was take off our spacesuits. Even in zero gravity those monsters were very uncomfortable.

Once undressed, instead of three of us in the spacecraft now there were six! The suits seemed like they were alive. They were floating all over— arms and legs everywhere! It was a jungle of arms and legs, ours and the suits. We finally got them stowed in special places beneath the left and center couches, and then it was time for our first meal.

In Apollo the food came in small plastic bags. It was wrapped individually and by meal, and these packets were stowed in the food locker. I took out DAY ONE, MEAL ONE, and separated the three packages, one for each crewman. Mine was color-coded blue, Ken's was white, and John's was red.

One meal might consist of four or five different bags—soup, meat, vegetables, drink, and dessert. The food in these plastic bags usually was dehydrated, and to prepare it correctly it was necessary to add water. To add water we were provided with a small water pistol that fit in a valve on the top of the bag. On the side of each bag was a set of instructions explaining the food type, preparation time, and water quantity required. We could select hot or cold depending on the instructions on the bag.

For instance to prepare a bag of pea soup, the instructions said, "Pea soup. Add five ounces of hot water and wait ten minutes." So to make pea soup, I stuck the barrel of the water pistol into the valve and pressed the trigger five times. Each time I pressed, out would come one ounce of water—and sure enough the bag filled up.

Then I shook it up real good and let it go, and the bag would float around the spacecraft turning into pea soup while I prepared the next bag. The next bag might say, "Orange drink, add eight ounces of cold water and wait two minutes."

I was the chef for this first meal and prepared all the bags. Now it was time to eat.

I took some scissors and cut off the whole top of the bag of pea soup—or bottom of the bag—it really didn't matter which in zero gravity. If I wanted to, I could turn the bag upside down, sideways, or any which way, and the soup or whatever always stayed in the bag.

The only utensil we had was a spoon. Amazingly when I reached in the bag and pulled out a spoonful of soup, the rest of the soup remained in the bag. I could even turn my spoon upside down or twirl it all around, like conducting an orchestra, and the soup would stay on the spoon.

But if I snapped the spoon real hard like a whip, off came the soup and instantly it took the shape of a sphere. It was like a tiny green marble of pea soup floating around the spacecraft. The molecular forces inside the soup equalized and drew it into a spherical shape.

To eat it, there were two choices. I could reach up and touch it with my spoon, at which point it took the shape of the spoon again. Or what was a lot more fun, I could just float over and suck in a mouthful of pea soup! We were the original Pac-men—gobbling up soup in space. As you can tell, we had lots of fun with liquids in zero gravity.

The food was actually quite tasty. To give us variety, we had some normal, everyday-type food such as slices of bread, peanut butter, and jelly. We also had meat patties, but the problem with them was that the meat was cold and there was no way to heat it.

The docs were concerned about our intake of calories and liquids, so after each meal we were required to log everything we ate or didn't eat and to inform Mission Control. With this information they charted our energy level.

It was now almost twenty-one hours since we had been roused out of bed at the Cape and fifteen hours into flight. We were very tired from our long day. Our scheduled rest period had been delayed to allow us to check out the LM for the possible fuel leak.

We put the spacecraft into a sleep configuration by setting a few switches. This gave Houston control of the onboard computer and enabled them to do a few other things while we were asleep.

In the event of an emergency, one of us slept with a communications helmet on, so that we could hear the warning systems on board and hear Houston call to alert us to an impending problem. All the way to the moon, we were in constant radio communication with Mission Control. Also one of us always slept with our medical monitor activated; then the flight surgeons could monitor the medical condition of at least one of the crewmen during the sleep period.

John went to sleep like a rock; he and Ken had a unique ability to simply switch off. John slept down in the lower part of the spacecraft, called the equipment bay, while Ken slept above his couch, floating between the couch and main instrument panel.

My sleep station was below my couch. There was a space about eighteen inches deep between a storage locker on the floor and the bottom of my couch. I floated in and attached my sleep restraint to the underside of the couch. This restraint looked like a fishnet with a zipper. Once inside the bag, I could float up and down a few inches, but I was prevented from floating out from beneath the couch.

I eventually took a sleeping pill this first night, because I couldn't get my mind off the events of the day. But before I fell asleep, I opened some letters that I had found in my flight plan earlier in the day. They had been placed there by the backup crew and were from my family.

The boys had each drawn a crayon picture of the Apollo spacecraft. On the back of Charles's he had written, "We love you." Tom's card said, "Have a safe trip home." What a neat deal! I almost choked up when I saw the simply drawn pictures and scribbled words.

Dotty sent a card which pictured a sunset over the ocean with the words, "Tonight . . . wherever you are my thoughts are of you . . . good-night my love . . . sleep warm."

In her letter she wrote, "I liked this card because of its words, but also because the picture reminded me of the perfect time we had together at the beach house." Then she added, "When you look out at the moon and stars, remember we are looking at the same moon and stars and are close to you."

Dotty—ever the romantic. I don't think I've known anyone to whom sunsets, full moons, and starlit nights were so important.

Why, on our honeymoon, we were always racing to be in the right place to view the sunsets over the Caribbean.

Dotty, the romantic. Actually, how we met is a very romantic story. . . .

# 6

## *SNAKE BIT*

### *Cambridge, Summer 1962*

It was June 1962 when I arrived for graduate study at MIT, and in August of that year I met Dotty. When we met I thought I had great luck, but now I believe our meeting was providential.

I had been living in the graduate house during the summer with two Navy officers, Lee Geis and Ray Stoetzer. We were older than the regular kids in graduate school, so we decided that we wanted to live in an apartment.

For the fall term we arranged to rent a place in an old house on Lee Street in Cambridge. Four single girls were living in the apartment at the time, and two of them were real cute, so Lee and I had an occasional date with them. One night in late August, we went over to find out when they were moving out and we could move in.

"We've got a house full," one of them announced. "Three girlfriends are here staying with us. They are sorority sisters from the University of North Carolina who have recently graduated and come up here to live. They just came in from job hunting and are kind of tired. But if you want to wait around, you can meet them."

Lee and I decided we'd wait, and we waited and waited. Finally they came out, and boy! one of them just knocked me over! She was a real cute, little, blue-eyed blond with the most infectious smile, and I was instantly taken by this southern belle. Something clicked—like a light went on in my mind and in my heart—and I knew there was something special about this young lady that I had to get to know. Her name was Dotty Claiborne and she was from Atlanta, Georgia.

I discovered that Dotty had just returned from a summer trip to Europe. "Hey, I just got back from Germany," I said excitedly. There was an immediate rapport between us, and we found lots to talk about as we discussed our favorite spots in Europe.

Before the evening was over, I said, "I'm leaving tomorrow to visit my parents, but when I get back I'll cook you a fried chicken dinner." I knew this suggestion would hit the spot since she was from Atlanta.

"We don't have an apartment yet; I don't know where you can reach us," she answered.

"I'll find you." And I knew I would.

Summer school was over, so the next day I went home on a couple of weeks' leave. As soon as I saw my parents, I told my mom I had met the girl I was going to marry; I was sure that Dotty was the one for me, because I had never felt this way about someone before. Mom started asking me all sorts of questions about Dotty's family, questions I couldn't answer.

When I returned to Cambridge, Lee, Ray, and I moved into the Lee Street apartment. It seemed all I could think about was Dotty, and so I called around trying to track her down. It took a little doing, but I finally found where she was living. She and her friends had moved into an apartment on Beacon Street in the Back Bay area of Boston.

I telephoned. "Remember me? I'm Charlie Duke. I've promised to cook you dinner. When will be a good time to do it?" We set a date, and in a few days I cooked up a great meal of fried chicken, rice, and milk gravy. They baked the biscuits.

As we were washing dishes after the meal, I asked Dotty, "How would you like to go out tomorrow?" It almost floored her, because all along she had thought I was more interested in dating her roommate.

On our first date, I took her to the Navy Club at the Boston Naval Shipyard. It was a quaint place, right next to the old eighteenth-century sailing ship, *Constitution*. We ate dinner, danced, and talked for a long time. That date was the beginning of our whirlwind romance.

A few weeks later we were parked in a secluded spot by the Charles River, right in front of MIT. The skyline of Boston was beautiful across the river; it was a gorgeous night with the moon flickering on the water. We had been to a movie and were talking about the future. I was already seriously considering marriage, and I knew that Dotty was the one, but not knowing exactly how she felt I decided to test the water.

"You know," I said, "I think we might end up getting married." It wasn't a proposal, but it let her know that I was serious. She didn't say anything—I could tell she was stunned; she had just started her job as a secretary at Harvard Business School and wasn't thinking about marriage.

But I kept after her. I was hopelessly in love from the very beginning, and she wasn't going to get away. I think she thought she was going to meet a Harvard businessman, and here was this MIT engineer putting the rush on her.

Boston is a great place to be in love, because there's a lot going on and many things to do. We attended the Boston Pops concerts and pre-Broadway plays. We walked along the Charles River across from Dotty's apartment and watched the Harvard sculls gliding across the water. Later on during the winter months, we joined a group on a ski weekend to Sunapee Resort in New Hampshire. Every night we were together or spending an hour talking to each other on the telephone.

In October my dad and some of his friends were coming to New York City for the World Series. I really wanted Dad to meet the girl that I was going to marry (even though Dotty didn't know it yet), so I invited her to go to New York with me to see him.

The weekend didn't start off very well. We found the hotel all right, but were on the wrong side of the street. Since U-turns weren't allowed, we had to drive on and on and on. After fighting one-way streets and rush hour traffic, it was one and one-half hours before we saw that hotel on Thirty-fourth Street again. Boy, was I frustrated. Fortunately things got better; my dad treated us to a great time, and he adored Dotty.

The Boston winter set in, and we were freezing in our Lee Street apartment. The old house wasn't exactly airtight; the wind was blowing through the rooms so hard it felt as though all the windows were open. We discovered that the landlord had locked the thermostat and set it a little above sixty degrees.

"There has got to be some way to get the furnace running," Lee said. "It's like an iceberg in here."

MIT engineers are *not* to be overcome, so we devised a slick way to fool the thermostat. We filled a plastic baggie with ice and put it on top of the thermostat. Well, the ice drove the temperature down, and sure enough the furnace came on. From then on we were toasty warm.

It wasn't long before the landlord made the first of several visits. "I just can't understand why my heating bill has gone up here," he said as he checked the thermostat and found it was still set at sixty-two degrees.

"We don't know either," we answered, trying to look as puzzled as he. He never did figure it out, and we never let on that we were packing it in ice.

My courting and studying weren't compatible. Because I wanted to be with Dotty all of the time, my grades began to drop; I was spending more time courting than I was studying, and my grades were a disaster.

Under the Air Force program in which I was enrolled, I was required to maintain a B average. Those of us who had been out of school for five or more years were finding that very difficult to do. MIT was extremely hard—not only did we have to go to classes, but we had to study at least eight hours a day just to keep up.

About halfway through the first semester, I got a midterm report from the Air Force, stating I was on probation. I was told that if my grades didn't improve, they would consider eliminating me from the program. That would have been disastrous for my career. I knew Dotty and I were going to have to get married soon or I'd flunk out.

On Veterans Day, the eleventh of November, I decided it was time to propose. We had the apartment to ourselves, but before I could ask the question, one of my roommates returned. We retreated to my room and sitting on the edge of my bed, I asked Dotty to marry me. It wasn't very romantic, but she must have thought it was a good idea because she said yes. I was one happy guy.

We decided to spend Thanksgiving in New York City and look at engagement rings. I wanted to find out what type ring Dotty liked, because we were planning to get formally engaged at Christmas. We had a fun time looking at rings at Tiffany's—just window shopping—Tiffany's was way out of my price range.

The holidays came, and I was off to Lancaster and Dotty to Atlanta. On Christmas Day I fireballed to Atlanta, engagement ring in my pocket and stars in my eyes. Dotty's folks knew what was up and helped ease the tension, greeting me warmly. I liked them immediately.

According to southern tradition, a prospective groom must ask the father's permission to marry his daughter. Well, the time came and I was very nervous. I had been there only an hour, and here I was sitting in the living room before the fire asking Dr. Claiborne for his daughter's hand in marriage—a guy that he had known less than an hour and his daughter had known less than six months.

"Dr. Claiborne," I began hesitantly. "Dotty and I are in love and would like to get married." Anxiously, I asked for his permission and waited for his answer.

"Yes," he replied. "It is fine with Mrs. Claiborne and me for you and Dotty to be married."

Man—was I relieved! I don't know what I would have done if he had said no.

Immediately Dotty and her mom burst through the dining room doors where they had been hiding—ears glued to the wall, listening to our conversation. Dr. and Mrs. Claiborne left us alone for a few minutes, and there before the fire on Christmas Day 1962, I slid a diamond ring on Dotty's finger. We were now officially engaged.

It was none too soon. The Claibornes, knowing about our engagement plans, had organized a party for all the relatives to meet this young Air Force captain from South Carolina. That evening I was on display, along with Dotty's engagement ring, and met all the aunts and uncles and cousins. They were a great clan, and everyone welcomed me as part of the family.

For the next four or five days, I stayed in Atlanta with Dotty. One evening we were invited to a costume party and dance at the Piedmont Driving Club. Dotty and I decided to go as astronauts and dressed up in two of my olive green flight suits. We made big signs to hang around our necks; mine said ON THE MOON and Dotty's, IN JUNE. When we stood together, it read ON THE MOON IN JUNE—a great way we thought to announce our wedding, which we had set for June 1.

After we had put on our costumes, Dotty's mom asked, "Do you have any ambitions to be an astronaut, Charlie?"

"Oh, no," I said. "Not me!" Neither one of us realized that later those words, *on the moon,* would come true.

Being an astronaut wasn't in my plans at all. I really thought that the space program had passed me by, and that I would never have such an opportunity. Now that I was getting married and settling down, I was even considering leaving the Air Force when my commitment was up and returning to South Carolina to go into the insurance business with my dad.

After a few days we drove to Lancaster so Dotty could meet the rest of my family. Dad had told everyone how sweet she was, and they were all anxious to meet her. Mom gave her approval and was thrilled I was marrying into a fine southern family.

Then it was back to the books. In March Dotty gave notice to Harvard Business School and went home to help her mom with all the wedding details. That was okay with me because it gave me a chance to do more studying. We wrote letters every day, and fortunately every few weeks I was able to fly to Atlanta in one of the T-33s out of Hanscom Field.

Meanwhile, I began looking for a place for us to live. I finally found a little duplex on Dorothy Road in Arlington, a suburb of Boston. I thought it was really appropriate that I was marrying a Dorothy and we'd be living on Dorothy Road in our first home.

At the same time I was looking for our place, I was also trying to locate an apartment for Dotty's sister and her husband. Dick was going to be an intern at the Boston Children's Hospital beginning in July, and he needed something for Mary Anne and their little one-year-old son, Richard.

He had two requests: the apartment needed to be near the hospital and cost no more than $75 a month. You can imagine what was available in the

Boston market for that price! I finally found a place that fit all their requirements, but it was really a dump in a slum neighborhood. In spite of my concerns, they said they'd take it.

When they arrived later that summer, their new brother-in-law with great trepidation took them over to see their apartment. As we arrived, we were greeted by an old, disheveled woman in a dirty dress and unkempt hair sitting on the steps of the entrance, rocking back and forth and mumbling incoherently. A little shaken, we walked around her and entered the building.

It was extremely dark—the hall illuminated by only a single bare light bulb, dimly glowing. The apartment was even worse—bare light bulbs hanging from the ceiling, heavy stains in the tub and sinks, cracks in all the walls—it hadn't been repaired in ages. They were horrified and decided it was a lot worse than even I had described. Fortunately they were able to get out of the lease and found another place—still close to the hospital but for a lot heftier rent.

My grades improved slightly during this second semester. The first session I had made a B, C, and D; the first D I had ever received and it had really shaken me up. This time I made mostly B's and one C. Even though I was still on probation, the Air Force had mercy on me and gave me permission to stay another term, which was to begin the middle of June.

Relieved, I left Boston during school break and went home to Lancaster for a few days. Then it was off to Atlanta for the wedding festivities. On the day of the wedding, Dotty's aunt and uncle, the Willinghams, entertained with a brunch and swimming party at their home. Dotty and I startled everybody by jumping in the pool and swimming on our wedding day. We were relaxed; no cold feet for us.

That evening as people began arriving for the wedding, my twin brother Bill was ushering people into the church. A lady approached him and in a deep southern accent drawled, "This is the strangest thing I have ever seen. I didn't know the groom ushered at his own wedding!" It was one of many cases of mistaken identity.

The service was held at the Cathedral of St. Phillip's, a large Episcopal church in Atlanta. Dotty's uncle, Randolph Claiborne, who was then the bishop of Atlanta, officiated. The cathedral was packed with people; it was beautiful with all the flowers and bridesmaids, and the most beautiful of all was Dotty in her long white dress as she came down the aisle escorted by her father.

The next day we were off to Jamaica for our honeymoon. And that's when things began to fall apart.

First our tropical paradise hotel was right off the end of the airport runway, and three or four times a night these humongous 707, four-engine jets came roaring over our room nearly shaking us out of bed.

Then when we were taking our first swim in the beautiful, warm, crystal blue Caribbean outside our room, we glanced back and saw all these people gathered on the shore waving and yelling at us. We swam back in and were told, "Didn't you know there were sharks sighted out there yesterday, right where you were swimming? You'd better not swim in that water!"

*That* did it! We began to look around for another place to stay and moved across town to a lovely resort club. It was situated on a hill surrounded by a golf course, palm trees, beautiful view of the ocean, safe beach, and we were the only ones there. It was out-of-season, and the hotel was actually closed, but the manager felt sorry for us and decided to let us stay in their best room. *What luck. This is great,* I thought. *Now, we can enjoy our honeymoon.*

But that was not to be, because the very next morning I awoke sick as a dog from food poisoning. It was one of those deals that at first you think you are going to die, but then things get so bad you want to die and are afraid you won't.

The last two days in sunny Jamaica, I spent with my arms wrapped around the toilet instead of Dotty. Finally it was time to leave, so she helped me on the plane and we bade a fond farewell to paradise. That afternoon in Atlanta she got sick from the same thing.

Things continued to get worse and worse.

For our trip to Boston I had borrowed my dad's station wagon and rented a U-Haul. We loaded it with all our wedding presents and were no more than twenty miles outside of Atlanta when the engine overheated. I had left the radiator cap loose, and all the water had boiled off.

Well, we finally made it to Boston, but I was so uptight with having a new bride, studying, being on academic probation, and worrying about what was going to happen next that I broke out in hives. I was miserable for a week with a red rash, and itching and swollen all over. I've never had them before or since.

Then not two weeks later, Dotty suddenly discovered a cyst and was in the hospital for emergency surgery! The rest of our first month together, she spent in a hospital ward with ten other people and a nurse who wouldn't let me sit on her bed or even get close to her. Ten days in the hospital and two weeks nursing her at home—bachelor life was easier than this!

Unbelievably, less than a month later Dotty was bedridden again. She was making iced tea by pouring boiling water over some tea bags she had put into a glass pitcher. Well, as the hot water hit the pitcher, it literally exploded, showering her with the scalding water! Her slacks and socks were soaked, and she ended up with second- and third-degree burns on her legs and feet.

"This marriage is snakebit," I said. "There's no way we are going to make it through the first year."

I found myself trying to attend classes, study eight hours a day, and take care of a sick wife. School was getting harder and harder, and I was thinking, *Golly, we've been married a month and a half, and we've had three major catastrophes already. I'm not sure this thing is going to work. It seems doomed from the start.*

Things didn't get much better the rest of the summer. In August after summer school, we were on the coast of South Carolina, and Dotty had another major medical problem. We were now in our fourth trauma and had been married only three months. We seemed to be allergic to each other.

I wasn't doing much better at school—the B average continued to be out of reach as my grades hovered around C. I began to wonder if I would ever make it, but mercifully the Air Force continued to be patient.

MIT was the hardest school I had ever attended. Examinations focused on our ability to apply what we were learning, instead of memorization of facts as at the Naval Academy. I remember some tests when a good grade would be eight out of one hundred.

All of the tests were open book, so I would stagger in with my armload of books, although they didn't do me a bit of good because you had to know how to use what was in them. *I'm not sure I'm in the right room,* I'd think to myself. *I don't recognize a thing on this exam!* I would thumb through the books so fast trying to find something I could recognize, that the lab curtain would almost stand straight out from the breeze.

It was a very difficult time, and there were many days when I wanted to run from it all and get back to flying jets, but for some strange reason, my grades began to improve.

In September Dotty got a teaching job in Cambridge, and I devoted myself to my studies. By the time she got home from work, I would be buried in the books in my study room. I'd give her a "hello, welcome home" peck on the cheek and then go back to my studying.

Dotty was an incurable romantic. She would fix us a candlelit supper for two on our little screened-in back porch; the silver and fine china would come out, and she would serve us a gourmet meal. When she'd call me to supper, I'd run in, gobble it down, and then run back to the books.

I wasn't very romantic, but that was all she was going to get from me because of my academic probation. My job had to come first; Dotty would have to wait. I could tell Dotty was disappointed. The married life she had envisioned—the one Hollywood portrayed in movies like *High Society* with Grace Kelly and Bing Crosby sailing away in the sunset singing "True Love" or *The King and I* with Yul Brynner and Deborah Kerr embracing to the enchanted waltz, "Shall We Dance"—wasn't what she was experiencing. I wasn't Bing Crosby or Yul Brynner.

I thought she'd get over these romantic dreams, and we could get on with what was really important—my career—but her dreams continued to test our marriage. Not realizing what would result from our having two different goals, we began to gradually travel down two separate paths that over the years became farther and farther apart.

When we got married, we talked about the church we should attend. I had been raised a Baptist, whereas Dotty was a cradle Episcopalian. It really didn't matter to me, but Dotty had a deep love for her denomination—her grandfather had been a priest and her uncle a bishop—and so we decided to attend an Episcopal church in nearby Belmont.

I attended confirmation classes, studying their history, rituals, and doctrines, and after several weeks of lessons, joined the Episcopal church. I was happy to do that because there were some very fine people there and I enjoyed the reverence, beauty, and solemnity of the worship service.

At the beginning of the fall term, I needed to pick a thesis subject. To get a master's degree, you had to write a comprehensive thesis—it was worth twenty hours of credit and had a major impact on your grade point average.

I discovered that MIT was working on the Apollo guidance and navigation system for the NASA space program—an onboard system designed to guide the spacecraft without any assistance from the earth's tracking network. This project looked very exciting to me, so along with a friend, Mike Jones, we decided this would make interesting thesis work. We volunteered to do some statistical analysis on the astronauts' ability to track stars utilizing the Apollo telescope or sextant, as it was called.

While working on the thesis, I met some astronauts who traveled to MIT to see how we were progressing. One of the astronauts was Charlie Bassett, a former test pilot before becoming an astronaut. I remember thinking that being an astronaut would be the ultimate achievement for a test pilot.

"Being an astronaut you not only get to fly," he enthused, "you get to work on the design of the spacecraft." My forte was operational engineering, so this interested me a great deal.

But even as I worked on the Apollo guidance system, I didn't have the foggiest notion and only the faintest dream that one day I would be an astronaut—especially an astronaut flying to the moon in a spacecraft that would be outfitted with the production model of the very equipment we were working on at MIT. Years later, however, the statistical analysis that Mike and I performed was used in the navigation system aboard the Apollo spacecraft.

While astronauting was distant, working on this thesis did make me anxious to get back to flying. I decided that I would volunteer for test pilot school when I graduated. Then I would be able to use my engineering knowledge and also pursue my love of flying.

Some friends told me about the test pilot school at Edwards AFB, California, which in those days was called the Air Force Aerospace Research Pilot School. I applied, realizing that my qualifications were at the barest minimum. I felt like my prospects of getting selected were either slim or none.

But miraculously, a few months later the orders came down assigning me to the class of '64-C (commonly called '64 Charlie)—to begin in August 1964. I was elated. I was going to be able to continue my flying in the hottest jets and also be able to use my engineering training.

It was then that I began to think that maybe I had a chance of becoming an astronaut. The thoughts weren't racing through my mind, but for the first time it seemed like a possibility.

Mike and I completed our thesis in the second semester of our last year, doing a good piece of work. We got an A, finally bringing my average up to a B, and the Air Force approved my degree. I was mighty relieved and proud when I was awarded my Master of Science diploma in May 1964.

With great excitement Dotty and I left Massachusetts and headed for California. Passing the city limits, we let out a shout, "We are away from the snow and are on our way to sunny California!"

While we had enjoyed many things about Boston, New England had been a real change for us from the sunny South. The weather that winter had been atrocious with snow storm after snow storm. And the Boston drivers were faster and crazier than anything at the Indy 500.

But mostly I was overjoyed at leaving the books behind and getting back to flying. I was *really* looking forward to the test flying at Edwards; the more I had read about it and what was going on, the more excited I had become.

All the latest aircraft were being tested there, and I would have the opportunity to fly a lot of different, high performance jets. Also I was to be on the same base with some of the real heroes of the Air Force—one being Chuck Yeager, who was commandant of ARPS (Aerospace Research Pilot School).

Dotty was excited, too. She had never lived on an Air Force base or been to California. Her love of travel and sense of adventure filled her with great anticipation. Little did she grasp what was waiting for her at Edwards, in the middle of the Mojave Desert.

# 7

# '64 CHARLIE

My reporting date at Edwards was not until the middle of July, so that gave us a few weeks' leave. We planned on camping while we traveled cross-country and loaded up our little red Chevy Corvair Monza with camping gear and clothes, shipping the rest of our goods to California. The car was jam-packed, but at least we weren't dragging a U-Haul.

We headed south to spend a few days with our parents. Then it was— "Go West, Young Man." Our first real stop was Colorado Springs, followed by camping in the Rockies and spending the Fourth of July at Mesa Verde National Park. In Flagstaff, Arizona, we attended their big annual Indian Powwow and then drove on to the Grand Canyon for a few days of camping and riding mules down into the canyon.

The next day it was on to Las Vegas, where we decided to splurge by checking into a hotel. I'm surprised they gave us a room; we looked so bad in our grungy, dirty clothes. That shower felt great, but we almost clogged the drain with the dirt that came off! That evening I hit the craps tables with a vengeance and managed to lose a quick hundred dollars.

Now it was time to report to Edwards. I was really excited as we loaded up the car for this last leg of our journey.

Well, the five hour trip is entirely across the desert and being the middle of July, you can imagine how hot it was. It must have been 110 degrees— and no air-conditioning! It was like a blast furnace with our windows open, so we drove with them closed.

I had heard that if you put a canvass water bag out on the front of your car, it will keep you cool as the water evaporates and blows through the vents. It didn't work for us. The only way we found to survive the heat was by continually soaking our shirts in water, so every hour we'd stop to wet them down again.

As if this welcome wasn't bad enough, things got worse. About halfway to Edwards, we drove into a *sandstorm*—a full-blown, first-class, can't-see-ten-feet sandstorm! I thought all the paint was going to get sandblasted off the car. We were both wondering what in the world we had gotten into, and what was it going to be like living in the desert?

But when we pulled into Edwards and I saw all those super flying machines, I forgot about the heat and the sand. Man, was I excited. I couldn't wait to strap into one of those jets and light the fire once again. "Look at that," I exclaimed to Dotty. "A whole rampful of F-4s, 104s, 38s, 106s!" I was drooling.

We headed toward our temporary quarters and drove through one of the housing areas. Well, it looked like a refugee camp. The homes consisted of prefabricated shacks, and there was not a blade of grass and hardly a tree in the dirt yards. The 110-degree heat, the sand, and now this! Dotty started crying; she thought if this was where we were going to live, she wanted to go home to Mom. This was not the type of adventure she was seeking.

The more excited I got about airplanes, the more depressed Dotty became. Her rosy dreams of married life began to crumble as she realized how in love I was with flying. She didn't know where she fit in. Living at Edwards was a tough time for Dotty, but I was ecstatic and figured she'd eventually adjust to being married to a fighter pilot. I was thrilled to be back in the cockpit.

When we discovered Dotty was pregnant, I was overjoyed—both at having our first child and hoping this would keep Dotty busy and happy. We were assigned a three bedroom, green stucco house—number nine Sixteenth Street—with trees, grass, and a fenced-in backyard. It was basic military housing, but our first home, and we began getting settled in.

Edwards Air Force Base was really out in the boondocks—smack in the middle of the Mojave Desert. In all directions was barren rolling terrain; a lot of sand, cactus, and small scrub brush. The largest plant was a weird looking thing called a Joshua tree. It looked like a prehistoric relic or stick people—with bare branches twisted in awkward ninety-degree angles.

The closest town was Lancaster, 35 miles away. Lancaster wasn't exactly a metropolis—population was about twenty-five thousand and the largest store was Sears. If we wanted to go to a real city, we would drive the 110 miles to Los Angeles. In fact driving to Los Angeles for dinner on Saturday night became a real treat for us, even though it took almost two hours to get there.

I began flying immediately. Classes weren't to start for a month, so I was assigned to base operations where I logged sixty-five hours in thirty days. After two years of eight hours per month, I was in hog heaven. Then it was time for the class of '64-C to begin.

On the first day of school, the fourteen of us filed into the auditorium to be introduced to the staff. Our commandant was the famous Chuck Yeager, first man to fly faster than the speed of sound and ace fighter pilot. We all looked in awe as Colonel Yeager sauntered into the room, dressed in his flying suit, sleeves casually rolled up.

He was a real life hero, a test pilot's test pilot. In the trade he had a reputation as a great stick-and-rudder man or a guy with good hands. In those days Yeager wasn't making commercials or writing books, so his name wasn't a household word, but to us young aspiring test pilots, Yeager was the best.

In a slow West Virginia drawl, Yeager announced, "Yaw'll have a tough year ahead."

That turned out to be an understatement. It was more than a tough year; it was almost an impossible year. The school was demanding and competition was intense. There were some top-notch pilots in our class with a lot more experience than I had, and everyone wanted to be the best. Class '64 Charlie included an ex-Thunderbird pilot, a Ph.D., an exchange pilot from Argentina, plus top Navy and Air Force pilots, and a Marine Corps officer.

Flying at Edwards was fantastic, but it was a different type of flying than I had ever done before. Most people think of test pilots as daredevils—taking an aircraft out to the limits not knowing what to expect. But that's really not the way it is.

Test flying is precision flying; you plan every step, every detail, every maneuver. For instance, we may plan a data point at 35,000 feet and 350 knots. At that point we could deviate only plus or minus ten feet and plus or minus 2 knots. It was very demanding, and I had many new techniques to learn.

One of the most thrilling missions we flew was in the F-104 Starfighter, in what was called the *zoom maneuver*. After suiting up in a partial pressure suit, we would take the F-104 up range from Edwards a hundred miles, turn around, and come smoking in at Mach 2—twice the speed of sound, which was as fast as a Starfighter would go.

On cue from radar control, we'd pull the nose up into a forty-five-degree climb and let it go as high as it could. The engine afterburner would blow out at 65,000 feet, and then at 72,000 we'd shut down completely and continue coasting on up to about 85,000 or 90,000 feet. From that altitude you could see the pale blue of the upper atmosphere and a very distinct curvature of the earth.

Going over the top we'd experience a moment of zero gravity and float in our seats against our seat belts; everything would feel very light. Then the nose would start down, and we'd begin accelerating back toward earth. If the engine didn't restart on the way down, we were right over Edwards and could make a dead stick landing onto the dry lake bed. The lake bed gave plenty of room because it was over seven miles long, compared to two miles for a typical jet runway.

That whole mission from takeoff to touch down took about thirty minutes. I loved these zoom flights. There was something about the partial-pressure suits, the speed, and the altitude that all combined to give me a real thrill of adventure that wasn't present on other flights. I felt like I was a baby or budding X-15 pilot.

The X-15 was a rocket-powered research plane that had been flying for a number of years. It was carried aloft by a B-52 bomber, then at altitude was dropped off, and its engine ignited to propel it to the fringes of the atmosphere or to speeds of Mach 5 plus. A number of X-15 pilots had already qualified as astronauts by flying this machine to an altitude of over fifty miles. One day I hoped to fly it, but for now I was content with the zooms.

These zoom rides were not just for kicks but to learn precision flying and high-altitude control techniques. The thought back in those days was that we'd eventually have not only spacecraft but an airplane that could go into space. In less than twenty years this became a reality when John Young and Bob Crippen flew the NASA space shuttle to a landing on the Edwards lake bed.

Occasionally we'd get airborne with no specific mission plan. During these flights my favorite experience was to get down on the tree tops and go roaring up the Kern River gorge. After fifty miles or so, the gorge would spit us out behind Mount Whitney, the highest point in the continental United States. The high Sierras were beautiful, especially in the wintertime, and I'd scream around over the snowpack, enjoying the isolation of the area. I never thought about being hip deep in snow if I had to eject.

Then I'd climb to altitude and circle like a vulture, waiting for an unsuspecting Navy jock to come out of the Naval test center at China Lake. When one did appear, we'd bounce one another and have at it in a dogfight before returning to Edwards.

All areas of flying were being tested at Edwards, not only hardware. During our year's training, the Air Force flight surgeons instituted a study to determine stress levels in pilots at various stages during a flight. It was decided that the students at the test pilot school would be the subjects of this study.

To generate the data, we were to be instrumented with respiration and EKG (electrocardiogram) sensors. The data would then be registered on a small tape recorder that was fitted in a pocket of our flight suit. Our only problem with this was the fear of being grounded due to some irregular heartbeat under stress. We all had friends who had lost flying status due to a few strange wiggles on their EKG.

To overcome our reluctance, Jim Roman, the doc in charge, agreed to keep the data confidential. He also hired two gorgeous young ladies to be his lab assistants. It was their job to apply the sensors, check out the recorders, and debrief us after the flight. When we saw those beautiful creatures, all the fighter-test jocks on base stood in line to volunteer.

This study was one of the first in attempting to understand how the heart responds under stress. It was a great success and in the end resulted in saving many flying careers—because the docs realized a few squiggles on the EKG may not be abnormal.

Everyone in our class were close friends, but as in any large group there are always special buddies. Among ours were Joan and Stu Roosa, Sam and Beth Armstrong, and Fran and Hank Hartsfield.

Stu's nickname was Friendly Forty-Eight-Pack, because he could out-drink anybody. While Stu played hard, he also worked hard and was very talented. We'd try to drive each other to perfection. Stu and I found we had a lot in common—both liking Coors beer, flying, hunting, and playing golf.

Sam liked golf, too, and occasionally the three of us would play on the Edwards course. Sam wasn't very good, but he loved to hit the ball hard. He'd swing so hard he'd almost come out of his shoes! Whether it was a driver or a nine iron, he hit it as hard as he could and spent a lot of time in the desert looking for his ball. Sam is now a three-star general, but it was ability, not golf, that carried him to the top.

Hank was the brain of the class. He had a Ph.D. and wowed us with his engineering talent. Hank eventually ended up as an astronaut.

We had great party times—most fighter pilots like a good party, and our class was no exception. Pancho's Happy Bottom Riding Club of Yeager's earlier days had burned down by then, so everybody took over the Officers' Club on Friday afternoons for beer call and then on to other places, continuing the party.

One of the greatest times we had during the year was at Joe and Shirley Wuertz's house, celebrating the birthday of the U.S. Marine Corps. Joe was the epitome of a spit and polish Marine officer, but off duty he loved to party .

We all arrived in casual clothes, ready to hang one on after a week's worth of studying and flying and were speechless when Joe paraded out in his full formal dress uniform with dress hat, polished saber, and spit-shined boots. Everyone stood at attention, singing "Happy Birthday" to the Marines and "The Marines' Hymn." After the formalities Joe, and most everyone else, commenced to party.

I found out that too much partying can lead to some embarrassing moments. After a big blast one Friday evening, the following morning our class was to leave at 5:00 A.M. on a trip to visit other Air Force bases. I pressed on until around 2:00 A.M., then went home to get a couple hours of sleep.

Early that morning when the alarm went off, I could barely open my eyes and instantly went back to sleep. Then all of a sudden I woke up with a start and shouted, "Oh, no, I'm going to miss that flight!"

I was the donut collector, so I rushed to the base dining hall to get the donuts and roared down to base operations. I jumped out of my car, donuts in one hand and suitcase in the other, and ran down the ramp trying to catch the airplane. The pilot already had the engines running when I thundered up. Fortunately he had mercy and ordered the crew chief to open the door, so I threw on my bag and they jerked me in. I had made it, but only by the skin of my teeth! Had I missed that trip, I would have been in deep trouble.

At six months from graduation, the competition grew stiffer. Each one of us had giant size egos, and each one thought that he was the greatest. Muhammed Ali had nothing on us. We tried to be the best in flying, the best in academics, and the best in partying. We studied hard, flew hard, and played hard. Everybody wanted to be *numero uno* in every category.

While intense, it was friendly competition. We knew there was going to be only one top graduate to receive the Honts Trophy. The coveted Honts was awarded to the top graduate in each class—tops by averaging our academic and flying records.

Well, I wanted it as much as anyone else. The stronger ones helped the weaker ones in the academics, because we didn't want anyone to flunk out—but in the airplane it was every man for himself. At this stage it became apparent that I was one of four who was in the running for the top slot, so I pressed hard in the homestretch.

All this time Dotty was involved with the usual women's activities and getting things ready for our new baby. A few months after arriving at Edwards she had gotten a job substitute teaching in the local elementary school, but morning sickness and the tiredness that came with her pregnancy did her in, and she decided to give up working. As the baby grew bigger and bigger, we got more and more excited about the arrival of this new addition.

Dotty was having a few problems, and the doctor warned us that the baby might come early and come quickly. He advised us to carry a string around whenever we went off base, just in case I might have to tie an umbilical cord. Fortunately we were home when the day arrived, and on March 8, 1965, Charles was born at Edwards AFB Hospital. He was about six weeks premature and weighed five pounds, four ounces.

When they showed him to me the first time, I said, "My gosh, we've got a drowned rat!" He was really puny and his skin was all shriveled up. He was definitely not a beautiful baby, but he was ours.

Charles stayed at the hospital for two weeks after he was born, due to complications related to his premature birth. When he came home, I proudly taught Dotty how to change diapers. She didn't know anything about taking care of a little baby, but I had remembered from my experiences baby-sitting my younger sister.

Dotty's mom came out to help. I remember when I picked her up at the airport in Los Angeles and we drove to Edwards. As soon as we arrived, I think she wanted to turn around and go home. She'd never seen such a desolate spot.

Now that we had our first child, I began feeling like a family man. "Every family needs a dog," I said, so we bought a little puppy. That was the dumbest thing I ever did—paying money for a dog.

We ended up with a high-strung, AKC registered beagle named Mickey, who was in full tilt all the time. He thought he owned the place and chewed up the furniture, our shoes, and the wash on the clothesline. He even chewed up the rose bushes in the backyard. One day he jumped the fence and got me in trouble with the air police! That was the *last* straw. Mickey and I had a real battle and I won! From then on he behaved.

When Charles was three months old, Dotty decided to fix up our backyard. She had seen some beautiful white rocks in other people's yards and wanted some for a rock garden. One day I was flying low level east of Edwards and happened to fly over an old quarry, and there were those beautiful white rocks. I did a couple of circles to map the roads and flew back to the base.

That weekend we climbed into our Corvair with Charles and Mickey and drove to the quarry. It was about an hour's drive and located in a very isolated part of the Mojave Desert.

When we came to the dirt road leading back to the mine, there was a chain stretched across the road, and hanging from the chain was an old rusted sign which read, NO TRESPASSING—SURVIVORS WILL BE PROSE-CUTED. Well, that got our attention—but we had come so far that we took a deep breath and drove around the chain and on to the quarry.

The place was like an old ghost town, one of the scariest spots I'd ever been in my life. The wind was howling and blowing tumbleweeds in every direction out over the deserted property. The old tin doors of the dilapidated quarry buildings were creaking open and slamming shut.

As soon as I stopped the car and opened the door, our high-strung Mickey hopped out. But when our brave dog heard the quarry doors creaking, he quickly jumped back into the car. For the rest of the time he cowered on the floor and wouldn't get out again.

About that time Charles started crying, and Dotty and I began to get really nervous. Was someone hiding behind the shack, aiming a gun to shoot us? At breakneck speed we threw in a trunkful of rocks and tore out of there as fast as we could, never looking back. That was our first and last visit to the old rock quarry.

Graduation came and Pete Hoag was named top graduate and winner of the Honts Trophy—I was tied for second place. It had been so close between four of us that there was something like $^1/_{10}$ of a point difference in our whole year's grades. And our scores were higher than the scores of all the recent top graduates. We felt great about how we finished the course. Our big egos told us we were the cream of the crop, and like *Top Gun* we strutted our stuff.

I received an assignment to remain at the test pilot school as an instructor, teaching control systems and flying the F-104 and other airplanes. That was great with me; I was delighted to stay at this exciting place. Dotty wasn't quite so excited; Edwards was not her favorite place. She still hadn't gotten used to the desert with the sand and heat, but being a dutiful Air Force wife, she accepted her fate.

Edwards is a dream come true for a pilot. Even though I still wasn't involved in any of the advanced testing, it was thrilling just being a part of the Edwards scene. I enjoyed my job as an instructor. Chuck Yeager was a good boss, and he and his staff made the school a class act. Since Yeager was gone a great deal, traveling around the country as a spokesman for the Air Force, he delegated a lot of responsibility, letting us run open loop if we didn't foul up.

Many interesting test programs were underway at Edwards at that time. I remember the first flight of the XB-70, a huge supersonic bomber, which was the forerunner of the B-1. It had been assembled at Palmdale, an Air

Force facility a few miles from Edwards. When it was announced that the plane was being flown to Edwards for its first landing, about half the base showed up to watch.

Right on schedule the XB-70, I affectionately nicknamed the White Goose, appeared with a gaggle of T-38 chase planes. They made a low pass down the runway and then circled for a landing. It was awesome. The big white bird seemed to hang in the air, as it slowly made its descent to a smooth touchdown. We all let out a cheer when the main gear kissed the runway.

The most impressive airplane I saw at Edwards was the YF-12. It later became the SR-71, which is today the strategic reconnaissance plane for SAC (Strategic Air Command). In contrast to the XB-70, the YF-12 was pitch black. It had two huge engines buried in its delta wings and a long needle nose with a fuselage that flared out back to the wings.

The Black Bird, as it was called, accelerated down the runway with both engines in full afterburner and lifted off like it was climbing straight out of sight. The pilots wore pressure suits because of the high-altitude flying. The knowledge gained from the Black Bird and the X-15 helped develop the technology used later in the space shuttle program.

Another program useful for the shuttle was the testing done on strange looking machines called *lifting bodies*. These were planes with little or no wings, so they flew by generating lift from the body or fuselage of the plane.

A former Annapolis classmate, Jerry Gentry, flew one that looked like a flying bathtub. It was designated the H2-F2. The plane was towed into the air like a glider, then cut loose for Jerry to attempt certain maneuvers to test stability and control.

On one such flight Jerry almost bought the farm. The H2-F2 started oscillating, and he had to do a big barrel roll just a few hundred feet off the ground. Landing out of a barrel roll is not recommended for your everyday flight.

With all this research going on at Edwards, I heard a lot about the space program and was aware that NASA was getting ready to move out of Gemini and on to Apollo. I also knew that the Air Force had decided to have their own program, the MOL (Manned Orbiting Laboratory). The MOL program planned to use Titan rockets to launch a laboratory into space, our first space station.

I determined if either ever opened up and I had the opportunity, I would give it a go. I believed the best job I could have as a test pilot was to be an astronaut. Many of the ARPS graduates were already astronauts.

One September Sunday afternoon in 1965, as I was watching a pro football game on TV, I glanced at the *Los Angeles Times* and there on the front page of the paper was an article saying NASA was seeking more astronauts. It read like a want ad.

> NASA is looking for men. You must be a United States citizen, not over 36 years old, less than 6 feet tall, with a college degree in Math or Science and with at least 1,000 hours flying time. If you meet all the requirements, then please apply.

"Hey, that's me!" I exclaimed. I got really excited.

I talked to Dotty and she said, "It's fine with me. Whatever you want to do." I think one thing in the back of her mind was that, if I was selected, she would get to move to Houston and that would be a lot closer to Atlanta—and no more desert.

On Monday morning I went in to see Yeager and the deputy commandant, Buck Buchanan, to ask them how to go about applying for such a job. In the early days Yeager had not been very enthusiastic about the space program. In fact most of the test pilots had thought the astronauts were like monkeys—"Flip them a banana and they will flip a switch." They hadn't considered spaceflight was really flying. But by 1965 Yeager had changed his mind and thought astronauting was a good job, so he and Buchanan really encouraged me and said they would find out the procedure.

All that day the topic of conversation at school and on the flight line was, "Are you going to apply? Are you interested?" Everybody was sizing up their chances versus the competition.

A few days later Colonel Buchanan called me in to say there were going to be two opportunities to become an astronaut. One was with NASA in the civilian space program and the other, with the Air Force in the Manned Orbiting Laboratory. I started thinking about what to do. The Air Force hadn't had a very good record in the manned space program; previous attempts had been canceled. What if they canceled MOL?

I made up my mind to volunteer for the NASA program. Stu Roosa and some others at Edwards did the same. Our applications were sent to Air Force headquarters at the Pentagon, and those the Air Force considered qualified were forwarded to NASA.

In late 1965 I received a letter from NASA asking me to go to Brooks Air Force Base for a physical. If I passed the physical, then I was to report to Houston for interviews. I had passed the first hurdle and was on my way! But I was nervous about the physical, because I wasn't in very good shape, so I started to work out.

The time came, and those of us from Edwards went to San Antonio and spent a whole week at Brooks being poked and prodded and tested and analyzed from every angle, in every conceivable position, and from every opening of our bodies. They did tests that I couldn't pronounce, much less figure out what they were. Some were crazy things like pouring ice water in our ears to see if they could uncage our eyeballs.

The physical also included psychological testing. It was the first time I'd ever seen inkblots, and we all decided ahead of time that when we looked at those blots we weren't going to see anything sexy or perverted. So when the psychiatrist asked me, "What do you see?" I always said a flower or a cloud. Sometimes I just said it looked like an inkblot.

Of course there were IQ tests and all kinds of other problem-solving tests such as matching up round pegs with round holes and octagons with octagons—all to be done at top speed. These tests were designed to bring out our ability to make rapid, accurate decisions under pressure.

It was an exhaustive and thorough physical. Interestingly the eye problem that disqualified me from Naval aviation was never found. It hasn't been seen since that one physical at the Naval Academy. We all passed and headed back to base to wait for the next step.

After a few months it was time for the interviews and some more tests, which were to be held in Houston. I was nervous as a cat when I walked into the Rice Hotel in downtown Houston to report for my interview. I didn't know what to expect or exactly how to act. I didn't have to pretend on the enthusiasm; I really wanted the job.

Deke Slayton, who was the chief of Flight Crew Operations and one of the original seven astronauts, and John Young and Mike Collins were on the interview team. They asked questions like, "Why do you want to do this? What are your goals?" There were also a few technical questions, but mostly they wanted to know about our background and motivation. The longer the interview went, the more comfortable I became, but when I left I had no indication whether I was going to be selected or not. I just hoped for the best.

Following the interview there were more written tests. I will never forget that on the day of the tests we were told that two astronauts—Charlie Bassett, whom I had met at MIT, and Elliot See—had just been killed in a plane crash at Lambert Field in St. Louis. It had been extremely bad weather and while trying to land, they had crashed into the top of a hangar. They were in training for the Gemini program and had been scheduled to fly on *Gemini 9*. This tragic news put a damper on everyone's enthusiasm.

After the final testing, I flew back to Edwards feeling pretty good about my possibilities. Those of us at Edwards knew that we had a good chance because we were exactly the type of candidate NASA was looking for—the fighter-test pilot. Many of the first groups of astronauts had come from Edwards and Patuxent River, the Navy test pilot school.

I was aware that going to NASA would take me out of the mainstream of the Air Force, and therefore promotion into the ranks of general officer would be slim. For this reason not everyone at Edwards who was qualified applied, because it didn't fit into their career goals and ambitions. I knew this, but I wanted to be an astronaut and fly in space no matter what.

In April 1966, I got a phone call from Deke Slayton. "Charlie, I've got some good news for you. You've been selected."

I let out a loud, "Yahoo!"

"Can you report in May?" he continued.

"You bet!" I shouted. I couldn't contain my excitement as I realized that in less than one month I would be in Houston to begin training as an astronaut! I was just ecstatic over the news. I was at the office when the call came through and immediately called Dotty. She was thrilled, too.

Deke made some other calls to guys at Edwards, and within minutes it was all over the base who had been selected. We got a lot of congratulations and a lot of free drinks at the bar that night.

Several days later, April 4, 1966, Dotty's twenty-sixth birthday, NASA officially announced that nineteen new flight candidates had been selected, bringing to fifty the total active astronaut roster.

Of the nineteen that were selected by NASA, eight were from Edwards. Besides myself, there were Fred Haise, Joe Engle, Ken Mattingly, Ed Mitchell, Bill Pogue, Stu Roosa, and Al Worden.

We were all glad that we had chosen the NASA astronaut program instead of going for the MOL. As it turned out the MOL program was canceled about three years later, before ever launching one spacecraft. Some of our buddies at Edwards who had gone with MOL, Hank Harsfield being one, ended up at NASA when the program was canceled. They became the pilots of the early shuttle missions.

In my selection process, I believe that there were about 3,500 applicants, of which approximately 350 were actually serious contenders. Of the 350, there were probably 100 of us that ended up going for the physicals and the interviews.

Finally, nineteen were selected to make up the fifth group of astronauts to join the NASA space program. Out of the nineteen, nine of us went to the moon, and three of us actually walked on the moon.

My astronaut career had come about as a tiny seed was sown here and there. It had not been a burning life's ambition but was more the outcome of the course I found myself on. It wasn't until that Sunday afternoon when I saw the newspaper article, that I really caught a vision of myself as an astronaut.

To me being an astronaut was the best job I could have as a test pilot, and I had always wanted the top job. I had always been one to aim high. And since our group of nineteen had been selected in particular for the Apollo program, I realized that I might even have a chance to shoot for the moon!

# 8

# MOON-BOUND

### April 17, 1972—Mission Control

"This is Apollo Control, Houston, at 23 hours and 3 minutes into the mission. We presently show *Apollo 16* at a distance of 97,906 nautical miles away from the earth. Velocity now reading 5,322 feet per second. Standing by now, awaiting CapCom Tony England's wake-up call to the crew," reported NASA's Public Affairs Office.

"*Apollo 16,* Houston. *Apollo 16,* Houston. Good morning up there. How are you doing?"

"Great!" spoke up Ken. He was still wearing his headset from the night before. John and I were just starting to stir in our sleeping bags.

"Good show. Everything looks fine up there from down here."

"Oh, yes. It sure beats work," replied Ken.

"I'd hum something for you to wake you up," threatened Tony, "but I've got a tin ear."

After stowing my sleeping bag, I got on the mike to give our postsleep report to Mission Control. All food intake, fluid intake, all urine and bowel discharges—everything had to be recorded.

"The commander ate a sandwich and his orange juice that was in his suit, and all his meal for day one, and his PRD (personal radiation dosimeter, which registered the amount of radiation we received each day) is 22,028, and he had seven hours of sleep. Best ever in spaceflight! No medication. Three voids—34, 20, 18. Fluid intake: total, 21 ounces. Over."

"Okay. We got that, Charlie."

"Okay. For Ken—he had from meal C everything but the pecans, and he ate his sandwich and his orange juice. His PRD is 15030. Six hours in the eight-hour period, but was awake once every hour. Two voids—one time 41 seconds, the other one was lost due to a malfunctioning bag. Thirteen ounces, total liquid intake."

"Okay."

"On me now—for my meals, I had the sandwich and the orange juice that was in the suit. For meal C, I had half the spaghetti, all the ambrosia, and the cocoa. My PRD is 21,040. I got about five hours' sleep, got two voids of 20 and 25 with about a 20-ounce fluid intake. Over."

"Okay. I got it all," said Tony. "Sounds like you all slept pretty good."

"Well, it was off and on for me. I must have been—"

Tony broke in, "I tell you, I'd be so excited, I wouldn't sleep at all."

Thank heavens for sleeping pills. Without them, I wouldn't have gotten any sleep at all. The night before my mind had been going about 90 miles a minute. I was physically tired, but with the excitement of the day and the things we had seen and done, my mind was just whizzing from one thought to the next and thinking about the next day's activities.

Also I had had difficulty adjusting to floating around while sleeping, and I missed resting my head on a pillow. I kept thinking, *Where's my pillow? What's wrong with my head?*

In zero gravity when you go to sleep, you just close your eyes—and your head doesn't go anywhere. It just sort of stays there.

To feel some pressure on my head and to keep from floating around, I had wedged myself between the couch support and a stowage container on the floor of the spacecraft. During the night I had floated out of the wedged position, but by then it didn't seem to matter, and I was able to close my eyes and go back to sleep.

There were some advantages to sleeping in zero gravity. On earth you have to turn over regularly to relieve the pressure points and, if you go to sleep sitting upright, your head nods and you wake up with a crick in your neck. In zero gravity there are none of these problems. You simply stretch out your legs, close your eyes, fold your arms, and go to sleep. The head doesn't nod, limbs don't go to sleep, and you wake up feeling perfectly refreshed. The only difficulty I had was the initial psychological adjustment to sleeping free of pressure.

John glanced out the left window. "We can see the earth out there, and it's getting a good deal smaller. It's about the same size as the moon, almost, out the other window."

I was in awe. Just imagine, here we are—out one window we can see planet earth with its beauty, and then we can float over and look out the other window and see the moon.

Even though we were traveling faster than 5,000 feet per second (3,600 miles per hour), we could feel no sensation of movement at all. Spaceflight is totally different from flying an airplane. In an airplane you hear wind noises and feel the vibrations of the engine and the craft as it cuts through the air and clouds.

But in spaceflight you don't experience any of those feelings or hear any of those sounds. There is no spacecraft vibration as you move through space. And all that you hear are the noises of the ECS (environmental control system) fans with their gentle purr and the electrical system inverters humming away. After a while you get used to these particular sounds in the spacecraft and are instantly alert if the sound changes, because you know something has gone awry.

Each morning in space the first couple of hours were set aside for housekeeping chores—going to the bathroom, cleaning up, and eating breakfast.

I believe one of the reasons we had no female astronauts in the Apollo program was the lack of privacy and hygiene problems. Our bathroom, bedroom, workstations, and kitchen were all in an area that was about twelve feet in diameter. This meant that we didn't have any privacy, even when going to the bathroom.

One of the most commonly asked questions of an astronaut is, "How do you go to the bathroom in space?" No matter the culture, the age, or the education, someone always asks this question. I usually answer, "Why, we don't, that's why we walk so funny when we get back!" Some people actually believe me, but after a good laugh I admit the truth.

The best way to describe going to the bathroom in space is very, very carefully. It was terrible! Apollo's waste management system was very crude; it was not a triumph of technology and almost seemed to be an afterthought. What we had were some bags and a little urinal.

The urinal was situated in the lower equipment bay to the right of the couches. Normally to urinate you would float down to that area, open up a little valve at the base of the urinal, and void in this device which looked like a large cup with a baffle inside. A tube from the urinal led to the side of the spacecraft, where it opened out into the vacuum of space. Through this tube the urine would be sucked overboard and vented off into space.

It was an incredibly beautiful sight as the urine hit the vacuum outside, crystallizing into very fine droplets and creating a mist of millions of tiny rainbows. For a few minutes our spacecraft would be surrounded by these colorful rainbows, until the prisms of ice crystals floated off into space and disappeared. The same thing would happen when we dumped water overboard.

That was the normal method of urinating in space. However, most of the time on our flight, we had to collect our urine samples so the doctors could measure what minerals we were losing in spaceflight. This meant we had to use special collection bags, the same bags we used inside our spacesuit. They were very similar to hot water bottles.

To urinate into these bags, we used a rubber condom. Connected to the end of the condom was a one-way check valve, which was plugged into the rubber bag. When we began to urinate, the force of the stream would open the valve, and when we finished, the valve would close. We then stored these bags in a special container. Since the docs wanted to know how much fluid we were losing, we would time our voids and report them each morning during our postsleep report.

It was an even bigger challenge to defecate. All we had for that was a plastic bag, cylindrical in shape and about twelve inches long. It looked like a chef's hat except for a narrow, 1½-inch rim.

To defecate, you got to the lower right side of the spacecraft, and the other two guys floated as *far away* as they could to the other side. You wanted as much distance between you as possible. Then you unrolled one of the bags and removed the toilet paper and some tablets, which were used as a disinfectant and gas neutralizer. These you stowed in a small pocket on the side of the cabin until needed.

Next you got completely naked—clothes, rings, watches, everything—because you really didn't know what was going to happen when you tried to use the bag. You then took the bag, put it in the right position, stuck it to your bottom, and as you floated around on the right-hand side of the spacecraft, you hoped everything went into the bag.

The big problem, though, was that nothing went to the bottom of the bag. You are floating, the bag is floating, and everything else is floating! It was a real mess getting cleaned up. Anything you can imagine, happened! You can see why the other two guys floated as far away as they could; they didn't want to be around if everything wasn't in the bag. We had a lot of laughs with the old waste management system.

All this was a very time-consuming procedure. It took a full hour to undress, get the bags out, use them, clean up, seal the bags, stow them away, and then get dressed again.

We also had to save the fecal material. Because the docs were concerned about mineral loss such as potassium, they wanted to study all of our body wastes to understand how rapidly, when, and how much the body was losing these key minerals. It had been discovered on *Apollo 15*, the flight prior to ours, that the crew had lost a great deal of potassium. This, the doctors had surmised, was the reason for heart irregularities they had seen on two of the *Apollo 15* crewmen.

To prevent our crew from having these heart irregularities, the flight surgeons decided to add potassium to our food. It turned out we didn't have any heart problems, but the potassium acted as a laxative and caused us to almost run out of fecal bags before we returned to earth. After only a few days, we knew it was going to be touch and go whether we would have enough! It would have been a *disaster* to have run out of bags with a couple of days left to go.

Our second day out, when Ken was getting dressed after using the potty, he found everything except his wedding band. It had floated off into the spacecraft unseen by us. We looked and looked, but just couldn't find it. Ken had been a bachelor for a long time and had just gotten married a couple of years before. He really wanted to find it, so we kept looking for it all the way to the moon—without success.

There was no shower; the only way we could stay clean was to use a wet washcloth and soap. The rag bath was necessary because a lot of water floating around the cabin introduced the risk of an electrical short behind the instrument panel. We even had to swallow our toothpaste when we brushed our teeth, and edible toothpaste wasn't the greatest.

To take our bath, we'd get naked, take the water gun and squirt a little hot water on the rag to get it damp, and then we'd rub down as best we could. You can see that we couldn't get very clean. And since we didn't bathe every day, it wasn't long before the odors began to build up.

During training we had decided we wanted to shave every day, because it felt better and we looked better; so we had on board a little windup shaver. It operated like an electric model, but worked by a windup spring mechanism. The whiskers were collected in a small chamber behind the blades. Unfortunately something happened to the cutting edge of the shaver and instead of cutting whiskers off, it felt like it was pulling them out one by one. Ken and I stopped shaving completely, but John reverted to the backup which was a simple safety razor with shaving cream.

After these housekeeping chores, next came breakfast. Some months before the flight, our dietitian, Rita Rapp, had asked us if we had any special request. "Well, I really enjoy grits for breakfast," I told her. For a southern boy, grits are almost a necessity at breakfast time.

"We don't have a recipe for grits that can be used in space," she said, "but I'll sure try to make some up for you." She experimented for a few months and came up with some nice-tasting grits. I had them for breakfast on day two and they were delicious. As far as I know, I'm the only astronaut who ate grits in space. John and Ken had grits on their menu, but they never would eat them.

Once we had finished breakfast, Houston would read us the headlines, local news, sporting events, and any news of interest. This second morning CapCom read, "One of Vincent Van Gogh's best was stolen from the San Diego Art Gallery . . . and I've got an input from Dotty here for Charlie."

The wives weren't allowed to talk directly to us during a spaceflight, but they could call Mission Control and send us messages. I wondered what Dotty had to say. "I'm all ears," I responded.

"She says your five bird eggs have hatched, and so you've got five new, healthy neighbors."

I laughed. A few weeks earlier some wrens had built their nest in our mailbox, which was actually a basket right by our front door. When Dotty discovered five little eggs in the nest, she had put up a sign for the mailman and roped off the front door. Every day she had watched for the birds to hatch, thinking how unique it was to have the baby birds launch into the world the same time I was being launched to the moon. Now they were hatched and had begun their new adventure as I was beginning mine.

Another time, Mission Control was reading us the news and gave us the stock market quotations. When they were finished, John laughed and asked, "Charlie wants to know how Consolidated Jackpine is doing."

Don Peterson, who was the CapCom at the time chuckled, "Was that Consolidated Jackpot?" "Jackpine," I answered.

"Roger."

Well, Consolidated Jackpine is a fictitious stock, so we were just having some fun with him to see what would happen. "Probably lost three or four points again yesterday," John teased, just egging him on.

"Roger," said Don. "Charlie, I guess I haven't got those figures handy. We'll see what we can do."

"If you can find out, Pete," I laughed, "you're a better man than I am. I've been trying to find it for ten years." John, Ken, and I had a few chuckles among ourselves, then we promptly forgot about it.

The stock, Consolidated Jackpine, was something my fighter squadron had made up when I was stationed in Germany. There was one guy in our group who really enjoyed playing the stock market. He was always trying to buy some of the strangest-sounding stock you could ever imagine, and so we just thought up this stock for Jerry. "Hey Jerry," we'd needle him, "why don't you buy some Consolidated Jackpine?"

Ten days later when we'd gotten back after the flight, we were told that NASA had received many calls from people wondering where they could buy Consolidated Jackpine. Jerry could've had a *bonanza!*

The three-day flight to the moon was a busy time; we had a lot of activities scheduled. Besides the time spent housekeeping, there was a full program of things to do. We had to copy daily flight plan updates from Houston and make midcourse corrections to our trajectory; we had photographs to take of earth and space, utilizing various wavelengths, such as UV (ultraviolet) and infrared; plus a great many experiments to perform inside the spacecraft.

One such experiment we nicknamed the light-flash experiment. On *Apollo 11,* after their spacecraft had passed through the Van Allen radiation belts, Buzz Aldrin had reported to Houston that he saw flashes of light when he closed his eyes, rather like a flashbulb going off or a shooting star going across the front of his eyes. The flashes had appeared at an intermittent rate. The other two *Apollo 11* crew members had also seen these lights and every flight crew to the moon since then had observed them.

Houston designed the light-flash experiment to try to determine what they were. The theory was they were high-energy cosmic ray particles which were penetrating the spacecraft protective shield and then penetrating either the retina of the eye, the optic nerve of the eye itself, or the part of the brain that interprets sight.

The experiment consisted of a large box whose sides contained photographic plates, that we placed over our heads. One of the plates was in a fixed position in relation to the head, and the other plate was free to move slowly; it was like wearing horse blinders. The idea was that the particles would leave a track on the photographic plate which the scientists could then measure for quantity of energy and direction it was traveling. Hopefully this would yield clues to what kind of particles they were.

The first time I put on the box, called the ALFMED (Apollo light flash medical experiment device), and closed my eyes, all of a sudden, bang! There was a flash similar to a flashbulb going off inside my eyeball. Another one appeared as a shooting star moving from right to left. Surprisingly, I could see the direction from which these things came.

Though they lasted only a fraction of a second, they were long enough in duration for us to be able to describe them to Houston. "Okay, Houston. That one was from the right to left and it appeared as a very fine pencil line of light."

I was really intrigued. In fact if I just closed my eyes at any time during the flight, within a minute or two I would see one of these flashes. At one time when I was wearing the ALFMED, I must have counted thirty to forty within an hour. It was like a fireworks' display on the inside of my eyeball.

Once we got back and they looked at these photographic plates, the physicists confirmed that they were in fact high-energy cosmic ray particles. This was important to know, because these and other forms of radiation could be a problem during long-duration spaceflight.

On the journey to and from the moon, we kept the spacecraft turning. On the side away from the sun it could get very cold, and on the side facing the sun it could get very hot. This was detrimental to the spacecraft's systems, so to keep the temperature balanced we kept the spacecraft in what we called the *barbecue mode*. It worked the same way as when a chicken is grilled on a rotating spit, spinning over and over so it barbecues evenly.

As we were rolling around, the earth would come into view in one window and then disappear.

"Tony, you just went by my window, and the half-earth, man, is a spectacular sight!" I was speaking to CapCom Tony England.

"I bet it is," he replied. "I tell you, I'm green with envy."

"Well, I don't want to trade with you. How far out are we now, Tony?" I asked.

"Exactly 108,285.1," he answered. "Man, we've come a long way, baby!" I laughed. We were now more than 108,000 nautical miles from earth and moving about 4,912-feet-per-second velocity. The earth's gravity was slowing us at this point, but we could not feel the deceleration in the spacecraft.

As we looked out of the window, space was just black. We weren't able to see any stars because there is so much reflection off the spacecraft. A similar experience occurs on a clear, dark night in the city when you look up amidst the tall buildings and bright street lights; very few stars are visible. But we were able to see and identify some of the major stars with our telescope, because of the twenty-four-power magnification.

"And now . . . heeeere he is . . . every space jockey's best friend, disk jockey B-B-Bill Bailey. . . ."

I had just inserted one of my audio cassettes for a little listening pleasure.

"You have just punched your Bailey button. This is Bill Bailey and all you guys. To you Charlie, especially, and John and Ken and anybody else you got up there with you—we've got about two hours of real good entertainment lined up for you. . . ."

For our personal entertainment, we were allowed to take a portable tape recorder and two tapes each. I loved country music, so I called a good friend, Bill Bailey, who was a disk jockey for a popular country-western station, KIKK, in Pasadena, Texas.

"Bill, can you put together a couple of sixty-minute cassettes for me so that we can listen to some country music on our way to the moon?" I knew he had made some for Pete Conrad on *Apollo 12* and Stu Roosa on *Apollo 14*.

"Be glad to do that for you, old buddy. When do you need them?" he asked.

". . . We've got five great artists in the country-music business today that are all set to entertain you for two solid hours. Without further ado, here is the Porter Wagoner show. . . ."

A few weeks before launch, the cassettes had arrived and the music transferred to the official NASA tapes. I hadn't had a chance to listen to them before the flight, so I was looking forward to hearing them now.

*(Guitar music)* "Oh, Mama, I'm excited. I'm almost out of breath. What I saw, like to made me run myself to death . . . *Company's a'coming*, that's a song I recorded way back in the early fifties . . .

". . . and Colonel Duke, Captain Young, and Commander Mattingly, this is the biggest show of the Wagonmasters and Miss Dolly and me in our entire lives. The longest distance from home of any show we have ever played—and the smallest crowd that we have ever played for—but the most important audience in the world, and outer space!

"And this show is one of the highlights of my career and the most significant of my career also. There's no way to put in words how the Wagonmasters, Speck, Dolly, and I really feel this second, to be able to share in the smallest way this historic mission, and to be able through the sound of music to be a part of it, and to all of you gentlemen aboard.

"So I hope you'll enjoy the songs and each thing that we put down for you. Now here is a beautiful little lady to sing one of her big hit songs that I know you will enjoy titled 'Joshua,' Miss Dolly Parton."

"Thank you, Porter. *(Guitar music)* Mmmmmmmmm, mmmmmmmmm, Well a good ways down the railroad track, there was this little run-down shack, and in it there's a man I've never seen. . . ."

I loved it! Besides Porter Wagoner and Dolly Parton, there were Buck Owens and his group, Merle Haggard, Jerry Reed, Chet Atkins, and Floyd Cramer. Bill had called each one to ask them if they would do something special for us to take into space. They said they would be happy to, and so during their rehearsal sessions, they had put together these cassettes, especially for us.

Before the flight neither John nor Ken thought they would like country music. John brought his easy listening and Ken his classical, but during the flight we played these country-western tapes more than any other. They enjoyed them as much as I did. We especially appreciated how all the artists had recorded the music and messages personally for us.

". . . Joshua, Joshua, you ain't gonna be lonesome anymore . . . nahhhh, nahhhh . . . me and Joshua. Yeah, me and Joshua, and that's the end of my story, me and Joshua."

Another friend of mine, entertainer Don Rickles, did a series of tapes for me which kept us in stitches, and we played them over and over again.

Another part of our daily routine was performing preplanned exercises. The doctors realized that three or four days in space without any physical activity left the muscle tone very bad, also the cardiovascular system begins to weaken. Based on the experience of prior flights, we implemented some prescribed exercise routines. The idea was to get our heartbeat up to about 130 or 140 beats per minute and maintain that for fifteen or twenty minutes.

Since you can't jog in weightlessness or lift weights, the doctors had put on board an exercise device that exerted tension when we pulled against it. It was called the Exergenie; these devices were very popular in the sixties and early seventies.

Simple as it was, it actually provided us with a good workout. Ken was very rigorous in his routines; John and I probably not as much so, because we knew when we got to the moon we were going to get a lot of exercise during our lunar excursions in one-sixth gravity.

During this three-day trip to the moon we also took time to rehearse certain flight procedures. On the second day, we practiced the separation of the lunar module from the command module. This was to actually occur on the fourth day of the mission in preparation for landing. Once in lunar orbit we would have only limited time to put on our spacesuits, take our equipment through into the lunar module, put the docking system back in place, close the hatches, and prepare for separation. It was essential we have this routine down to a fine art.

John and I entered the lunar module for this exercise. As I floated through the tunnel into the LM, it felt strange at first because we entered upside down in relation to the instrument panel. After doing a 180-degree turn, I was in proper position and then being in the LM seemed like putting on an old shoe. After checking all the systems and finding everything okay, we returned to the command module to put on our pressure suits.

"This is Apollo Control at 54 hours, 44 minutes." The voice of NASA kept the press and the rest of the world informed of our activities. "The *Apollo 16* crew at this time is in the process of donning their pressure garment assemblies, without helmet and gloves. Young and Duke are then scheduled to reenter the lunar module. The exercise is part of a check of procedures that the crew will be using on the day that they perform the landing on the moon."

In zero gravity it was very easy to get dressed in our spacesuits. In fact it is the only place I have ever been, where I could put my pants on—two legs at a time. Holding my floating suit out in front of me, I simply stuck both legs in simultaneously. Next I put my head through the neck ring, then arms in, and closed the front zipper, which I could easily reach.

The second zipper, the one that actually closes the suit, began on my left hip, going around my back to my right hip. It was impossible to work this zipper by myself, so I asked John, "How about zipping me up?"

He floated around behind me and tried to pull the zipper shut. He pulled and pulled, but couldn't get it zipped.

"What the heck is wrong?" I exclaimed. "This suit just has to work! It worked two days ago, so why won't it zip?" I was really concerned. If it didn't work, we were in serious trouble as far as the lunar landing went. I needed this spacesuit to be able to walk on the moon; a multimillion-dollar mission couldn't fail because of a tiny zipper!

John struggled and struggled, but it would not close. It was like I had grown three inches and was stretching the suit apart. Finally John took a pair of pliers from our tool kit, clamped them onto the zipper, and braced his knee against my back. As I held onto the side of the spacecraft, he gave a good yank and pulled the zipper shut. Houston didn't particularly like that procedure, but it worked.

*Now would it work when we got to the moon?* I wondered. I was worried and asked Houston if I could make some adjustments on my suit. I knew how to do this, but because it was a complicated procedure they decided that we should take our chances and hope that it would work better in the one-sixth gravity of the moon.

I hadn't realized it, but in zero gravity your spine tends to stretch and the muscles relax; I had grown about a half inch. It was just enough to keep the zipper from closing easily.

*Man, I've come all this way,* I said to myself, *and now the suit's not going to work!*

I had come a *long way* and didn't want to miss it now. Not only all the thousands of miles we had traveled from the earth, but all the training, all the work, all of the years since I was selected to be an astronaut.

I had come a long way since 1967, when "Charlie Duke, fighter-test pilot" became "Charlie Duke, astronaut."

# 9

# *ORIGINAL NINETEEN*

*Man, I'm an astronaut. I've got it made!* I thought to myself as we rolled into Houston. *Have I come a long way—from small town boy to NASA astronaut!* I felt like I had truly reached the top, the ultimate for an Air Force fighter pilot.

We drove straight to the NASA Manned Spacecraft Center (renamed the Lyndon B. Johnson Space Center in February 1973), which is located about twenty miles south of Houston. The space center has the look of a college campus, various buildings scattered around a well-landscaped lawn, but it wouldn't win any architectural awards. We checked in with the guard at the gate and went directly to the astronaut office to sign in and report that we were there. Alan Shepard, who was chief of the astronaut office, came out to greet us.

We were just agog. Here was Alan Shepard—the first American in space—an authentic American hero! We were almost speechless and Dotty's eyes got real big. I was really impressed. *There's Deke Slayton, Gordon Cooper, Wally Schirra. Wow, and now I'm one of them!*

When Dotty and I got back to the car, she excitedly exclaimed, "Imagine, meeting Alan Shepard—a real astronaut!" I reminded her I was an astronaut, too, but I knew what she meant. Alan was a "real" astronaut because he had actually flown in space.

Our team was the fifth group to join the program. We called ourselves the Original Nineteen—a takeoff on the Original Seven, a title given the first group of astronauts who had been selected in 1959. Of the nineteen in our group, seven were Air Force, six Navy, two Marine, and four civilian. Our average flight time was 2,714 hours, of which 1,925 was jet time. Eleven had earned a master's degree and two held doctorates. We brought the total number of active astronauts to fifty.

Our group was selected in particular for the Apollo moon program, but it wasn't long before I began counting noses and realized there were a lot more astronauts than there were seats to the moon. Someone wasn't going to make it. And I was just a rookie, so far down the totem pole that my chances were bleak.

Since we all knew that everyone was not going to fly, the competition was terrific. I determined to give it everything I had. If Dotty had complained that I was a workaholic as a test pilot, I really became one now. I literally poured myself into my job.

Our family needed to get settled, but we didn't know where we wanted to live. So for the summer, we moved into the Cardinal Apartments in League City. It was about a four- or five-mile drive from NASA, and several in our group had decided to live there or close by. We figured this would be nice for Dotty and Charles since I would be working long hours and gone a lot on training trips.

We were really packed into our little apartment. We had only one bedroom, so at night we would put Charles to sleep in a little porta-crib in our room; then when we went to sleep, we would roll him through the door out into the living room. There he would sleep for the rest of the night.

Charles was now fifteen months old and still wasn't walking. I kept urging him along and finally one day in June in the yard of the Cardinal Apartments, he took his first steps. "Oh no! We've got Frankenstein on our hands!" I yelled. He was staggering around like a monster, his arms fully extended over his head. And that's how he walked for about a month. But he was a cute boy even though he did walk like Frankenstein.

Charles was growing like a weed and was a joy to us. But Mickey was a pill. He was becoming more and more independent, often being gone for days. Unfortunately his independence was his undoing as one day he was killed by a car. We decided no more dogs for a while.

We did decide to expand our family and once again Dotty was with child. Our second was due in May 1967. The apartment wouldn't hack it, so we bought a lot in El Lago next door to astronaut Bill Anders and decided to build.

In those days a young Air Force captain's pay wasn't so great, but thanks to *Life* magazine we received a bonus. The original seven astronauts had negotiated a contract with *Life* that paid them five hundred thousand dollars per year for their stories. The contract automatically included any future astronauts, so now with fifty of us active, we were to get ten thousand dollars each per year. This was a major windfall and allowed us the resources to afford a house.

Through family friends, we met a young couple in Houston, Glenn and Suzanne House. Glenn was a struggling young architect, and he agreed to do our house plans in his spare time—for three hundred bucks. We had seen a home in Atlanta that we had liked—a Williamsburg-type, so he designed something similar to what we liked. Dotty had lots of ideas on the interior details.

Meanwhile I was occupied with my work at NASA. Training started out with four months of academic studies, focusing on such subjects as orbital mechanics and spacecraft systems. We also studied the major constellations and stars needed to navigate in *Apollo* and took periodic trips to the University of North Carolina Morehead Planetarium.

In addition we began an extensive course in geology. NASA reasoned that if we were going to the moon, we ought to know what kind of rocks to pick up. None of us were real geologists. I could tell you the difference between a rock and clod of dirt, but that was about it.

Our geology instructors were some of the finest, consisting of professors from the top universities and ones who were experts in fieldwork. These same geologists later helped determine where the lunar landings should take place. A great many of them worked for the U.S. Geological Service and were based at an astro-geological laboratory in Flagstaff, Arizona. They commenced to make us into what I would call semiprofessional geologists. By the end of all my training, I had the equivalent of a master's degree.

Our geology course began with a couple of months of classroom work, learning the basic terms, and understanding the different ages of rocks. You can't learn geology just by studying a book, so we took a lot of field trips; in fact almost every three months there was a training exercise. The object wasn't to turn us into mineral or petroleum geologists, but to become field geologists who could accurately describe our environment in such a manner that 240,000 miles away on earth, the real geologists could gain a mental picture of the things we were seeing and collecting.

At first we thought of our field trips in terms of, "Ho hum, let's go out and look at some rocks." We soon learned that such trips can be demanding exercises. Though there were side benefits to be enjoyed by virtue of some of the locations that we visited, we worked hard.

Our first trip took place in the middle of June 1966 and was a hike to the bottom of the Grand Canyon. When Dotty and I had visited the canyon several years earlier, we had ridden mules from the north rim. This walk was to start from the south rim. Vertically, it's a mile to the bottom, so the walk must have been at least ten miles of zigging and zagging down along the side of the canyon. That's a long walk. Fortunately it's downhill the whole way. We passed through a whole sequence of geological formations—sandstones, limestones, shales, and so on, which comprise the geological column of the western United States.

It took us all day to reach the bottom, and by the time we got there most of us had feet that were just one big blister. My flying boots really didn't double as hiking boots.

Blisters and all, it was great to have arrived. I was surprised to find a virtual oasis of cottonwood trees and a grassy meadow in the bottom of the canyon. There was a little footbridge that crossed the Colorado River, and on the north bank lay a place called Phantom Ranch where we were to camp.

We were all ready to jump into the river to cool off, then were delighted to find that someone had been foresighted enough to bring some beer down for us to have a cool one. Once cleaned up and cooled down by a few beers, we enjoyed a hearty meal that had been prepared by the ranch staff.

It was a beautiful night—so we threw our sleeping bags on the ground and settled down to get some rest in preparation for the long climb back out of the canyon the following day. The moon was out and the walls of the canyon were silhouetted in its light. Lying in my sleeping bag, I was transfixed by this magnificent sight above me. I couldn't help wondering if one day I might actually set foot on that moon.

I was sleeping soundly when suddenly I awoke with a start! *Something ran over my sleeping bag!*

I sat up quietly and looked around. I don't know whether it was a male chasing a female or two males, but a pair of skunks were engaged in a big fight, running wildly about among our party of ten guys.

*We're really in trouble now,* I told myself. *If one skunk catches the other on top of our sleeping bags, we're going to get wiped out!* I stayed very still so that they wouldn't know I was awake. If I frightened them, they would surely have gassed us all. Eventually they ran off into the night.

Our next geology trip was to Bend, Oregon, a region which had experienced considerable volcanic activity in the past. It was generally believed that the moon was going to be volcanic, consequently much of our geology centered on volcanic areas.

In Bend it was summertime and hot as blue blazes; on top of that we were traveling in a bus that didn't have any air-conditioning. When we arrived at a spot, we would study the geology of the volcano—cinder cones, cinder fields, and lava flows—then we would return to the heat of the bus. We noticed that every time we stopped, two men would pull up in a big Lincoln, get out of their car and follow us. Then when we'd get back into our bus, they would get back into their air-conditioned car and tail us to the next place.

After a half day of this, Stu Roosa, Joe Engle, and I could stand it no longer and went up and introduced ourselves. Their names were Bob Perkins and Phil Waters from Coos Bay, Oregon, a town about three hundred miles away. Phil had a radio station and Bob owned a motel called the Timber Inn. They had read in the newspaper that we were going to be in the Bend area and, because they had a keen interest in the space program, had decided to come over and watch us. From that point on, Stu, Joe, and I got to ride in the backseat of that air-conditioned Lincoln. This chance meeting in 1966 led to a close friendship, and I count both men as two of my very good friends.

For our third geology trip during that first summer at NASA, we went to Alaska. We first flew to Anchorage, then boarded Alaskan Airlines and flew out to the end of the Katmai Peninsula. Here we climbed aboard an amphibian plane, a twin-engine Grumman Goose. It was a typical bush plane. There were no aircraft seats or seat belts, just an old sofa to sit on! The outside didn't look any better.

The pilot was an old, crusty, bush pilot who was anxious to show these astronauts how to fly. He started the engines, and without any checkout fire-walled the throttles and we were airborne. For the entire half-hour flight, he never climbed above fifty feet.

"Look at that bear!" he yelled back to us as he banked and headed after a huge Alaskan brown. I felt the guy was crazy but had to admit he was a fantastic pilot. After chasing the bear, he peeled off and finally landed on a lake near the mouth of the Brooks River. This was to be our base.

It was late August and at this time of year, there were only about four hours of darkness. Since it became light very early in the mornings, some of us decided to rise early to go fishing. Unfortunately we had missed the salmon run; they had spawned and were now dying—the Brooks River was full of dying red salmon. But the trout were biting well.

One morning I was wading in my favorite spot, when I looked up and noticed just ten yards from me was this *humongous* bear. He sat there staring at me, and so I just stared back at him. But when he grunted, I figured that I was in his fishing spot and wasn't about to argue, so I hurriedly backed away to go on down the river to a new spot.

As I was backing up, I accidentally stepped into a hole, instantly filling my waders with water. The river was swift and knocked me over, and I began tumbling in the current. *I just missed getting eaten by a bear and now I'm gonna drown,* I thought. *This ain't my day!* I finally recovered my balance, but was soaking wet in the ice water. That ended my fishing for the day.

The geology in this area of Alaska was fascinating. A huge volcano had blown its top either in the 1800s or around the turn of the century and had left hundreds of feet of ash and mud which had solidified. We chose this area because we thought we might encounter something similar on the moon.

All this time we were continuing our classes in spacecraft systems—*Apollo* guidance and navigation systems which I had worked on at MIT, propulsion systems, electrical systems—the many systems that keep the spacecraft operating. The courses we took were very interesting, and it was exciting to be part of that training every day. By the end of the summer, general academics came to an end, but occasionally we would have a week's worth of classroom training on geology. And we continued our field trips up until the time we launched.

We were also called upon to work on the final *Gemini* missions. This was a busy time in 1967—with *Gemini* flights in June, July, September, and November. At the same time the *Apollo* command module was being built, lunar modules were being made and checked out, and the basic understanding of the *Apollo* mission was being completed. Training was already underway for the first *Apollo* mission to be manned by Grissom, White, and Chaffe.

Part of the purpose of these last *Gemini* missions was to develop and hone to precision the rendezvous techniques needed for *Apollo*.

I was given an assignment on the flight control team for the last two *Gemini* flights. My title was booster systems operator, or something to that effect; it was an assistant position in the area of the Titan boosters. I assisted in the simulations that went into flight training, got to meet a lot of the flight control team, and then at lift-off was part of the team in Mission Control.

Even though my job was over after the first ten minutes of flight, it gave me a feel for Mission Control and appreciation of the important job these dedicated engineers performed. This was the first of many assignments in the trenches at the mission operations control room.

The first flight I worked on was *Gemini XI*. It flew in September 1967 and its crew was Pete Conrad and Dick Gordon. *Gemini XI* lasted three days; its main purpose was rendezvous with one of the Agena target vehicles, which had been placed into orbit for practicing rendezvous.

The atmosphere in Mission Control is one of intense concentration and professionalism. There are moments of frivolity when you can relax a little, but only when all is going well. In *Gemini*, the mission operations control room had five rows of consoles, arranged in theater style so that the back row could see the screens at the front of the room. The rows were called trenches and I was in the first trench, lower left side.

I remember I got very tense as I sat there, listening to the countdown for lift-off of *Gemini XI*, and imagined how the crew must be feeling. My team was responsible for a delicate time of the mission—we had to monitor the pressures and temperatures of the propellants. Things could go wrong in a hurry, so we had to be on top of the situation. Well, launch went well, and I breathed a big sigh of relief.

It was a tremendous thrill to be a part of the team. You almost felt like you were airborne with the crew. You had so much information at your fingertips and knew exactly what was going on. Once the booster shut down and the spacecraft was in orbit, my job was over. I performed the same job on *Gemini XII,* the last of the *Gemini* series. As they entered orbit, I thought, *Now it's on to the moon.*

In Mission Control, splashdown was pandemonium! Everybody cheered and clapped and waved American flags. And out of nowhere, fine cigars would appear and everybody would light up. It was like the birth of a baby—everybody was happy and congratulating one another and puffing on their cigars. You lit up whether you smoked or not, just to celebrate the successful completion of the mission. I hated cigars but puffed away to be one of the gang.

When everyone had completed their postsplash reports, the whole team would turn out for a big party to celebrate the end of the flight. In fact the whole NASA community celebrated. We consumed beer and booze like rocket engines gulping fuel.

After the crews got back and finished their debriefing and official visits, the astronaut office would hold what we called the pin party. These parties were astronauts and wives only—no one else was allowed.

The people responsible for the party were the backup crew. They would arrange for a private ballroom at one of the local motels and would organize the whole deal, including the entertainment, which was usually a funny skit meant to poke fun at the prime crew and their inevitable foulups in simulations and other phases of training. It was also the occasion for the prime crew to give out accolades and mementos to the backup and support crews who had helped on their mission.

Then if this had been the first flight for one of the prime crewmen, with great ceremony he would exchange his silver astronaut pin for a gold pin— the symbol of a "real" astronaut. The pin looked like a shooting star with a circle around the tail. It was always a proud moment for that rookie astronaut to get his gold pin at the pin party.

After the first four months of formal training, our group of nineteen were assigned engineering jobs. Stu Roosa and I were given the task of watching over the development of the *Apollo* Saturn V launch vehicle. This meant we traveled frequently to the Marshall Space Flight Center at Huntsville, Alabama, where the engineering and management responsibilities were under the control of Dr. Wernher von Braun

Frank Borman was the astronaut in charge of the whole area of propulsion systems, and Stu and I were placed under his leadership. It was great working with Stu. We had become close friends at Edwards when we were in the same class at test pilot school. In addition I was assigned the task for monitoring the lunar module propulsion systems.

*Apollo* was designed to utilize two spacecrafts. The lunar module with two men on board would attempt to land on the moon, while the command module would orbit the moon with one man. A series of flights had been planned—commencing with *Apollo 1* in January 1967; this was to be an earth orbital mission. Following a series of developmental flights, the first lunar landing was scheduled for the summer of 1969. If this failed, we would still have another go at it before 1970 arrived, therefore achieving President Kennedy's goal which had been set back in 1961.

The whole schedule got torpedoed in January 1967. During a countdown demonstration test for *Apollo 1,* there was a major fire in the *Apollo* spacecraft at the KSC (Kennedy Space Center), and Gus Grissom, Ed White, and Roger Chaffee were killed. Due to an electrical short, their spacecraft caught fire and they were asphyxiated.

The night of the fire I was in my hometown, receiving the Lancaster Jaycees Young Man of the Year Award. I was actually in the middle of my acceptance speech when I was called away from the microphone to be informed of the terrible news. It's hard to describe the shock and sense of loss which I experienced at this point. It was almost with tears that I walked back into the meeting, choked up and hardly able to talk, and announced the death of these three friends.

Of course everyone wanted to know what had gone wrong. I wasn't in possession of the facts, but I did know that the space program had suffered a tremendous setback. President Kennedy had committed the United States to landing a man on the moon by the end of 1969; this was our mandate from Congress. That evening with real sadness I told everybody, "Now it seems there is no way we are going to make it to the moon by 1970."

After the fire, it was as if the astronaut office was in a daze. I had been a pilot for almost ten years and had seen many friends killed in aircraft accidents, but this accident was different. How could it happen? The space program was invincible—no one was supposed to get killed in a spacecraft. I was devastated! What a blow to America's ego.

As I began to reflect on the accident, I realized that unlike fighter and test flying where you always felt you had a way out, there were some phases of spaceflight where no escape systems could operate. There were things that could happen to the spacecraft that you couldn't overcome. I knew if I dwelt on this I would become morbid in short order, so I drove those thoughts from my mind.

The attitude of—"Well, it's not going to happen to me" and "We've got to make sure it doesn't happen again"—was the one most of us took. Finally my desire to explore and my sense of adventure overcame any lingering doubts and fears that I might have had and within a few weeks, the shock of the deaths had passed, and it was full speed ahead.

Initially the belief was, "We're not going to make it by 1970; we'll never recover from this tragedy. The program schedule is dead in the water." But after the initial frustration and seemingly impossible hurdles were faced, it began to be, "Let's work like mad to make sure we get off on schedule. We've got to get this thing going again." Everyone at NASA came up to speed, as we plunged into the redesign of the command module. It was to be a major effort.

In total the Apollo program was grounded for almost two years. And there were no manned spaceflights over a period of two years from the last Gemini, *Gemini 12* in November 1966, to the first Apollo flight. *Apollo 1* had been scheduled for January 1967, but it didn't fly until October 1968, redesigned as *Apollo 7*.

Investigation of the fire and the decision-making process concerning redesign of components took a couple of months. As a result of the fire, the decision was made to redesign the command module hatch. The original spacecraft had an inward opening hatch. This is excellent during spaceflight for the pressure in the cabin firmly seals the hatch, preventing leaks. However in an emergency such as the fire, the command module overpressurized, making it impossible to open the hatch, and the crew was trapped. The new design was to be outward opening for rapid egress in a launchpad emergency. Other changes were also implemented, one of the most important being tighter management controls.

In addition NASA decided that a special committee be set up to review launch emergency procedures. Since Stu and I had been working on the Saturn vehicle and were as familiar with the operation at the Kennedy Space Center as anyone, we were selected to be the astronaut representatives on this committee, called the Emergency Egress Working Group.

Our task was to help redefine and develop procedures for escape on the pad so that this kind of tragedy wouldn't happen again. Over the next year we were very active, attending meetings weekly and developing new escape techniques and equipment.

Because of low morale and the concern for quality control following the fire, management recognized the increased need for a program to encourage esprit de corps. All along the astronauts had been periodically visiting the plants of contractors to give words of encouragement in order to improve productivity, safety, reliability, or whatever the need at that particular facility. Now these visits took on even greater importance.

NASA renamed the program the Manned Flight Awareness Program and developed an award system to recognize individuals at the various contractor companies who were doing an especially good job. Winners received a pin designed by the cartoonist Charles Schulz, which we called the Snoopy Award. This cute little pin showed Snoopy wearing a little spacesuit and helmet and a little life-support system. Top winners were promised a trip to Kennedy during launch. The program was very effective in motivating everyone to accomplish their tasks so that the Apollo goal could be realized.

Four hundred thousand people worked on the NASA space program, and while only three astronauts got to ride on the spacecraft, unless everybody did their job to the utmost of their ability, we weren't going to make it to the moon. Even though the part they worked on might seem insignificant, we knew full well that any little insignificant piece of equipment could be the difference between life and death.

I enjoyed these manned flight awareness visits for it allowed me the opportunity to meet people from janitors to packers, from engineers to managers, and from all levels of contractor and civil service involvement. We walked along the assembly lines and had meetings in cafeterias or wherever, in order to let each person know how important his job was. It was like being a cheerleader to spur everyone along.

Most of the people we talked with would never get to see a launch, and many of them really didn't understand the purpose of the component they were working on; they just knew it went into the spacecraft somewhere. Our job was to instill in them a consciousness that their jobs were important to the success of the space program—that it was a team effort.

Every one of those visits was beneficial—to the contractors and to the program. Attendance improved, absenteeism diminished, attention to detail, reliability, productivity and safety were all enhanced by our visits.

Another project that we did during those days to help promote the space program was to make public relations trips. The astronauts were sent out to speak at various functions and sell the NASA story. We called it being *in the barrel.*

When it was your turn in the barrel, you traveled for a week, wherever NASA wanted you to go, as their public spokesman. The number of requests for astronaut appearances was ten times more than we could fulfill, so it usually took congressional interest to get NASA to send us. Since Congress controlled the budget, we always obliged.

Astronauts were grand marshals in parades, speakers at planetariums, schools, conventions, you name it—we were there. Usually we had an opportunity to stress the value of the space program while thrilling everyone with the Gee Whiz of spaceflight.

For one of my times in the barrel, I was sent to Ocilla, Georgia, to participate in the Georgia Sweet Potato Festival. As was typical, I rode in their parade and was the featured speaker during their afternoon festivities. NASA sent along three large-scale exhibits which were displayed in the local auditorium. For a bonus I was given a big box of sweet potatoes to take home to Dotty; the best we have ever eaten. That was one stop in many places I visited over the next few years in the barrel.

Personally I enjoyed those trips. I'm a people person and I like meeting people. I also like selling a program I believe in, and I really believed in the space program. So it was a pleasure going out and selling it. Some of the other astronauts hated speaking and couldn't stand it when their time came up, but everyone pitched in, and once a year each astronaut was in the barrel for a week whether he wanted to be or not.

For our travel, we had a number of T-38s kept at Ellington Air Force Base. As astronauts, we did a lot of flying to maintain our proficiency and to get to all these various meetings around the country. Even though I missed the exciting test flying at Edwards, I loved every opportunity I got to fly the T-38. It was a fun machine, with spiffy performance and easy to fly.

While I was immersed in my job, Dotty was left the responsibility of building our new house. Glenn had completed the plans and we had chosen a local contractor. Finally in January, after much delay from a gully-washing rain, ground had been broken and the house begun. Since I was traveling so much, it was up to Dotty to supervise the building of the house.

She was under a lot of pressure. Being six months pregnant with our second child and chasing around after Charles, who was now in his terrible two's, just added to her stress. The builder tried to cut some corners, but she held his feet to the fire and things began to get very tense between the two of them. I was no help for I was gone the majority of the time.

The situation got so bad with the builder that while I was in Hawaii on a geology trip, he told her he was quitting and she could finish the house herself. She had no way of reaching me by phone to tell me we had lost our builder and what was she to do next. Fortunately by the time I got home, things had smoothed over and he was back on the job.

With the house half completed, on the first of May our second child, Tom, was born. Unlike Charles he was a full-term baby and chubby as a butterball. And whereas Charles was blond and blue-eyed, Tom had thick black hair and brown eyes. I was home for the delivery, but off on another trip as soon as Dotty and Tom got home from the hospital. My mom came out for a week to help out with Charles, but after that Dotty was on her own again.

It was a difficult time for her. She was recovering from delivery, had all the responsibilities of a new baby plus a very rambunctious two-year-old, and on top of that was making all the decisions during the final three months of completing the house.

I knew she was stressed, but so were we at the office. It wasn't a very sympathetic ear Dotty had when I came home—it was every man for himself. If I can do it, you can do it. "Just hang in there" was my response to her lament. That's what they had taught me at the Naval Academy. Finally in August, after much delay, we moved into our new home. At closing the builder was just as happy to end the deal as we were.

Dotty probably thought life would be more normal for our family once we moved in, but that wasn't to be. In fact the pressures just increased. During the summer and fall, we had two more fatal accidents in the astronaut office. Ed Givens, one of our group of nineteen, was killed in an automobile accident, and a few months later a plane crash took the life of another astronaut and friend, C. C. Williams. Funeral services came at a frequency that stunned everyone.

The years 1966 and 1967 had been a bad time for the astronauts—three killed in a fire, three killed in aircraft accidents, and one in a car accident! We seemed to be jinxed.

For a while everyone pulled a little closer together, mourning the loss of another life in the astronaut office. But the unspoken words of who might be next tended to create more barriers between husbands and wives instead of bringing families closer together. Of course you never thought it would happen to you; things like that just happened to the other guy.

With all these fatalities and the work overload of trying to get a man on the moon by 1970, marriages were strained in the whole NASA community. There had never been a divorce in the astronaut office. After all, we were the all-American guys—no one ever had any problems. It was thought that a divorce was death to your career and a chance to fly in space. But slowly and quietly the cracks were beginning to appear.

I increased my efforts at work determined to do as good a job as possible and let my marriage and family take a backseat. Little did I realize what consequences would come from that decision, and that the cracks forming in our marriage would bring us to near disaster.

# 10
## OVERCOMING PROBLEMS

Even though Dotty's life and mine were headed in two separate directions, things were progressing well with *Apollo*. In the months since the fire, the more we worked, the better it looked. By late summer 1967, people were more optimistic. A schedule had been established, and it looked like we could still make it to the moon on time and even have a few months' breathing room.

But then other problems began to surface. It seemed like one snag after another. *Will this thing never stop having problems?* I wondered.

A major difficulty NASA faced was with the *Apollo* lunar module ascent engine. Everything was going well with the descent engine, but the ascent engine, the engine that was to get us off of the moon, was not doing well in its qualification testing. The problem was combustion instability due to the engine injector design. The injector is the device through which the propellants are forced into the combustion chamber. There had been a number of failures.

In machines as complex as the *Apollo* spacecraft, it was expected that there would be technical difficulties, and the various crews were trained to work around these. But there was one system that could not fail—the lunar ascent engine! Once the astronauts were on the moon's surface, the only way off was through the successful firing of this engine.

So in August 1967, NASA Apollo Spacecraft Program Manager George Low formed a special committee to review the design of the ascent engine injector to determine if it was going to qualify or whether we needed to go with an alternate. Since I had been working all along on the Saturn and lunar propulsion systems area, I was asked to join the team as the flight crew representative.

When our committee started its investigation, NASA had already made the decision to hire an alternate contractor to have an ace in the hole. A backup injector would be needed, if the prime contractor's engine did not complete its tests properly. Many times our team traveled to the prime contractor, which was Bell Aerosystems in Buffalo, New York, and to the alternate contractor, Rocketdyne in California.

While we were assured by Bell Aerosystems that the problem could be remedied, I had a growing feeling of uneasiness about their injector. The more I studied the test results, the more uncertain I became of its ability to perform unfailingly.

In May 1968, decision time had come. George Low called us to a meeting in his office to discuss the various possibilities. Should we stay with Bell or go with Rocketdyne? Bell had been working on this design for five years, and time was rapidly running out. This injector was a major component, involving a very large contract, and to switch this late in the game was no small matter.

The discussion was quite lengthy and at the end, Low went around the room and asked each person how they felt and what they recommended we do. As each person responded, it became apparent the committee was leaning toward Rocketdyne. I was one of the last to speak.

"What does the crew think, Charlie? Which one would you rather ride? Which would you feel comfortable flying?"

As the astronaut assigned to this committee, I would be speaking with the authority of the astronaut office, so I did a lot of soul-searching before making my recommendation. I felt that if we stayed with the current system, there was a strong possibility that we would have a disaster which would shock the world. But if we went with the alternate contractor and the engine was not ready in time, we would miss making it to the moon by the end of the decade.

I knew that whatever the crew thought carried great weight, so I sensed that what I said would help swing it one way or the other. It seemed like all eyes were on me as I made my recommendation.

"I believe we should go with the alternate contractor. Rocketdyne has done a great job in the last few months—their design is solid, test data look good, and I believe we'll have a good engine."

After further debate, it was decided—we would use the Rocketdyne injector in the Bell engine and it would be assembled at Rocketdyne. History shows it was the right decision. We never had a moment's problem with the ascent engine in the lunar module.

This was the first time I was involved in a major decision that affected the spacecraft. I had been involved in other decisions—emergency procedures on the launchpad and guidance systems of the Saturn V, allowing the crew to manually fly into orbit—but this was a major engineering decision, and I was excited to be a part of it.

My participation was just an example of the total astronaut involvement in engineering design and development. While none of us were really responsible for the designs, we were key players in the development of the systems. Our opinions were highly valued from an operational standpoint.

Management wanted to make sure that from a crew perspective the systems would operate and were understandable.

At the same time that we were attempting to resolve our hardware problems, we were having to deal with problems of a totally different nature, but which were just as important to the success of the program. NASA was being attacked by politicians, scientists, and the press; articles were being published that were highly critical of the Apollo program, especially because of the fire and the deaths of the three astronauts.

Some people believed it was a big boondoggle and a total waste of money—money which should instead be spent on welfare or some other way. Others, in the scientific circles, felt that the manned program was sapping a lot of funds away from the unmanned flights, most of which were set to explore deep space—Venus, Uranus, Mars, and other planets. These programs had taken back burner to all the hoopla of manned flight, and people were jealous.

Then there were many scientists who thought we could get the same return for a cheaper investment by sending unmanned vehicles to the moon. I vigorously defended manned spaceflight. For two very important reasons I believe man is an essential element in space exploration. First of all man is an adaptive control system, one that can adjust to unexpected circumstances and bring about mission success in the face of failure, whereas a machine could come up against unprogrammed anomalies and not be able to work around them.

The second reason is more intangible—it has to do with man's psyche. Mankind wants to experience this adventure through another man's eyes. The sense of adventure and interest is greater with a human on board than with a robot. We can personally identify with a man challenging the heights, not a machine.

In spite of all the problems, NASA continued to move forward and the time came for the first unmanned launch of the big new Saturn V rocket. The previous Gemini missions had all flown on Titan rockets. These were intercontinental ballistic missiles modified for manned flight. Apollo, with its millions of pounds of fuel necessary to reach the moon, needed a much larger vehicle. The Saturn V and its companion the Saturn IB were the first vehicles designed from the start to carry men into orbit.

Dotty and I, along with most of the astronaut office, flew down to the Cape to view this historic launch. Everything had to work from here on out if we were to make a 1969 landing. It was one of the most impressive experiences that I've ever had.

On November 9, 1967, we watched this enormous Saturn V ignite and lift off, trailing a white plume of flame many times longer than the vehicle. By the time the spacecraft had left the pad, the sound of the engines had reached the viewing area three miles away. It was a deafening roar, and you could even feel the sound as the air and ground reverberated around us.

Those five Saturn engines were enormous—each producing a million and half pounds of thrust—each with fuel lines thirty inches in diameter! They were gulping down fuel and oxygen in tons per second. It was the largest rocket that had ever been launched and to be there and watch the first one go off was a great thrill.

This launch was the culmination of years of dreams and hard work. Many people had committed their time and energy to achieving this successful launch, and as our group of nineteen became more involved in Apollo, we became friends with some of these people who were the legends of the space program. A few were now NASA managers, but in the early days had been the pioneers that had gotten the whole program started.

One was Bob Gilruth, part of the original team from early Space Task Force days and now head of the NASA Manned Spacecraft Center. He was a great administrator and a highly qualified engineer. I loved his management style, which was easygoing yet direct and honest.

Dr. Gilruth was a warm, kindly man—like a gentle Daddy Warbucks. In fact he sort of looked like him—balding with a little bit of gray hair on the sides of his head. He usually wore a beige Stetson and always had a smile. He was like a father figure, someone I could go and talk with about any problem on Apollo. I knew he would listen, and, if he felt like I had a good case, do something about it.

Then there was Chris Kraft, who at this time was the Director of Flight Operations and in charge of the mission control team and mission planning. His mission control teams had supervised every manned flight and were true professionals. If anyone could get us to the moon and back, it was Chris Kraft.

Since Stu Roosa and I were working on the Saturn V and monitoring its development, I got to know the people at the Marshall and Kennedy Space Centers. I was really impressed with Dr. Wernher von Braun, the Director of the Marshall Space Flight Center, Alabama, and Kurt Debus, Director of the Kennedy Space Center, Florida. Under their leadership this Saturn V, one of the world's most complex machines, had been successfully built, tested, and launched into space.

Wernher von Braun and Debus were old friends from Germany and had worked together on the German missile programs. They were the developers of the V-2 in World War II and had years of experience in flying rockets. At the conclusion of the war, they were brought to America to work on our rocket program.

The first time I met von Braun was at Marshall, where I had gone to attend a Saturn V design review. I was immediately taken by his commanding physical appearance, very dignified and much like a college professor. Then after hearing him speak, I was filled with deep admiration for his technical abilities. He probably had more corporate knowledge of flying rockets than any person alive at the time.

The date was now set for the first manned launch of Apollo, renamed *Apollo 7*. Lift-off would be in the fall of 1968. Although this mission wasn't to use the big Saturn V, since the astronauts would remain in earth orbit, this was to be the first flight of the newly designed command module. The crew of this first Apollo flight was Wally Schirra, Don Eisle, and Walt Cunningham.

As the time approached, I could feel the tensions beginning to build in the astronaut office. Wally helped lighten the air with his one-liners, which we called the Schirra gotcha's. He loved practical jokes and was always involved in something to help boost morale.

On October 11, 1968, the day of the *Apollo 7* lift-off, tension was max. It was all business at the space centers in Houston and Kennedy; not that we were so concerned for the astronauts' safety—everyone had a positive attitude about that—but just that this thing had to work or we were in deep trouble schedulewise. Everyone was hoping for a good flight. Fortunately everything went well, and all mission objectives were accomplished. The Apollo spacecraft passed with flying colors.

It was the first time a TV camera was taken on board and the crew gave a great space show, cracking jokes and demonstrating zero gravity. But for some reason they all caught colds and used up their supply of Actifed. This was to be the beginning of many medical problems on Apollo flights and gave birth to the astronaut Actifed commercials.

NASA had decided that if *Apollo 7* was successful, the second Apollo flight would be sent on a lunar orbit mission. It was a risky decision to go into deep space and orbit the moon this early in Apollo, but it was a bold stroke to add impetus to the program. Things were progressing well, and, with all things considered, it seemed the best choice to make.

Launch was set for December 1968. The Duke family had been very excited when our next-door neighbor, Bill Anders, was selected to be on the prime crew along with Jim Lovell and Frank Borman. Jim and Frank were also good friends, as I had worked on projects with both of them; so even though I wasn't part of the team, I felt close to the *Apollo 8* mission.

On December 21, Dotty and I were back in the viewing stands at Kennedy to watch this first flight to the moon and the first manned launch of the Saturn V. There was a holiday spirit in harmony with the Christmas season. Everyone had a great deal of enthusiasm and excitement about this flight. No one seemed apprehensive. The attitude was all upbeat in spite of the inherent dangers; we were just glad to be on with the show

The launch went off fantastically and after the cheering had subsided, I jumped into my T-38 and flew back to Houston to spend the next couple of days in and out of Mission Control. The flight passed each major milestone, and things looked super.

Early Christmas Eve as *Apollo 8* approached the vicinity of the moon, I was in the Mission Control viewing area. The viewing room of Mission Control was packed to capacity. In fact it was standing room only, so many people had squeezed in to observe this tremendous event—the first human beings to orbit around another planetary body.

When the moon's sphere of influence began to accelerate the spacecraft toward its rendezvous, I began to worry. This was the first time any manned craft had approached the moon.

*Were the equations really accurate? Would they reach the correct orbit, or would they impact onto the moon's surface?* Question after question kept popping into my mind.

We were aiming for an orbital point sixty miles above an object that was almost 240,000 miles away. There wasn't much margin for error. The computers, the tracking—all said right on target—but, *What if we're off by just less than 1 percent. They would impact the surface instead of orbiting!*

When *Apollo 8* went around the back of the moon and we had LOS, it got very quiet in Mission Control. Even in the viewing area with no responsibility for the control of the mission, the tension was so thick you could cut it with a knife.

During the forty-five minutes *Apollo 8* was out of contact with earth, questions kept running through my mind. *Was the spacecraft on the correct trajectory? Did the burn go well? Would we have contact at the right time?* A burn was needed to slow the spacecraft down in order for it to enter lunar orbit.

I watched the clock count down to AOS (acquisition of signal). AOS . . . minus one minute. AOS . . . minus thirty seconds. *Would we hear them? Is it going to be successful?*

Right on—to the second—the Manned Spaceflight Network communications guys shouted, "AOS! We have a signal from the spacecraft!" Soon after that we heard the crew's voices as they announced that the burn had gone well.

Mission Control erupted with cheers, and everybody patted one another on the back! Even those of us who had nothing to do with the mission were taking congratulations from each other. It was really an exciting time, that early morning on Christmas Eve.

Then we all got quiet as the crew began to describe what the lunar surface looked like from orbital altitude. They were wild with enthusiasm and apparently bouncing off from window to window to get the best vantage point, as they described the different hues and colors and craters and rills and valleys and mountains.

They broke out the TV and started panning the camera around the moon's surface. We received the TV pictures back in Mission Control, but the resolution wasn't so hot and it looked like a big blob of black and white. Nevertheless we were all excited, and I know billions of people around the world were watching this first TV show from the moon.

Late that night the crew announced they had a special message for the world from lunar orbit. Each taking a turn they read, "In the beginning, God created the heaven and the earth. . . ." They were reading from the first ten verses of the Bible, the creation story from Genesis. ". . . And God saw that it was good."

It was a very moving moment on this special Christmas Eve. And the world was brought closer together as we listened to these words from Scripture read to us by Borman, Lovell, and Anders, and glimpsed a breathtaking view of the earth from moon orbit.

Following the success of *Apollo 8*'s voyage, *Apollo 9* was scheduled to take the newly built lunar module up for its maiden spaceflight. The lunar module had not yet flown in space, and it was necessary to begin checking it out in anticipation of the first moon landing. All was proceeding well— each new step being critical to the success of achieving our goal.

Two months after the flight of *Apollo 8,* on March 3, 1969, *Apollo 9* launched with the lunar module and put it through successful maneuvers of separation and docking. *Apollo 10* was now commissioned to test the lunar module around the moon.

I was really excited. *Apollo 10* was the first mission I was to be involved in as a crew member. In the summer of 1968, I, along with Joe Engle and Jim Irwin, had been assigned to the *Apollo 10* support crew. Tom Stafford, John Young, and Gene Cernan were in training as prime crew and the backups were Jim Lovell, Fred Haise, and Ken Mattingly.

Each Apollo flight was manned by three crews. The prime crew was to be the actual flight crew. The backup crew went through all the training and was ready to go if some mishap occurred to the prime crew. The support crew had no flight or training responsibilities but were responsible for taking the load off the prime crew in procedures development, spacecraft testing, and a whole pile of other tasks that had to be done before flight. We were the go-fers of the team.

My responsibility on support crew was to develop the lunar module checkout and activation procedures which would be utilized in lunar orbit before undocking. I believe the reason Tom selected me was because of my experience in the lunar module systems, especially the ascent and descent propulsion systems.

On this mission the crew were to enter lunar orbit, separate the lunar module from the command module, and verify all the procedures to be used up to the moment of descent for lunar landing. They would not attempt a landing. Their job was to check out all the techniques up to landing and then confirm the rendezvous scheme that would be used on the ascent from the lunar surface.

It was great working with *Apollo 10*. Being in the thick of things was a tremendous thrill for me and gave me a real sense of satisfaction. I didn't know whether this job would result in a flight crew assignment or not, but I knew I was getting close and so hit it with all the enthusiasm I could muster. I was given a relatively free hand in procedures development, and therefore gained a great deal of experience and confidence on the support crew.

To develop the lunar module activation procedures, I worked with a team of engineers who were lunar module experts. At first we had to work out everything on paper, because there were no simulators available to us—the *Apollo 9* crew had priority on those. It wasn't until after their mission in March 1969, that we were able to verify our procedures on the simulators. With the *Apollo 10* launch scheduled for May 1969, it was tight and therefore a busy time for us.

In addition I was selected to be one of the *Apollo 10* capsule communicators—the individual in the mission operations control room who talks to the spacecraft. Mission Control is a building full of people who are all directly involved in some aspect of the flight, and obviously it would not be feasible for each of them to talk to the crew. So information is funneled through a flight director who then authorizes which communications should be relayed to the crew by the CapCom.

The responsibility of CapCom required that I participate in a great many hours of flight simulations. In fact the whole Mission Control team spent hours simulating their portion of the flight.

I enjoyed working with Tom, John, and Gene. Tom was a take-charge type of guy and very decisive. He would take all of the inputs that were available to him on a certain situation, such as training or the flight profile, and quickly make a decision. Not only was Tom a very competent astronaut, but he also had a political flare. He was constantly on the telephone with a lot of things going. He was busier than a one-armed short-order cook.

Gene was the same way. In fact we used to tease them that we were going to install a phone in the lunar module simulator. It seemed like they had a thousand phone calls a day. John, on the other hand, was very laid back. He was a quiet individual who methodically mastered the command module systems and procedures.

Most of this final simulator training was done at the Kennedy Space Center, therefore I was spending a great deal of time in Florida. In order to see more of the family, I decided to take them to Cocoa Beach; it was April and a perfect time for them to swim and enjoy the sun. So about a month before launch, we packed the car with kids and our new dog, Booster, and drove from Houston to Cocoa Beach, renting an apartment right on the ocean next to the Holiday Inn.

Let me tell you about our great new dog. A year earlier Dotty and I had decided to get another dog for the family. This time we made a decision that we were not going to get a thoroughbred or pay any money for a dog; we wanted a mutt. All our lives growing up we had both owned mutts, and they had been good dogs, gentle and a joy to have—unlike our high-strung, thoroughbred Mickey.

When we saw an ad in the paper that said, "Come get free dog," we eagerly jumped in our car and drove over to see if one of these might become ours. There in a box were the mother, who looked like an English terrier, and five or six little puppies. One of the puppies was pitch black with a little white spot. He was the only male and the cutest, so we picked him. We gave him the name Booster, because I was working on the Saturn booster rockets.

Booster turned out to be a wonderful dog. He was really a Heinz 57, looking like a labrador in the head and feet with a dachshund's legs and body. Everyone teased us because he was so funny looking. They would ask, "What happened to your dog's legs?" It looked like he had forgotten to get in the leg line.

He went with us wherever we'd go. He had a special place in the car—on the floor of the front seat under Dotty's feet. In the years to come he flew in light aircraft, floated on an inner tube down the Guadalupe River, sped around in our little johnboat on Clear Lake, and attended all of the boys' baseball, football, and soccer games. Everyone knew and loved Booster—he was a very special dog.

Now Booster and all the family were together at Cocoa Beach. I enjoyed having the family there—being able to come home to a good meal and taking the boys out on the beach. Unfortunately right after we moved in, training for *Apollo 10* changed and I found myself flying back to Houston for weekly mission simulations in Mission Control. But the kids enjoyed the ocean, and we were seeing more of each other than if they had remained in Houston.

About a week before launch, the crowds began to arrive. Every motel was bursting with people and parties. There were at least three or four parties we were invited to every night. It was a real festive time with everyone seeing friends from around the country.

One of the most memorable affairs was one given by an oilman from Denver. He rented a huge yacht from Miami and sailed it up the Indian River to Cocoa Beach. All the guests were ferried out to the yacht in small boats and then wined and dined in first-class style.

Because I was to be CapCom at *Apollo 10*'s lift-off, I had to fly back to Houston the day before launch—but my parents had driven down from South Carolina and they, with Dotty and the boys, went out to the VIP viewing area where they watched the lift-off of *Apollo 10*. Charles was four and Tom two when they saw their first launch—too young to have any memory of this historic occasion. According to Dotty, they spent most of their time running around, hoping to see an alligator in the marshes at Kennedy.

While *Apollo 10* was still en route to the moon, the *Apollo 11* space vehicle was moved to pad 39A. *Apollo 11*'s designated mission was to attempt man's first landing on the moon. The goal of "landing a man on the moon and returning him safely to earth within this decade" was now looking like a real possibility.

The *Apollo 10* mission was flawless save for one wild unplanned maneuver in the lunar module. All eyes were now focused on *Apollo 11*.

The launch of *Apollo 11* was scheduled for July 16, only seven weeks after *Apollo 10* splashed down in the Pacific. This would give us six months before the end of the decade. Then to help ensure a successful landing within 1969, NASA scheduled launches every two months after that to take advantage of every possible opportunity.

Since we had never attempted a manned lunar landing before, there might be numerous unforeseen factors—even though thousands of man-hours had been expended trying to plan for every contingency. There was always a chance of difficulties arising during the flight of *Apollo 11*, which would mean that they would not be able to land. Therefore it was essential that *Apollo 11* get off as early as possible in order to give us a second chance with *Apollo 12*, and even a third with *Apollo 13*. No major failure could be tolerated.

Neil Armstrong, Buzz Aldrin, and Mike Collins were to be the crewmen of *Apollo 11*. Little did I know that I was going to have the opportunity to play a role in this mission, the most exciting venture in the history of man!

# 11
# "ONE GIANT LEAP"

"Charlie, can you help us on *Apollo 11*?"

It was the voice of Neil Armstrong, the man who had been selected to be the first person ever to set foot on the moon. I could hardly believe my ears.

"You bet!" I answered in shocked amazement.

"We'd like to use your experience in the lunar module activation procedures' development," Neil explained. "I guess you will also be CapCom for the lunar landing."

I was elated—What a thrill! What an honor and responsibility to be a member of the *Apollo 11* team. The eyes of the world were going to be on this first lunar landing. Something like five hundred million people would watch it live on TV, and I would be a part of the drama in Mission Control.

We worked hard in the control center for the two months leading up to the flight. Three shifts had to be trained so that Mission Control could be manned around the clock. It was necessary to do countless simulations to tune the system and train ourselves to be able to respond in an instant to any malfunction that could occur in actual flight. We went through every phase of the mission, but descent and landing got the most emphasis.

During these training sessions, the mission operations team was in the control center in Houston while the crew was in the simulator at Kennedy. Simulation engineers purposely designed malfunctions into the systems to test our skills. Suddenly lights would flash in the spacecraft and in Mission Control, indicating a problem. We had to master every emergency procedure and be innovative as we solved new problems. These sims were so real, it seemed like the flight was actually in progress.

As on previous flights, the *Apollo 11* crew selected names for their spacecraft—the command module was called *Columbia*, and *Eagle* was the name given for the lunar module. The mission patch showed an American eagle descending onto the surface of the moon and carrying an olive branch in its talons.

On July 16, 1969, launch day had finally arrived. My shift was not on duty, so I was able to be at Kennedy to attend the lift-off of this first landing on the moon. Dotty joined me, and we participated in a few of the parties and saw a lot of old friends. It was a thrill, and everyone from the astronaut office who could was there for this historic moment. After a flawless launch, I immediately flew back to Houston to man CapCom on the next shift.

Three days later the big day had arrived—the day that everyone had been working toward—the first landing on the moon! *Apollo 11* entered lunar orbit, and Neil and Buzz moved into the lunar module to power up and prepare for undocking and descent. I was in Mission Control as Cap-Com.

We were right on schedule with all systems go. The lunar module descent engine ignited, and the *Eagle* started on its way down to the surface. This was the first time such a maneuver had ever been attempted, so we were spring loaded for any problem.

I was relaying all pertinent info such as fuel state, trajectory analysis, and systems performance. Everything was looking good. A few minutes into the descent and just minutes before landing, the crew started to incorporate the landing radar data into the onboard computer's guidance equations.

*"Program Alarm,"* barked Neil. "It's a 1202!"

When I heard that I couldn't believe it. My first thought was, *What's a 1202?* We'd never seen a 1202 alarm in any of the simulations before. This was impossible—but there it was! The rules said that if there was a malfunction in the computer program, we were to *abort* the flight. The tension lever went off-scale high!

I took a quick glance at Steve Bales, who was responsible for the guidance and control system in the lunar module. He was looking rock solid as he analyzed this situation—Not a hint of panic.

Then almost instantly, he spun around and shouted to Flight Director Gene Kranz, *"GO,* we're GO on that alarm!" I heard the instruction and, without waiting on the word from Kranz, relayed it to the lunar module.

Steve Bales had remembered from somewhere that a 1202 alarm meant the computer is being called upon to do too many things at once and therefore is forced to postpone some of them. It was not an abort situation. Mission Control radioed a correction to the crew, who entered the procedure into the computer.

At three thousand feet, the computer flashed another alarm—"1201!" It was another overflow condition, another "GO" from Steve Bales, that I quickly relayed to the *Eagle*. There were two more warning lights—each one overruled by a "GO" from Bales.

As we got down to the last few hundred feet of descent, things were really hectic in Mission Control. People were checking their systems advising Flight Director Krantz, "It's GO"; I was relaying all this to the crew; everything looked good and go.

Then Neil started reporting landing site problems. At six thousand feet when Neil and Buzz saw their landing area for the first time, the *Eagle*'s automatic guidance system was taking them into a large number of big boulders! It would be an impossible place to land. Neil took manual control and maneuvered the craft over the rock field to an area which looked like a suitable landing site.

While Neil was trying to maneuver the *Eagle,* I continued to pass up all the information that was flowing to me at CapCom. About this time Deke Slayton, the Director of Flight Crew Operations, punched me in the side and said, "Charlie, shut up and let them land."

I got real quiet and except for a few essential check points stopped my running commentary with the lunar module. We all listened as Buzz gave information to Neil about altitude, rate of descent, and forward velocities.

"540 feet, down at 30 [feet per second] . . . down at 15 . . . 400 feet, down at 9 . . . forward . . . 350 feet, down at 4 . . . 300 feet, down 3½ . . . 47 forward . . . 1½ . . . 13 forward . . . 11 forward, coming down nicely . . ."

I began to get anxious. The manuevering was using up a lot of fuel, and the fuel state was becoming critical. They had to land quickly or we would reach an abort point in the mission. My next fuel call was 30 seconds, and they had to be on the ground before that 30 seconds had ended or my next call would be ABORT.

Buzz continued, "200 feet, 4½ down . . . 5½ down . . . 5 percent . . . 75 feet . . . 6 forward . . . lights on . . . down 2½ . . . 40 feet, down 2½, kicking up some dust . . . 30 feet, 2½ down . . . faint shadow . . . 4 forward . . . 4 forward . . . drifting to right a little . . . okay."

"Thirty seconds," I shouted.

"Contact light! Okay, engine stop . . . descent engine command override off." Right as I called thirty seconds, we heard Buzz say, "Contact!" At that point the lunar module landing probes touched the surface, turning on a blue light in the cockpit, and Neil shut the engine down.

"We copy you down, *Eagle*!" I cheered.

"Roger. Tranquility Base here. The *Eagle* has landed!"

"Roger, Tranquility. We copy you on the ground. You've got a bunch of

*113*

guys about to turn blue! We're breathing again! Thanks a lot!'' I sank back into my chair, took a deep breath and looked at Deke—we were grinning from ear to ear. This was my greatest experience, until I had the opportunity to land on the moon myself almost three years later.

By this time there were great shouts, and clapping erupting from everyone in Mission Control. Gene Kranz got order very quickly and said, ''All right you guys, settle down. Let's get back to work. There's a lot we've still got to monitor to make sure that we are go on the spacecraft.''

Instantly we got back to our consoles. All I could think was, *Boy, that was close.* We were within thirty seconds of aborting due to the low fuel state, yet the crew and the ground had pulled it off in a very professional manner. All the training and practice had paid off. We were able to weather the storm of problems without a hint of panic.

The *Eagle*'s stay went perfectly. Millions of people all over the world watched as Neil took man's first step on the lunar surface—''That's one small step for man, one giant leap for mankind.''

The enormity of this achievement hit me later when I began to reflect that this feat had occurred less than ten years after the first man had gone into space. It was a tremendous accomplishment and the culmination of years of planning and training and managing. All of us felt a great sense of pride and fulfillment to have been a part of this flight. Everyone was popping their buttons, our chests were so swelled with pride.

After the *Apollo 11* crew returned to Houston, all the astronauts were invited to a postflight debriefing at the Lunar Receiving Lab. This was the facility at the NASA Manned Spacecraft Center where all the moon rocks were brought for inspection and cataloging, and where the crew was kept for a three-week quarantine following their mission. The quarantine was established as a precaution to safeguard the human race from any potential problems from ''moon bugs'' or strange diseases that might be brought back from outer space.

At the debriefing, Neil, Mike, and Buzz sat behind a plate-glass window in the quarantine facility, while the rest of us assembled in a room on the other side. This was an opportunity for us to ask the crew any questions we had concerning the flight.

When the debriefing was completed, Deke Slayton got up and began to review the next few missions. We already knew Pete Conrad, Al Bean, and Dick Gordon were to fly on *Apollo 12*, but the *Apollo 13* crew had not yet been announced.

''*Apollo 13* will be Jim Lovell, Fred Haise, and Ken Mattingly,'' Deke said. ''The backup crew will be John Young, Charlie Duke, and Jack Swigert.''

"Hot dog!" Was I excited!! Not only was I to be on a crew, but I was to be *lunar module pilot!*

I had heard a rumor that I was to be on the *Apollo 13* backup, but as command module pilot. The command module pilot doesn't get to land on the moon but remains in orbit. Instead Deke was announcing that I was to be the backup lunar module pilot and as backup crew to *Apollo 13*, normal rotation called for us to be the prime crew of *Apollo 16!*

I knew that if all went well, and I didn't break a leg, and they didn't cancel the program, *John and I were going to land on the moon!*

I wish I knew how an astronaut is selected for a crew, but it is probably one of NASA's best-kept secrets. There are no tests or interviews, just a simple straightforward announcement that you have been chosen. I do believe that part of the process is that the director of flight crew operations would select the commander, and then together they would select the rest of the crew.

Once a crew had been agreed upon, the names would be sent to the director of the Manned Spacecraft Center. If he approved, the names were then forwarded to NASA headquarters in Washington, D.C. I never heard of a selection being overruled, but if it was, it was done before any announcements were made.

From July 1969 on, I was involved in training full time with *Apollo 13*. The backup crew had to be ready to go if anything happened to prevent the prime crew from flying. The launch date was originally scheduled for late 1969, but since *Apollo 11* had made a successful landing, the program was stretched and *Apollo 13* was reset for April 1970.

We continued our geology trips, practiced the lunar surface activities, did simulator training in both the command and lunar modules, and a host of other activities. We had to memorize all the procedures for our scientific experiments and documentation of lunar samples. Hundreds of hours were spent in training, not only in shirtsleeve environment but also in spacesuits.

On the prime crew were Jim "Shakey" Lovell, Fred Haise, and Ken Mattingly. Jim had flown in Gemini twice; this was to be his second flight in Apollo, having flown earlier on *Apollo 8*. Ken and Fred were both contemporaries of mine and had not yet flown in space. Ken was a Navy pilot and Fred a former civilian test pilot.

Backup was John, Jack Swigert, and me. I had gotten to know John well, having worked with him on *Apollo 10,* and I was delighted to be a part of his crew. Jack was another contemporary from our original nineteen. He was a happy-go-lucky bachelor—always looking for a party and a good time, yet a hard worker and competent pilot.

At the very last moment a week before launch, when the docs discovered I had caught the measles and had exposed them to the crew, Ken was replaced by Jack and Jack flew instead on *Apollo 13*. This was the first time someone on backup crew flew in place of a prime crew member.

When *Apollo 13* launched on April 11, 1970, I was still at home sick and watched the launch on TV with the family. I was feeling very badly about all of the problems I had caused with the change of crew. Well, the mission proceeded according to plan. Then all of a sudden at fifty-five hours into the flight, on April 13, the crew heard a *thump* and felt the whole vehicle shake violently!

"Houston, we've had a problem," said Jim, amazingly calm. "We've had a main bus B disconnect." A bus disconnect is complete loss of electrical power to half the spacecraft. It turned out to be more than a problem. It was a potential catastrophe!

I was home when I heard this announcement, and sick or not I knew I had to go to Mission Control to assist in any way I could. They were in deep trouble and John, Ken, and I not only knew the mission, but understood what the crew was thinking and how they would respond. So I quickly got dressed and spent the next thirty-five hours assisting in any way I could, developing procedures, time lines, and maneuvers to get them safely back to earth.

Ken never talked about his feelings, but I think during this time of emergency he really felt he should have been there, so he worked doubly hard to come up with the solutions that would bring them back. It must have been sort of the feeling of a commander that has sent his army to war and had to stay home because he'd gotten sick.

The thump heard by the crew and the vibration they felt had been a liquid oxygen tank explosion. A heater in the tank had failed and caused the tank to overpressurize. The relief valve could not keep up with the increasing pressure, so the tank exploded. For such events Apollo was designed with redundant systems, having basically two of everything, so there was another oxygen tank. Unfortunately, debris from the exploding tank had severed the line to the other tank, and all that oxygen was lost, too.

With the loss of oxygen, the electrical power generators (the fuel cells) dropped off the line, because the electrical systems needed oxygen and hydrogen to generate power. This resulted in the main bus B warning, which was the first of many warning lights. Within minutes, the warning panel was lit up like a Christmas tree.

From the initial report—"Houston, we've had a problem"—things began to deteriorate rapidly and became a bucket of worms. The command module lost all normal power and was now operating on the reentry batteries, which had a maximum life of eight hours. Fortunately the command module was still attached to the lunar module, which had its own oxygen supply and electrical system, and this oxygen supply was designed to last four days, or approximately 96 hours on the moon.

But there was an upsetting predicament. It would take another 30 hours to get to the moon, where they could take advantage of the moon's gravity and swing around, then another 80 hours back to earth—a total of 110 hours. The spacecraft would run out of oxygen, and the crew would be lost in space! Things looked grim!

While the crew moved into the lunar module and prepared for their return to earth, the mood in Mission Control was one of impending doom, but that didn't stop us from functioning at our peak efficiency, trying to work out solutions to these problems. We wanted to make things last as long as possible, so that we could at least give them a fighting chance at reentry.

I wasn't one that was praying in those days, but I found out later that there were many people praying for the safety of the crew and for wisdom in these decisions that we had to make.

As the hours passed, things began to look better and better. The oxygen usage was less than we had anticipated and the swing around the moon was precise; no precious minutes were lost. Forty hours after the accident and with *Apollo 13* on its way home, we realized that they had it made unless we made some procedural foul-up. We began to breathe easier.

One possible foul-up could happen at reentry. The timing of separation from the lunar module, which had been their life support, was critical. John, Ken, and I manned the simulator working out these separation procedures and the proper time line necessary for the crew to perform. All these procedures, pages of them, were voiced to the crew.

After almost one hundred hours in the lunar module, the crew reentered the command ship to power up for reentry. There was some concern about the status of the entry batteries, and things really got tense as other problems arose and were overcome just in time.

The most critical was the alignment of the inertial platform used during reentry. Jack had difficulty finding the stars used in the alignment, and the crew barely got into the correct attitude in time. You can imagine how anxious we were during loss of communication, as the spacecraft hurtled through the atmosphere. Had they made the window? Would they burn up by coming in too steep, or instead skip out of the atmosphere and be lost in space forever?

When they came out of blackout, *wow*, a great cheer went up! And there was tremendous shouting everywhere, as the parachutes came out and *Apollo 13* splashed down safely in the Pacific. That night was one of the biggest and wildest splashdown parties we ever had.

President Nixon came to Houston to welcome the crew and gave them and the Mission Control team the Presidential Medal of Freedom, the highest peacetime award given by our country. The successful recovery of the *Apollo 13* crew was a tremendous example of teamwork by Mission Control, NASA contractors, and others.

The *Apollo 13* crew were disappointed that they didn't get to land on the moon, but they were thankful to be alive. Jack Swigert later called me Typhoid Mary, and Fred said it was all my fault—that my germs had caused it. Of course they were just teasing, but my measles did result in some new NASA procedures.

When I exposed the measles to the prime crew, NASA realized that there was a considerable risk of astronauts becoming sick during flight because of viruses contacted here on earth. We had already experienced colds, flu, and other illnesses in space. "Maybe we should have quarantine for three weeks before each mission," someone suggested.

So it was decided—*Apollo 14* would have three weeks of quarantine before the flight and three weeks following their return. The medical authorities were still not certain that the moon was free of all germs, although they had not seen any moon bugs from *Apollos 11* or *12*.

Fortunately after *Apollo 14*, it was decided that since there was no life whatsoever on the lunar surface, quarantine would no longer be required following splashdown. The *Apollo 14* crew had been stir crazy by the end of the two quarantine periods. They were the only crew to have three weeks of quarantine both before and after their flight. I was greatly relieved we didn't have to endure that.

# *12*
# *"SWEET SIXTEEN HAS ARRIVED!"*

*April 19, 1972—Translunar Space*

"Apollo Control, Houston at 66 hours, 16 minutes into the mission. We now show *Apollo 16* at 19,304 nautical miles away from the moon, and now traveling at a speed of 3,643 feet per second (2,484 miles per hour). Although we've had no conversations with them, our data here in Mission Control indicate the crew is awake, waking up on their own. We will stand by with the air-to-ground line up to pick up the conversations between the crew of *Apollo 16* and CapCom Hank Hartsfield, should it occur."

We were already up and working, in great anticipation of the busy day ahead of us. Today we would enter lunar orbit and fly within *eight* miles of the lunar surface!

Sleep last night had been fitful for me—each of us had awakened early. Not that we were nervous, but there was certainly an air of eager expectation.

As we began to prepare the breakfast meal, we took quick glances out the window to watch the approaching moon. It was growing in size tremendously. Only a crescent was bathed in sunlight, the rest was in the soft light of earthshine, the reflected light from the earth. This gave the moon a softness and yet an eeriness as the shadows tended to meld together into the dark gray of the lunar surface.

The spacecraft had been performing flawlessly for the last day, so we were looking forward to lunar orbit insertion with great confidence. There was nothing that would indicate we were going to have any problem whatsoever.

"We're ready to copy the menu now—food," broke in CapCom.

It was Ken's turn to give the vitals. "Okay, Henry. The Happy Gourmet says that on the commander you can delete the grits. On mine you can scratch the peaches, scrambled eggs, bacon squares, grits. And for Charlie, he's been good—he eats everything!"

CapCom Henry Hartsfield, who was also a southerner and lover of grits, chuckled. "Charlie, you're going to have to work on those guys about the grits."

Ken continued, "And you'll be happy to know that we shared our peaches with Casper. He ate just about as much of them as we did."

"Roger," replied Henry. "That sounds kind of like it didn't work out too well."

"There's a lot of peaches still on Casper's face, I'll tell you that," exclaimed Ken. "Like when you open that can, you get them all at once." We hadn't been too successful with the canned fruit, which was experimental food for the later skylab missions. Every time we opened a can, the contents exploded all over the place, making a mess in the spacecraft. It was tough getting it cleaned up, what with all the sticky syrup, but finally a wet towel did the trick.

The moon's gravity was pulling us now. When we had been in the earth's sphere of influence, which extended out about 206,000 miles, the spacecraft was constantly being slowed down by the earth's gravitational pull. Beyond this distance the moon's influence began to accelerate us, the crossover point coming at around sixty hours after lift-off.

As we drew closer to the moon, we began to prepare for LOI (lunar orbit insertion). Before this occurred we had to expose some experiments which Ken would be performing during lunar orbit; these were stored inside the service module in an area called the SIM BAY (scientific instrument module bay). Casper shuddered as we jettisoned the SIM BAY door. What a sight!—the sun reflecting off the door as it tumbled away into space.

At about seventy-four hours from lift-off, we got into position to make our burn into orbit around the moon. In order to enter lunar orbit it was necessary to slow down; we were going too fast. If we did not decelerate, the gravity of the moon would slingshot us back toward earth. We needed to burn retrograde for six minutes, fifteen seconds to slow us down and attain LOI.

Our spacecraft was now positioned in such a manner that when we ignited the engine, our velocity would decrease in the right direction to put us in the appropriate orbit. Our objective was to achieve an elliptical orbit around the moon that was 60 by 170 nautical miles. This meant 60 miles at its low point or perigee and 170 at its apogee or high point.

As we accelerated toward LOI, we observed our first lunar sunset. Unlike on earth where the sun set with beautiful gold and orange colors, in lunar orbit the sun simply disappeared. Now you see it; now you don't!

We were now in darkness, racing toward a huge object we couldn't see. We would be in LOS during the burn, so had to completely trust that the tracking network had put us in the correct trajectory. A trajectory error of .025 percent would splatter us all over the back side of the moon, but we had great faith in the pros of the flight control team, and so the thought of error never entered our minds.

"*Sixteen,* you're go for LOI," reported CapCom.

For the past hour, we had grown quieter and quieter as the tension began to mount. This was a big maneuver. If we blew it, the mission was lost and maybe our lives! I wasn't scared, but felt tight—like I was spring loaded.

"*Sixteen,* we're a couple minutes from LOS. See you on the next pass."

"Okay, we'll be there," said John confidently. Now we were on our own, out of contact with Houston, as the earth slid behind the moon—and only minutes from LOI.

*Ignition!* Twenty thousand pounds of thrust in the service module engine roared to life, and we decelerated into lunar orbit.

That six minutes seemed an eternity as we monitored the spacecraft performance. I was glued to the engine and electrical system gauges, while John watched the computer, and Ken eyed the flight instruments.

*Shutdown!* The computer issued the command right on schedule. We had indication of a perfect orbit, and Ken, John, and I sighed with relief. *Apollo 16* had just become the heaviest object ever placed in lunar orbit—over 100,000 pounds.

Almost immediately, we maneuvered the spacecraft to put our windows forward, so that we could see the surface of the moon when we came out of darkness. Then—*instant light!*—and we experienced our first sunrise!

There was the moon beneath us with its awesome beauty—*absolutely breathtaking*! A wave of pride swept over me as I looked at this far side of the moon unseen from earth; only the Apollo astronauts had seen this view. We were speechless! I wasn't prepared for this *incredible* sight.

Just sixty miles below us was desert upon desert upon desert of foreboding, barren, gray terrain. The surface was very mountainous and pockmarked with craters of various sizes and shapes. It was mostly gray in color, although some of the rocks were absolutely jet black. The back side was a lot rougher than I had imagined. There didn't appear to be a level place to land, and I was glad we didn't have to attempt a landing here.

As we glided silently across the surface of this stark landscape, I was reminded of the movie *2001: A Space Odyssey*. It was an eerie feeling, our spacecraft floating quietly across this lifeless terrain. There was no sound save for the hum of the inverters and the ECS fans.

Yet while it was lifeless and barren, there was a beauty about this wasteland. It was spectacular and I was nearly overwhelmed emotionally. I couldn't believe I was actually here, only miles above the moon. Our photographs pick up the barrenness and the craters and the hills, but they just don't capture the emotion that you have in real time.

The stillness was broken when simultaneously we each called out to the others, "Look at *this*! Look at *this*!" We began talking all at once, excited because we'd seen something especially interesting. We'd quickly float over to that window to look at this specially significant crater or ridgeline or fissure, and then float back to our own window.

Acquisition of signal came right on time, and this confirmed again that we'd had a successful burn.

"Hello, Houston," announced John. "Sweet *16* has arrived!"

"Roger, *16*. Copy you loud and clear."

"Pete," I exclaimed. "Super, double, fantastic burn! If you're ready, I'll give you a burn status report." (During LOS, Mission Control had a shift change and Don Peterson took over CapCom from Hank Hartsfield.)

"DELTA-TIG was 0-06:15.1 burn time plus 2803.9 DELTA-V; residuals, plus 0.2, minus 0, minus 0.1. DELTA-VC is minus 5.5; fuel, 376, OX, 371; 150 unbalance, decrease. Okay, at ignition, we got a momentary SPS light; then it went out," as we continued to give the report.

"Roger. Copy."

"And as you can see," said John, "we're in 170.4 by 58.3 according to the old computer, and that baby just rifled it right down the line. Everybody is looking out their window. Three guys, each got a window, staring at the ground. Boy, this has got to be the neatest way to make a living anybody's ever invented."

Then John asked, "How'd the S-IVB look?" Three days earlier when we separated from the third stage of the Saturn rocket, it had been placed on a trajectory to impact the front side of the moon, to act as a calibrated seismic impact experiment. This meant that when the S-IVB hit the moon, it would register on the seismic experiments already in place and would give us precise data to calibrate future meteorite impacts.

"It hasn't happened yet. It's about another nine minutes or so."

"I trust we're not getting there the same time it does." We didn't want to be in its way when it came zooming in for its crash landing.

"I trust," Don chuckled. "It's going to hit on the southwest corner of Reinhold." That crater was a long way from us. A little while later CapCom announced the the S-IVB had made impact, but we never were able to see it.

John, Ken, and I continued floating from window to window, describing everything we saw to Houston. "Pete, Tsiolkovsky out my window—it's a spectacular sight!" exclaimed Ken. "Looks like a marshmallow float—a central peak floating in the top of a hot chocolate. I tell you, all that time spent with Farouk really's going to pay off, because it does look like old home."

During our training, we had worked with a lunar geologist named Farouk El-Baz. He had given us photographs of our orbit track across the moon, and we had studied them for hours. We were really excited because we were seeing features that we recognized from the maps.

There was a set of variable-power binoculars on board that we could use to get an even more detailed picture of the lunar surface. But in zero gravity, we found we had difficulty holding steady enough to see on the high power setting, and we ended up using only about 10X magnification. Yet even that brought the surface very close, and we were able to see the smaller fissures, rilles, and rocks on the central peaks of the large craters. On this front side of the moon we were climbing to 170 miles altitude from our perigee of 59 miles.

We continued our running commentary to Mission Control.

"The submerged craters in Smythii remind me a lot of coral atolls."

"We're going to get a close-in picture of Humboldt here."

"We got Petavius with its central dome."

"Some of those central domes are exceptionally dark," said John, "and they have exceptionally dark material running down a white surface."

"And apparently this line of secondaries down here that cross the Mare of Icarus," I cracked, "gives you the impression that there have been a couple of great big chickens walking across there."

"That was courtesy of Charlie Duke, our airborne geologist and chicken farmer," laughed John. I was having a great time describing what we were seeing.

"Houston," I continued, "we're coming up on Theophilus now. Central peak's in the shadows, and as we approach the terminator, looking out toward the horizon, it really looks rugged."

Ken added, "In this lighting, you can see the crater Descartes, and it stands out much bigger than you would expect because of the low sun angle. And in fact I had to look in to my map in order to make sure that was what I was looking at."

We were approaching the terminator now, the divide between daylight and darkness on the surface of the moon. First the shadows began to get longer and longer, and this made for a very dramatic moonscape. Then at sunset the bright mountain peaks instantly disappeared and now we were looking at the surface of the moon in earthshine.

In earthshine the moon was pale blue and the shadows were subdued, much like a bright moonlit night on earth. This continued for a few minutes, until it began to get darker and darker with an approaching earthset. When the earth set, it was instantly dark and we couldn't see any of the lunar surface. But with earthset we did begin to see the stars. Stars don't look any different from the moon than they do from earth; they were just little dots of light as we looked at Scorpio, the Big Dipper, and the other constellations.

We were unable to see our landing site on this first revolution, because it was situated on the terminator and was still in darkness. We had to wait on our next revolution for the moon day to progress and the terminator to move westward, before we were able to identify the valley where we were to land.

When we came around the moon a second time, we were amazed at the amount of terminator movement. The first time around, Descartes just barely showed up as a crater, but now we could see it clearly and took pictures of the bright ray material that had been thrown from the site at the time of meteorite impact. Ken thought he saw Palmetto and Gator, two smaller craters that marked our landing site. He had studied the orbital maps a lot more than we had and was able to get a good view of our landing area.

But now we were approaching another critical maneuver, and we gave our full attention to the task at hand. At the end of this second revolution, we had to do another rocket burn to reduce our orbit from 170 miles over our landing site to about 8 to 10 miles. The DOI (descent orbit initiation) burn was a very sensitive maneuver and like the LOI burn, it was to be performed on the back side of the moon while we were out of radio contact with Houston.

The burn was to last 24 seconds. The problem was that if it lasted 26 seconds, just 2 seconds longer, we didn't lower our orbit to 8 miles, we would *impact* the moon! So the burn time had to be very accurate, and the performance of the engine was extremely critical.

As we approached this maneuver, you can imagine we double-checked everything. I had a stopwatch, John had a stopwatch, the computer had a clock, and there was also a digital clock in the spacecraft. Each of us was ready to manually shut the engine down should it burn over the allotted time.

"*Sixteen,* Houston. We're about two minutes from LOS."

"Roger. Two minutes from LOS," responded John to CapCom.

"About twelve from the burn," informed CapCom.

"Roger."

LOS began and we became very tense. We wanted to make sure this thing worked exactly right, since we would have no monitoring from Mission Control. Outside the spacecraft, it was total darkness, which only increased the drama we were feeling.

"DOI!" The burn started right on schedule, as the computer sent the ignition signal.

At twenty seconds I began counting, "Twenty . . . twenty-one . . . twenty-two." If I said twenty-five and the engine had not shut down automatically, Ken was going to stop it manually. We were going to let it burn only one second over. "Twenty-three . . . twenty-four . . . shut down!"

Fantastic! It shut down on schedule, and the computer said we were now in orbit 10.9 miles by 59 miles. But we had to verify that; there was no way to know for sure. We couldn't tell by just looking out the window, even though we had now entered daylight and could see the surface of the moon. Suppose we had a computer error or a sensing error and the engine actually overburned and lowered our orbit so that we were going to impact?

For verification, the plan was to put ourselves in bailout burn attitude and wait for AOS from Houston. The resumption of radio contact was one way to confirm our orbit; we knew what time we were supposed to reacquire signal, and any deviation in orbit would change that acquisition time. If we were late, it meant we had overburned and could be headed for impact.

Also Houston was prepared to track us for a few minutes to verify the orbit. It would not be precise, but it would be enough to say, "Yes, you're go" or "No, you're impact. Bail out!"

Right on time, we had acquisition of signal. Now the orbit was confirmed by two means. We waited for Houston to confirm what our computer was saying.

*"Apollo 16,* Houston. You're good on the short arc. You have a STAY, and we show you 59 by 10.7."

We had *made* it! We didn't need to bail out! Our elliptical orbit was near perfect. We all breathed a sigh of relief and began looking out the windows again.

"Henry, it feels like we're clipping the tops of the trees," Ken exclaimed.

It did feel like we were right down in the valleys. I couldn't believe how close we were to the surface. I'd had similar thrills flying low level up the canyons in the Sierra Nevada Mountains in California, at three hundred and four hundred miles per hour. But this topped that! We were rocketing across the surface at about three thousand miles per hour in this low orbit, with mountains and valley whizzing by. The mountain peaks and craters went by so fast, it gave you the same impression as looking out your car window at fence posts while traveling seventy miles per hour.

We updated the computer for tomorrow's activities, and then it was time for our eat period. While John and I ate, we passed food over to Ken who was still busy performing some experiments with his service module SIM BAY.

I continued to be concerned about my suit fitting for the lunar landing the next day, and so inquired of Houston, "Anybody thought any more about my suit?"

"We thought about it, and smoked it over," responded Houston, "and we kind of think maybe we ought to do nothing unless you have some real bad trouble tomorrow."

"Like if we can't get it zipped?" I asked incredulously.

"Can we use my pliers on it to pull the zipper closed?" questioned John.

"Talked with the suit people," replied CapCom, "and they don't want you using the pliers on the zippers."

I was really concerned, but Houston didn't seem too worried. They told me that Dave Scott on *Apollo 15* had lots of trouble fitting his suit in zero gravity too, but on the moon in one-sixth gravity he had had no problem at all. I made a decision then to take no chances. When we dressed in zero gravity for the lunar landing tomorrow, I was not going to wear all my undergarments in order to keep the bulk down. Houston agreed.

With that we went to sleep and tried to get some rest for the big day tomorrow. It was the day we had been working for—*our moon landing*! I was keyed up in anticipation of the next day's activities, so I took a sleeping pill before floating down under the couch.

"This is Apollo Control. We've lost radio contact now with the spacecraft as it passes behind the moon on the fourth revolution. The crew is scheduled to begin a nine hour rest period while on the back side of the moon, and we would expect to hear no further word from them until the end of that rest period."

# 13

# 16 TRAINING BEGINS

A moon landing doesn't just happen. The crew doesn't just simply show up the day of launch, put on their spacesuits, wave to the crowd, and launch to fame and fortune. Preparation for a particular flight entails many long hours of hard work. Training for the flight of *Apollo 16* took exactly two years.

With the splashdown of *Apollo 13,* John, Ken, and I immediately started into an intense schedule, even though the *16* flight and crew had not yet been officially announced. We were to spend the next two years working over sixty hours each week preparing for our lunar mission.

Following the flight of *Apollo 14* in February 1971, a backup crew joined us—Fred Haise as backup commander, Ed Mitchell as lunar module pilot, and Stu Roosa as command module pilot. All three had previously flown in space. Hank Hartsfield, Tony England, and Don Peterson were selected as our support crew and would also serve as CapCom.

Our mission was designated for a three-day stay on the moon. Up to then the crews had spent, at the most, only a day on the surface. This extended stay allowed for three excursions, and we would even carry a car, called the lunar rover, which would further our range of exploration. Our lunar module was modified to have more oxygen, more batteries, more water, more everything.

Since John and I were going to be the ones to land on the moon, we trained together for all phases of the flight. Because we trained so much together, we became very good friends. John and I were like the Bobbsey Twins. We knew what the other was thinking, just like brothers. We knew each other's mannerisms and idiosyncrasies, and strong and weak points.

John had a great sense of humor with a dry wit, like Will Rogers. He was always coming up with these one-liners that would stop you in your tracks, they were so hilarious. He was a brilliant engineer and had a tremendously keen mind, but he didn't appear that way. He acted more like Elmer Fudd, just a good old country boy who sort of shuffled around. He never gave the impression that he was a brilliant engineer.

In fact he liked to convey, for reasons unknown to me, that he was a klutz. He had a slow southern drawl and was sort of an aw-shucks kind of guy. He'd come into briefings and say, "Well, Ah guess it's 'bout time ta start. What're ya'll gonna tell us ta-day?" People who didn't know him were thrown off guard. You knew they were thinking, *Man, this guy's not so bright. He ought to be with* Ned and the First Reader, *instead of senior astronaut.*

But John's slow-motion movements and talk didn't affect his keen engineering mind. He had an uncanny knack for always asking the right questions. So when he began asking these very penetrating questions about this or that system or experiment or whatever, it didn't take the briefers long to realize that they had a real tiger by the tail.

While John and I were working on lunar activities, Ken was training by himself. Ken was a good balance for our crew. John and I were always the eternal optimists. When problems occurred, we would look at the bright side, while Ken would say, "Wait a minute; what if . . ." He was a what-if guy on everything. He looked at every conceivable scenario or possibility that could go wrong.

Since Ken was always looking for something to go wrong, he was ready to respond instantly in any emergency; he had already considered the alternative. He was very serious minded, a deep thinker, and added a lot to the crew. The three of us developed into an extremely cohesive team. Although I worked well with Ken, I never had an opportunity to develop as close a relationship with him as I did with John.

Our training covered basically three areas: practice in the simulators, geology, and lunar surface activity. The first year John and I concentrated on the development of the lunar rover and on geology, because we hadn't been assigned our lunar landing site. Also the Apollo experiments package that we were to use on the moon was still being finalized.

Occasionally we would get time in the simulators in Houston. They weren't the same caliber as the ones in Florida because they weren't kept in the latest configuration, but they were good enough to learn the basic systems and procedures. The *Apollo 15* crew had first claim, so the simulators were not our top priority.

Geology was a priority. John and I made it a rule that we would train at least one day a week on geology. Sometimes we combined two or three days for a field trip, traveling all over the world to geologically interesting places. We studied all types of rocks from Sudbury, Ontario, to Meteor Crater, Arizona. On every trip I would bring home a collection of the most interesting specimens and with great enthusiasm display them to Dotty and the boys, expecting the family to ooh and aaah over them.

There were olivine bombs from New Mexico—which looked like cannonballs, until you broke them open, exposing a matrix of beautiful green crystals. And then there were Pele's tears from Hawaii, my favorite—which were little pieces of black glass formed from molten lava that had been thrown high into the atmosphere and then taken the shape of teardrops as they cooled on the way down. These little shards were named after the Hawaiian goddess of fire and were very fragile and beautiful.

To be honest, the kids didn't get turned on by my rocks. They would look at them, nod, and run off to play. But Dotty was interested. In fact she got so interested in geology that she decided to enroll in a course at the local junior college.

This first year of training, the development of the lunar rover consumed a lot of our time. Originally our crew was to be the first to utilize the rover, so we assumed the responsibility of monitoring its development. We participated in many design reviews, especially as they related to the operational systems. Later the rover was rescheduled to *Apollo 15* for it first flight.

The first time I saw this moon buggy, I thought to myself, *This thing ain't gonna work!* It looked like a bunch of klutzes had designed it. But I was wrong—it turned out to be a tremendous machine. The only problem we had occurred on *Apollo 15* when the crew had a very difficult time fastening their seat belts. Other than that, the rover went through its entire three missions without a major change.

The rover was a battery-operated electric car with four-wheel drive. The batteries also powered the TV camera and navigational system. It had

*Charlie, 8 years old (on right), with twin brother, Bill, and parents in San Diego.*

*Charlie as a midshipman at Annapolis, in front of the chapel.*

*Dotty and Charlie's wedding picture, June 1, 1963, Atlanta, Georgia.*

*Preparing for a high altitude flight in a F104 at Edwards AFB, 1965.*

*Geology field trip near Taos, NM.*

*Zero G training aboard a KC-135, affectionately called "The Vomit Comet."*

*Charlie and John at Kennedy Space Center driving the Lunar Rover training vehicle.*

The Dukes at the base of the launch platform 39A the day after roll-out of Apollo 16.

*Two months before launch, the Duke family view Charlie's actual spacecraft in the "white room" on top of the launch pad. Left to right: Charlie, Tom, Charles, Dotty, Guenter Wendt.*

*Charlie, Ken Mattingly, and John Young at the second roll-out, February 9, 1972, Cape Kennedy.*

*Last spacesuit check at International Latex Corporation in Dover, Delaware.*

*Launch pad the evening before lift-off.*

*Family anxiously watching the first moments of lift-off.*

*April 16, 1972—Apollo 16 as it clears the launch tower.*

*Charlie saluting the flag with the LM, Orion, in the background.*

*Tom* (left) *and Charles looking at their daddy on the moon, on the special TV set up in the Duke's garage during the flight.*

*Charlie collecting lunar rocks on the rim of Plum Crater.*

Apollo 16 *moments before splashdown in the Pacific Ocean, April 27, 1972.*

*Charlie being helped out of the command module by Navy frogman, minutes after splashdown.*

*Dotty and neighbors welcome home Charlie at the Duke's house in El Lago, Texas.*

*The specially designed* Apollo 16 *patch.*

*Hometown parade during "Charlie Duke Day" Lancaster, South Carolina, May 1972.*

*Family photo Charlie left on the moon.*

*Copy of the family picture that was left on the moon; Charles, 7 (left), and Tom, 5 (right).*

*Family photo taken at home in 1986.*
Left to right: *Charles, Charlie, Tom, Dotty.*

two seats and looked a lot like a cross between a jeep and a golf cart. On the back end was a stowage area for our lunar samples and a place to carry the tools we would use during our surface exploration.

Each wheel had its individual electric motor, which meant you could even drive with one wheel if all the others went out. The outer part of the wheels was made of wire, like a piano wire. The inner part was a piece of flex steel that acted like a shock absorber.

To control the rover, we had a T-shaped handle that was positioned be--tween the two seats. To go forward, we pushed the handle forward; to stop, we pulled the handle back; to go left, we pulled the handle left; to go right, we pushed the handle right. The car was highly maneuverable with four-wheel drive and four-wheel steering. We had a turn radius of ten feet and could climb hills up to a 25-degree slope.

The rover was designed to fold up like a giant suitcase. It was stowed in a frame on the outside of the lunar module, and then once on the moon, through a series of pulleys and cranks, we could slowly lower the car to the ground. As it came out of its stowage area, the chassis would automatically open by spring action and the wheels unfold, so that when it reached the lunar surface it was completely assembled. Folded it was five feet long, unfolded ten feet.

Another phase of our training involved learning to operate in one-sixth and zero gravity. It was essential that we be at home in the zero gravity of space and the one-sixth gravity we would experience on the moon.

For this NASA utilized a Boeing 707. The forward area of the plane was stripped of all its regular seats and lined entirely with rubberized mats. Then special mock-ups of all of our lunar module gear were constructed to carry for use aboard the 707. We had different hardware for each flight since we couldn't carry all of the mock-ups at one time. To assist us we had technicians, instructors, photographers, and a doctor.

After takeoff and climb to altitude, the 707 would fly parabolas, which was like being on a continual roller coaster. The pilot would dive down, then pull up the nose to a 45-degree climb, and then push over. During the pushover, we would experience zero or one-sixth gravity depending on the rate at which we went over; then we would go into another dive and start all over again.

We dived, pulled up, and pushed over continually—each time experiencing either zero or one-sixth gravity for forty-second intervals. During these forty seconds we practiced walking, collecting rocks, and doing our experiments.

Harder on us than the zero gravity were the Gs we felt as we pulled out of each dive. As the pilot recovered at the end of a dive, we would experience 2½-times gravity. This meant that in our spacesuits we weighed around 900 pounds. To alert us, a bell would ring and two support technicians would grab us and slam us to the floor, since we were dressed in our spacesuits and weren't able to get into position on our own. It was like Kareem Abdul-Jabbar slam-dunking a basketball! That's the way I felt when I hit the floor. Then the 2½ Gs would flatten us as we spread eagled.

When the airplane reached the 45-degree climb and the Gs came off, I'd think, *Oh oh, here it comes again!* The bell would ring and then the same guys would flip us upright, so as not to waste any of the forty seconds. This made me feel like my eyeballs were spinning around like numbers on a slot machine. The technicians would hold us for a couple of seconds until we got everything caged and our equilibrium returned. Then we would start training again.

Some of the astronauts had iron stomachs and could do a couple of hundred parabolas, but my limit was always fifty-seven. When I'd had enough I'd yell, "Stop! That's it! One more and I'm going to throw up!" Then I'd ask the pilot, "How many did we do?" "Fifty-seven," he'd answer. We went up dozens of times, but every time when I called a halt it would be right on fifty-seven parabolas.

Everyone else had to hang in there—the crew was in charge, so we called the halts. I'll never forget one poor photographer who went on all the flights. Every time he got sick on the very first pushover, turning pea green and looking like a limp dishrag. We used to say he was "in the bag," as he'd be holding his camera in one hand while barfing in the other. If a crew did two hundred parabolas, he would be sick the entire two hundred!

Another way we practiced working in zero gravity was in a huge water tank. We were made to be neutrally buoyant, which meant our spacesuits were ballasted with weights so that we wouldn't float either up or down. This enabled us to work for an hour or two in conditions that were very close to zero gravity, but the airplane was the closest to the real thing.

Training was hard work, so we wanted to be in shape. NASA didn't have a set PT (physical training) program. No one said to you, "Here's the astronaut physical fitness routine for this week: Do one hundred push-ups and run two miles." The attitude of management was more a matter of, "Here's the gym. You're grown men. You know that you have to be in shape, and so do what you want in order to achieve that."

They provided us with an excellent facility and in the early days we had a physical training instructor, an Air Force sergeant named Joe Garino. I got together with Joe, and we came up with a program that would build my stamina. Most of the time I jogged, working my way up to two or three miles a day. I was never a speed-demon but averaged six and a half minutes per mile on a three-mile run. A few of the astronauts were down in the five-minute range, including Ken who was in marathon shape.

Some played handball, while others played racquetball, squash, or pedaled a bike. We could do as little or as much exercise as we wanted. One of the guys was quoted as saying, "The good Lord gave me only a certain number of heartbeats, and I'm not going to waste any of them exercising." He hardly ever came to the gym.

Finally the time had come to announce the launch date and crew of *Apollo 16,* and I anxiously awaited the press release from NASA. A lot of people had been kidding me, "Well, you'll never make it because you got the measles, and Typhoid Mary will kill off all the crews. They'll never pick you." I wasn't worried about that. But I was worried that there might not even be an *Apollo 16* mission.

There had been some comments in Washington that it was too risky to continue the moonflights. With *Apollo 13*'s near disaster—what might happen next? It was argued that since we had made two successful landings, we ought to quit while we were ahead, before we lost a crew on the moon. Much to our relief, wiser heads prevailed and it was decided to continue the program. Management did decide to cancel the last three proposed flights, *Apollo 18, 19,* and *20;* but primarily for budget.

On March 4, 1971, came the following announcement: "The space agency named the crews Wednesday for the *Apollo 16* mission to the moon, scheduled for launching next March. Navy Captain John W. Young, 40, will command the mission. It will be his fourth spaceflight. His command module pilot will be Navy Lieutenant Commander Thomas K. Mattingly II, 34, who was to have been the command module pilot on *Apollo 13.* The lunar module pilot for *Apollo 16,* who will explore the moon with Young, is Air Force Lieutenant Colonel Charles M. Duke, Jr., 35. He was the backup lunar module pilot of *Apollo 13.*"

I was really going to get to *fly!* I knew this would be the most exciting flight I'd ever make. To fly two of the finest machines ever built by man, to experience zero gravity, and to walk on the moon would be the experience of a lifetime. I was so excited I felt like I would explode.

Dotty, too, was thrilled and pleased that I had been selected. She was aware that many in our group were not going to get to fly on Apollo and, knowing how much it meant to me, she was glad I would have the opportunity to go. Our boys didn't have much reaction; I think they sort of expected it. Our neighbor, Bill Anders, had flown and so had so many others they knew. It was really no big deal to them.

Two of the proudest people were my parents. My mom and dad were patriotic Americans and faithful South Carolinians. They loved to brag about all their children, and made themselves available for every interview with the press. They both got personalized license plates for their cars—one said "Apollo 16," the other "Moon 16"—and they kept those plates for years, long after the flight was over.

At that time, I was the only astronaut from South Carolina, and so when the announcement came out the whole state—the politicians, the press, and especially my hometown—were all as proud as they could be.

My hometown paper, *The Lancaster News,* printed the story with a slightly prejudiced slant: "Lt. Colonel Charles M. Duke, Jr., of Lancaster and two other astronauts were named Wednesday by the U.S. space agency to fly the Apollo 16 lunar landing mission in March 1972."

Lancaster even had signs made—THIS IS THE HOME OF ASTRONAUT CHARLIE DUKE—and posted them at the city limits. A committee was formed to prepare for a Charlie Duke Day celebration on my return from the moon. It seemed as if everyone in Lancaster began to organize their schedules so they would be at Kennedy Space Center when their boy flew to the moon.

# 14

# *DRESS REHEARSAL*

"Let's invite all the family to the launch of *Apollo 15,*" I suggested to Dotty one day. "I can be with them to explain everything that's going on. It'll be like a dress rehearsal for *Apollo 16.*"

In July of 1971, I had the idea that it would be nice to have our parents, brothers, and sisters and their families experience the drama of lift-off before it actually happened on *Apollo 16.* Most everyone was able to come, and the trip really helped them have a deeper appreciation for Apollo and the activities of the astronauts.

First I arranged a special tour of the VAB (Vehicle Assembly Building) where the stages of *Apollo 16* were being stacked, one on top of the other, and the family was able to see and touch the big Saturn V rocket that I was to ride into orbit. Next I took them through the astronaut quarters, the simulator and other training areas, and they watched John and me as we practiced our lunar surface activities.

We also visited the main launchpad, 39A. The area was a beehive of activity preparing for lift-off, and while we couldn't get on the pad because of security, we were able to drive around the base and get a good view of *Apollo 15*. We did drive onto the adjacent pad, 39B, where I was able to show them the flame trenches and explain the major phases of countdown and lift-off.

The next day at launch, we all went together to the private astronaut viewing area, located on the Kennedy complex not far from the VIP stands. As the final minutes clicked away, I described what the crew was doing and what was happening in Launch Control. In the back of my mind, and probably in the back of everyone else's mind, was that at the next launch I would be on top of that beauty, heading for the moon. Lift-off was spectacular, and we cheered the spacecraft into orbit.

Now it was full speed ahead in our training for *Apollo 16*. Since we were the next up, we began to spend more time at Kennedy. John, Ken, and I got so familiar with the command and lunar modules, we could have flown them blindfolded.

As with each previous flight, we selected names for our spacecrafts. John and I considered a number of choices for the lunar module, ranging from ships to star constellations. For a while our first choice was Beagle, after an old sailing ship, but we rejected that since it sank on one of its voyages. "That may be a bad omen," we reasoned. We finally settled on *Orion* because it is a prominent constellation and easy to pronounce and transmit to Mission Control. For the command module Ken chose the name *Casper*, of Casper the Friendly Ghost cartoon character fame.

The lunar module was really an ungainly machine. At first sight I thought, *Man, that is the most horrible looking flying machine I've ever seen!* It didn't have a pointy nose or any wings. It didn't have a heat shield like the command module. It didn't have anything that looked like a plane, and it was built on Long Island, New York. I didn't think anybody above the Mason-Dixon line knew how to do anything.

I was wrong. I have flown twenty-two different models and types of aircraft in my Air Force career, and I quickly learned that the two spacecrafts I was to fly in Apollo were probably the finest flying machines I'd ever strap onto my rear-end. They were tremendously exciting. And even though these New Yorkers didn't talk like southerners, the engineers and technicians who worked on the lunar module at Grumman-Bethpage were some of the finest, most capable people I'd ever met. My prejudices were quickly dispelled when I saw their workmanship.

The lunar module was a unique design. It didn't have to operate in an atmosphere and didn't have to survive reentry at nearly 8 Gs. It was designed for one purpose in mind—to land two astronauts on the moon, to keep them alive while they were on the lunar surface, and then to return them safely to lunar orbit.

The LM was built with two stages, the descent stage and the ascent stage. The ascent stage contained the crew cabin and the engine to get us back into orbit once our lunar stay was complete. The descent stage contained the main engine, which provided the propulsion power for the lunar descent and landing. Then, other than being the storage area for our oxygen and electrical supply and other consumables, the descent stage had done its job.

The landing gear on the descent stage had four legs, which made the whole thing resemble a giant spider. To prevent the lunar module from sinking into the moon dust and tipping over, enormous plates were attached to the bottom of each leg. They looked like big saucers and enabled the weight of the lunar module to be distributed evenly across the surface of the pads at landing. On every moon mission, none of the modules sank more than an inch or two in the soft lunar soil. It was an expert design.

The descent stage was covered with what looked like Reynolds Wrap. Actually it was an orange material called Mylar, which was layered aluminum foil with insulating material inside. This provided protection from the heat of the sun and maintained the temperature of the interior of the descent stage.

Whereas the descent stage was heavy and sturdy looking, the ascent stage appeared fragile and weak. It was constructed of a lightweight aluminum, painted flat black and gray.

One day I was walking around the ascent stage and poked the side. It was like punching a beer can. I was really shocked how flimsy and fragile it seemed. *Hey, is this going to hold pressure?* This was to be our home on the moon for three days, and it had to maintain pressure to keep us alive, for we weren't planning on wearing our spacesuits while inside the spacecraft between moonwalks. Fortunately once the ascent stage pressurized, it became rigid and was a very secure vessel.

The crew cabin in the ascent stage was quite small. Two astronauts with all our gear on would barely fit in; there was only about twelve inches between us when we were fully suited. It was so crowded that we couldn't even get dressed at the same time. John would help me with my suit and backpack, and then I would assist him. With our backpacks on we couldn't even stand up straight—the packs hit the top of the cabin.

*Man, there's just no way we're going to get suited up in this thing,* I thought. But after one hundred hours of training, we had mastered the technique.

Once our spacesuits were off, it was very comfortable. John stood on the left side and I on the right, with the instrument panel in the front center. We each had a set of flight controls that enabled either of us to fly the machine.

There were no seats. Since the lunar module was designed for use in the zero gravity of lunar orbit and the one-sixth gravity of the moon, it was decided that we didn't need any seats. In orbit and during descent we would be anchored to the floor by a restraint system to keep us from floating around in zero gravity. Then on the lunar surface—since we would weigh so little, twenty-five pounds for me—we wouldn't get tired standing up.

There were two large triangular windows in the crew cabin, one on the right and one on the left, so that each crewman had a clear view looking forward. These were slightly larger than the front windshield of an automobile, providing us with quite a good view. Also there was a very small window, approximately six inches wide by a foot long, overhead the commander's station.

Now that we were the next crew to launch, we were able to have first crack at the simulators at Kennedy. NASA had redone the trainers into the configuration of our spacecraft and had been meticulous in keeping them exact, so that we would be familiar with our actual spaceship.

Everything was identical, right down to the fine details. The decals were all the same, the switches were all correct, the instruments were identical, the stowage boxes and experimental items looked like actual flight items. We even had patches of Velcro in the right places. No detail was left out. When we later climbed aboard the actual spacecraft, we felt, *Well, we've been here before.*

Simulator training was thorough and was to familiarize ourselves with the spacecraft operations and all the details of our flight plan. Our instructors were responsible for making sure we could overcome any emergency that we might encounter during our flight. They were very knowledgeable of spacecraft operations and could easily recognize the weak points of the crew.

This training was very demanding, especially in the critical phases of flight, such as the final few hundred feet of lunar descent. If something happened with the engines or attitude control system at those times, you had only seconds to respond or you would crash onto the moon.

In the lunar module we had as our chief instructor Charlie Floyd and his team. To learn our flight systems and emergency procedures, the instructors would insert various simulated emergencies into the spacecraft. As we worked through these emergencies, things would get very real; and if it appeared we were crashing on the moon, our hearts would beat faster and the adrenaline would start to flow. It seemed like the real thing.

"There we go again!" we would scream. "Splat—Blood all over everywhere! Well, we bought the farm again!"

The sessions got to be a game between us and the trainers. If we made it, it would be one for us. If we crashed, it would be one for them. At the end of the week, we'd total up who'd won for the week and then we'd have a few beers on the losers. John and I must have crashed on the moon a thousand times.

"Well, that's one for us," our instructors would quickly remind us. "Yeah, you've got us on that one," we'd answer, disgusted. Then we'd review what happened and where we went wrong.

But if we overcame a serious emergency and were able to make our landing it would be, "*Apollo 16* scored again. How about that one, sports fans?"

John was a tremendous partner and great to work with, and we rapidly became a cohesive crew, mastering the systems as a team. Even though John was the most experienced astronaut in the office, he never let his ego get in the way. Some mission commanders wanted to do everything themselves, but John wanted us to develop as a team, dependent on one another.

While John and I spent most of our time in the lunar module, Ken became the expert on the command module. Yet there were times when the three of us worked together mastering launch, reentry, and on-orbit procedures. I remember one simulation in the command module where Ken and I were practicing our return from the moon.

The emergency we were simulating was total loss of communication with earth, thus requiring us to navigate our way home using onboard procedures. There were programs in our computer designed for this contingency, which we could update with navigational marks on selected stars and planets.

We peered through our sextant and could see the constellations—the Big Dipper, the belt of Orion, Scorpio, Cassiopia. We didn't see all of the stars that can be seen on a good clear night, just the main ones that were necessary for navigation. Throughout each phase of simulated flight, every scene out the windows was coordinated with the location and attitude of the spacecraft.

Well, we were a few minutes from reentry and everything looked fine on the computer. We separated from the service module, but instead of reentering the earth's atmosphere, we went right by entry interface and just *zipped* on by the earth. Our supercircular velocity acted like a slingshot and hurled us off into space. Had that happened in real life, we would have been lost in outer space!

Looking over at Ken, I jokingly said, "Our Father who art in heaven," then began singing, "Rock of Ages, cleft for me."

We all laughed, but thank heavens it was just a simulation. That exercise pointed out to me very realistically that Mission Control was a very important part of the success of any mission. John, Ken, and I were only part of a much larger team.

We were now only about six months from our launch, and a few important decisions still had to be made—one was the *Apollo 16* landing site. All the Apollo site selections were based on obtaining maximum data from the moon. The decision was to be made by the scientists on the Site Selection Board.

If you think of someone traveling to the earth for the first time, you can see what a difficult problem this was. Where would you select to obtain the fullest picture of the earth, if you could make only five landings and could travel only a very few miles around your landing site?

Would you select one of earth's many deserts or a mountain region such as the Himalayas, the jungles of South America, or a site near the Grand Canyon? There is tremendous variation in the terrain on earth, and the same was thought to be true of the moon.

As you view the moon, some areas appear dark and others light. The ancient astronomers thought that the dark areas were oceans, so they named them *mare* and *oceanus* (Latin names for sea and ocean); the light areas were thought to be land or highlands. In a way the ancients were right. The light areas did turn out to be the highlands, and the dark areas are oceans of volcanic lava. At some stage of the moon's history vast seas of lava flowed, and since the minerals in the lava absorb light, these areas appear darker.

The Site Selection Board debated the merits of at least four different sites. John and I didn't get involved in that process except to make sure it would be smooth enough for a problem-free landing. We hoped it would be geologically exciting and unique. About six months before flight, our landing area was chosen—it was to be in the Descartes highlands. Most of the other Apollo missions had explored the mare or edge of the mare, so it was decided that we should go to the mountains.

The Descartes highlands was specifically selected because, according to photographs, it seemed to have two different types of rock which were believed to be two kinds of unusual volcanic material. We were certain that the rocks there would be different from the rocks in the mare. The area

*137*

was named after the sixteenth-century French mathematician and philosopher, René Descartes, and lies basically in the middle of the moon, ten degrees east and ten degrees south of center.

Choosing our precise landing spot in Descartes was difficult. The best photographs of our landing area were taken from lunar orbit by *Apollo 14* at an altitude of sixty miles, but even with these pictures it was not possible to see an object that was less than forty-five feet in diameter. We were able to identify large craters, hills, and boulders, but not smaller rocks and craters.

We finally chose a place that was surrounded by several major lunar features, but which itself appeared to be fairly smooth. The various craters and mountains surrounding it would enable us to recognize our site once in lunar orbit, and hopefully the spot would be smooth enough for a safe landing.

Based on these photographs, NASA constructed a scale model of the landing area for our simulator training. A TV camera was mounted above the model, and this was plugged into the lunar module simulator. According to the flight instructions we issued in our simulator, the TV camera would move around over the model. If we wanted to travel to the left across the lunar surface, we banked the spacecraft to the left, and though it appeared that we were moving, it was actually the TV camera gliding over the model. The results were extremely realistic.

Besides training in the simulator, a great deal of John's and my time was spent practicing lunar surface activities—driving the rover, taking pictures, collecting rocks, setting up experiments. All of this activity was done in our spacesuits, which made it extremely hard work.

The suits were bulky but more than that, they were very heavy—each suit weighing 55 pounds. When added to the 95-pound training backpack, all total on the earth I weighed 307! The real flight backpack was even heavier at 150 pounds, but because of the one-sixth gravity on the moon, my total weight there would be only 60 pounds.

These lunar surface training sessions lasted four or five hours, and we were exhausted when we finished. With our heavy spacesuits, plus the stiffness of our suits when they were inflated, these exercises were physically demanding. Especially difficult was learning to emplace the many experiments assigned to our flight. Most of these experiments weighed ten to fifteen pounds, and carrying them in our bulky spacesuits and trying to erect them with our large cumbersome gloves required many strenuous hours of training. We hoped it'd be easier on the moon.

The design of these experiments was fantastic. Some of them reminded me of a Rube Goldberg contraption. If you pulled pin A, out flopped leg

B, that tripped over bracket C, and caused pin D to be pushed into socket E. It looked squirrelly but it worked. We had to learn the sequences so well, that when we arrived on the moon we would know exactly what to do. There was simply not enough time to stop and say, "Wait a minute, what does page five of the instruction book say?" Time was too valuable on the moon to read manuals, so we spent hundreds of hours practicing these sequences until they were automatic.

Learning to drive the lunar rover was another task we had to master. We couldn't very well drive it on the highway, so we had a special road constructed through the swamp next to our training building at Kennedy. Since dense foliage and brush surrounded each side of the track, we had to use our imagination to visualize we were on the barren terrain of the moon.

With our simulated Mission Control directing our activities, we would drive along through the brush until we'd suddenly come upon the edge of a simulated crater, replete with large boulders and volcanic materials. We would climb out of the rover, turn on our TV camera, and begin our routine of collecting rocks. The geologists were back in the training building, and together we'd go through a lunar sampling pattern similar to those we would follow on the moon.

"Houston," I'd radio, "we've discovered this very unique crystalline rock. It's five centimeters in diameter and is egg shaped. It has a fine-grained matrix with greenish crystals about two millimeters across and it's very similar to olivine." Then we'd number the rock, put it in a plastic bag, and drop it in our sack.

Our greatest nuisance during these lunar surface training sessions was that it was hot as blue blazes in our spacesuits. The direct heat of the sun wasn't the problem, it was our internal body temperature. Normally when we work and our bodies generate heat, we perspire and our perspiration evaporates keeping us cool. But inside our spacesuits, our perspiration wasn't able to evaporate, and the flow of oxygen was insufficient to cool us down. Therefore we became extremely hot while training for four or five hours and became very dehydrated. We could literally pour the sweat out of our gloves when we finished and needed to drink what seemed like gallons of Gatorade to replenish the liquid we had lost.

Because the same problem would occur on the moon, the spacesuit engineers developed a cooling system that would remove the heat we generated while we worked. The system consisted of a set of long underwear into which were woven plastic tubes that coiled around our legs, arms, and body. These water-filled tubes came together in a manifold located in the middle of our stomach, which then plugged into a hose that led to our backpack.

Once installed, we switched on a pump located in the backpack, thus circulating water through the tubes. The water would pick up our body heat and carry it to the life-support system on our back where it was exhausted to space—the same principle as the coolant system in a car engine.

As designed, this system worked only in space, so in training we improvised by circulating the water through a cooler filled with ice. This cooler was carried around by one of our technicians while we worked. We were attached by a long umbilical cord, and everywhere we walked, he walked. In space the system was very efficient. On maximum cooling it would get so cold inside our suits that we would be freezing; it was almost like being inside a deep freeze, therefore I was usually set on minimum cool.

We each had three spacesuits—one for training, one as the prime or flight suit, and the third as backup. We didn't know which of the latter two we would wear in space until the day of launch. Generally it would be the prime suit, but if it failed the final leak check, we could then don our backup. The suits were expensive—custom-made, costing about $50,000 each. The nature of the suit necessitated that all of the measurements be exact for each individual astronaut. You couldn't just say, "Give me a size 39 long."

As backup on *Apollo 13,* I had made numerous trips to the manufacturer, ILC (International Latex Corporation) in Dover, Delaware, for suit fitting. ILC is most famous for making ladies' bras; a strange combination, ladies' bras and spacesuits. I don't know about the bras, but our pressure suits were great.

On my trips to Dover, I visited all the people working on my suit, not only the design engineers but also the seamstresses; expressly making a special point to talk to the little lady sitting there at her machine sewing the zippers into my spacesuit. It was a highly important job she had—if that zipper ripped out on the moon, I was instantly dead! Therefore I got to know the suit people well and encouraged them all. At the time of lift-off, I was totally confident that my suit was flawless.

When you look at the spacesuit you see only the white exterior with various protruding knobs, inlets, and outlets. This white exterior is not the pressure suit itself, but a thermal protection garment made of fireproof Beta cloth, a very finely knit material. Then beneath this exterior are layers of what appear to be aluminum foil, serving to protect the astronaut from the heat of the sun and small meteorites that might impact him while on the moon or walking in space.

The pressure suit is underneath all of this and consists of a rubberized material with nylon outer and inner liners. The outer liner keeps the pressure vessels from stretching, while the inner layer provides a smooth or slick surface. Attached to the pressure vessel are a series of cranks, pulleys, and cables that keep things aligned. Once inflated the suits were extremely stiff, so the system of cranks and pulleys was designed to facilitate movement. Each system had to be individually adjusted for each astronaut.

The suits were pressurized with 100 percent oxygen that circulated through the suit. Without this circulation, it would be like being in a closed refrigerator, and we would rapidly use up the small amount of oxygen inside our helmet and asphyxiate.

We had to wear numerous articles underneath the spacesuit. The first thing we donned was a big diaper called the FCD (fecal collection device). If we had to defecate while on the lunar surface, it was impossible to return to the lunar module. If you had to go, you had to go! The diaper was like a girdle, with the rear side made of very absorbent material. We would have had a terrible time getting cleaned up had we been forced to use the diaper, so thankfully it was never used on any mission.

The front of the diaper was cut away to allow for the attachment of the urine collection device. The urine bag was shaped like a hot water bottle and snapped onto the diaper. It was attached to the body by means of a roll-on condom and had a valve which opened and closed to permit one-way passage of fluid.

Over the diaper we wore our set of long underwear, which was called the LCG (liquid cooled garment). Finally came a drink bag and a food bar. These were Velcroed to the LCG at chest level and were for use during our excursions on the lunar surface.

During these remaining six months before launch, John and I continued our geology training. Our last trip was to Hawaii in December of 1971, and in a sense it was to be our final exam. Hawaii was an interesting place geologically because of its volcanic activity. On the big island of Hawaii, there is an active volcano, and many times we were there when it erupted.

Because this was going to be our last geology trip, several of us decided we would invite our wives along, so that they could observe our training. Dotty and Mary Haise, Fred's wife, were especially excited about going, since they had taken a year's course in geology at San Jacinto Junior College.

As we made our plans, we had a big disappointment when we realized we would miss the roll-out of our Saturn V from the VAB to our launchpad. Rollout was a special time, and we hated missing it, but Ken went down to the Cape by himself to represent the *Apollo 16* crew, and we left for Hawaii.

The group all stayed at the Volcano House, a small hotel in the Volcanoes National Park. A few times the gals came out and watched us practice, but most of the time they went off to explore by themselves. One day they got real adventurous and took a trail from Volcano House down into the crater of a nearby volcano, Kilauea Iki.

Unfortunately on the second day of the trip, I became ill with a severe case of the flu with a temperature of at least 104 degrees. When we returned to Houston from Hawaii, I never could shake the flu. Amid the Christmas activities and working hard, I continued to experience a tightness in my chest and a dry cough.

On New Year's Eve we partied into the wee hours, then the next day, I hopped into my T-38 and flew from Houston to Cocoa Beach to resume training. Driving to the Holiday Inn, I felt terrible.

The following morning I was to report to Kennedy Space Center but was so sick I couldn't even get out of bed. I telephoned the astronaut office and asked if someone could pick me up and take me to the doctor. When the doctor saw me, he took an X-ray and immediately sent me by ambulance to the hospital at Patrick Air Force Base. I had double pneumonia and was confined to the hospital for a week.

*Oh, no,* I thought to myself, *this is going to foul up everything. First the measles and now this. Typhoid Mary strikes again.*

We were scheduled to fly in mid-March, and I was worried that I would not be well enough to go. I knew that management would have no qualm about replacing me on the crew, and, if they did, there would be no more chances to fly to the moon. Fortunately for me, something happened to delay the launch.

While I was still in the hospital, some technicians were running a test on the attitude control system of the command module. During the test they overpressurized the system, causing it to be damaged. In order to fix it, the entire launch vehicle had to be hauled back into the assembly building, which meant a month's delay in the flight. Instead of a March 17 launch date, the flight was postponed until April 16.

You can imagine the sense of relief at this news! I was very thankful! This gave me another month to get back in shape and to continue training. Barring a major accident or screw-up on my part, there was no question that I would be aboard *Apollo 16* as it launched for Descartes.

# 15

# COUNTDOWN

"Hey, Daddy! Look—there comes your rocket!" exclaimed Charles. "W-W-Wow! It's really big!" chimed in Tom.

The monstrous crawler with its huge cargo of launch platform, launch tower, and rocket appeared and slowly rolled out the door of the white, fifty-story superbarn named the VAB. In spite of the cloudy day, the brilliant black and white striped Saturn V glistened aboard this machine that looked like a gigantic Caterpillar tractor.

Charles, Tom, Dotty, and I were watching the Saturn V, with the *Apollo 16* spacecraft poised firmly on top, make its journey to pad 39A. Since we had missed the first rollout in December, we were thrilled to have a second opportunity to view this exciting event.

The transporter's massive steel-link treads rolled over and over as they slowly crawled their way along a road made of eight inches of river rock. The 3½-mile trip to the launchpad would take six hours. The total weight of the crawler and its load was nine thousand tons.

It was a cold, blustery day. The wind was blowing hard, and the boys pulled their knit hats farther down over their ears.

The cold outside contrasted with the warm feeling of closeness I was experiencing with the family this day. These times were rare because I traveled so much. The times I was home, I just seemed to disrupt their routine; Dotty and the kids seemed to have their own life and I, mine. Out of necessity they had learned how to get along without me. Actually I was glad they had—there was too much on my mind getting ready for flight to be bothered with domestic responsibilities.

But this day was different. It felt really nice to have the kids there and see them so excited and to see Dotty enjoying herself so much. With great pride, I showed the family all over the space center and introduced them to all the people I had been working with these past two years.

I took them to the astronaut quarters where they met Lou, the cook, who gave them one of his famous cookies, and then in our weight room the boys enthusiastically tried out the various gym equipment. We visited the suit room where they were allowed to try on my actual space helmet and touch my spacesuit. Then a real treat was riding in the lunar module simulator. As a family I flew them through a practice landing on the moon, and they were thrilled to see the simulated view of our landing site.

The day after rollout, I received permission to take them out to the pad for a close-up view of our *Apollo 16* command module. I had never seen the family so excited! We took the long elevator ride up the launch tower that was now beside the Saturn V and walked carefully across the swing-arm. From our vantage point four hundred feet above the ground, we had a magnificent view of the space center.

After crossing the swing-arm, we entered the white room and were greeted by the spacecraft checkout crew. Guenter Wendt, who was the chief of this team, supplied little white smocks and hats made especially for the kids. They were then able to peek into the hatch of the command module and see the couch where their dad would be lying during lift-off. All the complex instruments and switches awed them. It was a special moment for us all.

Next we went over to the training building, where they could watch while John and I practiced getting the rover off the LM, putting up the flag, and deploying our experiments package. I felt it was really important to explain as much as I could to Dotty so that she would know what was going on during the various phases of our flight. I was thankful for this time together, for after this my schedule got so busy I barely had time to say hello.

About two months before lift-off, the prime and backup crews were called together for a briefing at the flight surgeon's office in Houston. The doctors were concerned because of some heart irregularities that had shown up on two of the crew of *Apollo 15*. Their mission had been the first to stay three days on the moon, and since *Apollo 16* was to also stay three days, the doctors wanted to make sure we didn't experience the same medical problems.

Because they felt that the problem was due to a loss of potassium, the docs had decided to add large doses of potassium to our food. In this way they hoped to maintain a proper level in our bodies. But as a safety measure, they had also decided to add some new medication to our in-flight medical kit. If serious trouble arose, we would have syringes of this special medication which we could inject directly into our hearts.

One of the doctors got up to explain the procedure. "Here is one of the syringes that we want you to use." That syringe got our attention! It was about three inches long and about the size of a 12-gauge shotgun shell. The needle was not exposed.

"Take the syringe and place it right below your sternum, or breast-bone." He showed us how to count down a certain number of ribs to get to the right place. "Press hard and a needle from inside the canister will fire into the heart and inject the medicine." We didn't much like this idea and expressed our feelings to the doctors.

"Well, there's really nothing to it," they answered. "We'll give you a demonstration." They had a Styrofoam ball about the size of a large orange. One of them took the ball in one hand and the syringe in the other and pressed the syringe against the Styrofoam ball.

And as he pressed hard, *bam*—the thing went off! And as the needle fired the medicine into the ball, it blew the whole back end of the ball off. It was a shower of Styrofoam.

There was stunned silence in the room. I looked around and all six of us—the prime and backup crew—were as white as sheets!

"Doc—look what happened!" I said incredulously. "Is that thing going to do that to our hearts?"

Once the shock had subsided, we had a good laugh and kidded the doctors with, "What are you trying to do, kill us? If you think we're going to use that, you're crazy. It's a lethal weapon."

The doctors tried to assure us that it wouldn't happen that way to the soft tissue of the body. But even though we agreed to take the medicine with us, we had made up our minds that we weren't going to use it. All six of us made a silent vow, *I don't care what the doctors say. I don't care how sick I am. No one's going to fire that thing into my heart, while I'm out in space!*

Our relationship with the doctors was good, but in the early days of the space program, there had really been an adversarial relationship between the astronauts and the flight surgeons. They had experienced some difficult, and often hostile, times.

The problem originated because no one knew exactly what was going to happen to the body in the space environment. The docs, being supercautious, designed all these crazy tests and medical experiments to build a data base. A few doctors even looked at the astronauts as their guinea pigs. Naturally the astronauts began to resent this treatment, and when some of the tests resulted in guys being removed from flight status, the hostility increased one hundred fold.

Deke Slayton was among those grounded. Then after Al Shepard flew in Mercury, he was also grounded because of an inner-ear problem. In Deke's case his military career was affected, and he left the Air Force to remain at NASA as a civilian. Fortunately for both men, they later medically requalified and flew in space—Al walking on the moon on *Apollo 14* and Deke flying on the *Apollo-Soyuz* mission.

In the early Mercury program, the docs had placed extensive instrumentation on the crews during flight. There were the brain sensors—tiny pins that were inserted just beneath the scalp to measure brain waves. There were rectal thermometers. There were the forty-five electrocardiogram leads to measure the heartbeat.

"We have to do this or we will not have the necessary medical data to avoid a potential problem," the doctors would argue.

"Well, you're not going to stick that thing in me," the astronauts would counter. It had been a big pain! So there was a running battle, because the doctors wanted to do more and the astronauts wanted them to do less.

By the time I came on board, we were subjected to considerably less medical examination during flight than in those early days. Sufficient information had been gathered by then, to render several tests unnecessary. We still measured heart rate and respiration, and collected urine and feces—but blood pressures, temperatures, and brain wave measurements had been abandoned, except for specific in-flight medical experiments.

The hostility had evaporated, and there was a good give-and-take relationship between the flight surgeons and the crew. If we did have a problem, there was a nurse, Dee O'Hara, who always had a sympathetic ear. She was tough, but she was also sensitive and would do anything to make sure her boys got the best medical care.

Actually I had a great respect for the doctors, and realized they were superconservative because they had our best interests at heart. They were fine, conscientious people who took excellent care of us and our families. If we had a child who was sick, they were ready to help all hours of the day or night; more than once I can remember them meeting Dotty and Charles or Tom at their office in the middle of the night to handle an emergency.

Now that we were just a couple of months from launch, there were a number of personal decisions to be made. Three major ones were: who to invite to lift-off, what to put in our PPKs (personal-preference kits), and what patch to have for *Apollo 16*.

Each crew selected their own special flight patch. John, Ken, and I had several basic ideas we wished to incorporate to commemorate our mission: patriotism, teamwork, and the moon. We wanted these ideas, plus the mission number and the names of the crew, to be displayed on our patch, and talked with a NASA graphic artist who designed exactly what we wanted.

Basically the design was a brown and white eagle with wings outstretched, perched atop a red, white, and blue American seal, over a gray lunar surface background. To show teamwork, the yellow NASA wishbone symbol of flight was placed on top of the seal, and then across the seal were written the words *Apollo 16*. Circling a blue and gold border were our names—YOUNG, MATTINGLY, and DUKE—and sixteen white stars to emphasize outer space and the number of our flight. We were very proud of this patch, which to us symbolized *Apollo 16*.

The second decision that had to be made was what to put in my PPK.

Each astronaut was allowed to carry an eight-ounce kit of personal items. There were some restraints—we couldn't take flammable or explosive material or anything that was not in good taste, but other than that we could carry whatever we wanted. Actually we each had two kits—one for the command module and one for the lunar module.

What was I to put in these kits that would be special and would commemorate the flight in a proper way? Dotty and I thought and thought about what to carry. We decided to have some special jewelry made for all the women in our families. Also we contracted with the Robbins Company, a jewelry firm in Attleboro, Massachussetts, to strike some gold and silver medallions in the design of our patch. This had been a tradition of each spaceflight for a number of years.

Another tradition was to carry small 3-inch by 5-inch nylon flags. I decided to carry flags of the United States, South Carolina, Georgia, and a few other states, plus many foreign countries. Next I offered to take some things for relatives and dear friends—a silver dollar, a cross for my sister Betsy, and a prayer banner from our church, Saint John's.

I took some stamped envelopes or first-day covers which others before me had carried. I put in twenty-five of them, autographed by John, Ken, and me. Later on there was a big public scandal about unauthorized envelopes that had been taken to the moon by *Apollo 15* and later sold by the crew. As a result of that publicity, *Apollo 17* and subsequent flights were not allowed to take any envelopes on their missions, but everything I carried in my PPK was approved by NASA.

Another special item I carried were two silver medallions commemorating the twenty-fifth anniversary of the U.S. Air Force. I thought it would be nice to say "Happy Birthday" from the moon, since I was the only Air Force officer that was to be in space during their anniversary year. I suggested a medallion and NASA approved, as did General Ryan, Chief of Staff of the Air Force, and Dr. Seamans, Secretary of the Air Force.

The Air Force got excited and provided two special silver medallions with the understanding that I would leave one on the surface of the moon and bring the other one home. This I would present to the Air Force at a special ceremony after my return.

A unique idea was suggested to me by Jim Irwin, who had flown on *Apollo 15*. He told me he had left a picture of his family on the lunar surface. I talked with Dotty and the boys about it, and they were delighted about having a picture of the Duke family on the moon.

So one day, Ludy Benjamin, a NASA photographer and good friend, came over to our house in El Lago and took a picture of the four of us. On the back of the picture I wrote, "This is the family of astronaut Charlie

Duke from planet Earth, who landed on the moon on the twentieth of April 1972."

Then we all signed it and put our thumbprints on the back. My plan was to leave this picture on the moon, so that some future astronaut might find it and see the family of astronaut Duke, who had been there many years before.

As the end of March approached, our flight plan and procedures were well established. On the way to the moon, we were essentially following the pattern set by those who had gone before us, but once we arrived on the moon, the procedures were different. Each flight had different objectives, a different type of traverse, and different experiments. We had worked out the details of our lunar excursions in coordination with the engineers, the scientists, the geologists, and management.

These procedures had evolved over several months through a series of meetings. Since everybody had the same motive, which was to maximize the return from the flight, we didn't have any major disagreements. We all presented our different ideas on how to do this, eventually reaching a common mind. Outside of the lunar experiments, the most important thing was returning lunar samples for analysis, so the geologists had the greatest impact on our lunar surface time line.

The time line called for us to land on the moon and remain there for seventy-two hours. Fifty-one hours would be spent in the lunar module, and twenty-one hours would be outside working on the lunar surface. These lunar excursions would be divided into three EVAs (extravehicular activities) of seven hours each.

Upon landing we were to place the spacecraft in a low-power configuration so that the batteries would last for the duration of our stay. Then we were to put on our life-support systems, check them out, open the hatch of the spacecraft, and descend the ladder to the lunar surface for our first EVA.

After this EVA we were to climb back inside, take off our suits, resupply our life-support systems, eat a meal, and sleep for eight hours. The next day we would have breakfast, suit up again, go back out on the surface for another seven hours, then return to the lunar module and repeat the same procedure. This was to be our pattern.

Because we had the lunar rover, John and I wanted to drive out ten or twelve miles from the lunar module. But management disagreed, saying it was too far. They felt that if once out there and the car broke down it would be too great a distance to walk back.

"We'll show you that it can be done," we retorted. We had a machine at NASA called a centrifuge. John and I got into our pressure suits and stepped into a special sling that hoisted us off the ground until we weighed one-sixth of our normal weight, simulating lunar gravity. Then attached to this hoist, which was suspended from the centrifuge, we started walking around the circular room, finally breaking into a lunar-type jog. We jogged for three hours! I had never run that long in my life before and covered at least ten miles.

Despite the fact that we proved we could cover this distance in our spacesuits without much difficulty, management still responded, "No way, we're not going to let you go that far; there's just too much risk compared with the extra geology we'd get." As a result, our traverses took us to a maximum of five miles from our landing site.

Three weeks before our launch, the quarantine period began. I said good-bye to Charles, Tom, and Dotty and flew to Kennedy. All the crews moved into the astronaut quarters so our whereabouts could be closely monitored. We were not permitted to leave the site except to fly.

Training continued during the quarantine period, but only an essential group of people were allowed to come into contact with the crew, and if any of them got sick they were immediately removed from the list. To ensure a secure quarantine, NASA also spent a great deal of money providing a special filtered atmosphere in our training facilities. All the precautions worked. There was not a repeat of the measles panic.

Although we could not come into contact with our children, we were allowed to see our wives provided they were not sick. Therefore Dotty followed in a few days, after she dropped the boys off in Atlanta. They would stay with her parents until they all came to the Cape about five days before launch.

Since the astronaut quarters were not very private and wives were not permitted to live in, John and I got permission one weekend for Dotty and Susy to stay with us at a special facility called the *Beach House*. Ken's wife, Liz, was pregnant at the time and unfortunately wasn't able to travel to Florida for the launch.

The Beach House was located on KSC grounds, about a mile or two from the launchpad and situated right by the Atlantic. It was the only remaining house of the many beachfront cottages that had been on Cape Kennedy before the government bought the land for the space center. It was reserved for the astronauts to use as a retreat house, a private place where we could get away to read and relax.

What a great time we had! John and Susy were newly married, and all of us enjoyed this opportunity to have a minihoneymoon. Susy and Dotty got along great and became the best of friends. It was wonderful getting away from the stress of training and being able to unwind a little bit. We walked along the beach and talked about the mission and relaxed with only a little work to do. Lou supplied us with plenty of food and beer. Friday night we grilled steaks and then on Saturday invited Ken and the backup crew out for hot dogs on the beach.

Late that night Dotty and I drove over to the launchpad so she could see *Apollo 16* bathed in the bright floodlights. For a minute she got choked up and a little apprehensive, knowing in only eight days I would be aboard and on my way to the moon, but mostly her attitude was positive. She was proud I had been selected and happy for me that I was going to get to fly on the trip of a lifetime.

After the weekend John and I moved back into the crew quarters and Charles and Tom arrived with Dotty's folks. All the family moved into the VIP quarters at Patrick AFB, and the kids had a ball, swimming in the pool and playing on the beach. NASA assigned the families bodyguards because of some terrorist threats, and they took right to the kids, becoming like favorite uncles to Charles and Tom. Then each day more and more friends and relatives arrived—every one of our brothers and sisters plus many cousins, aunts, uncles, and friends came to see me off.

Five days before lift-off, we were placed on a low-residue diet so that our systems could get flushed out. The food was tasty enough, but the medical requirements during these five days made eating a real pain. We had to weigh all our food before we ate it, then weigh what was left over, so the doctors would know exactly our intake. Plus every time we voided, we collected the urine in a big beaker, and with each bowel movement we collected the feces. All this was turned over to the doctors for the sake of medical science, but to us it seemed like just another weird idea.

In addition we were tested for our reaction to potassium and the drugs in our medical kit. Among the drugs tested were sleeping pills. Even though our bodies would be tired, the docs knew that our minds would be keyed up, and maybe we'd need some help in getting to sleep. It was essential that the doctors knew that we could be awakened and could overcome the effects of a sleeping pill, just in case a real-life emergency occurred in space.

So one night we took a pill and went to bed. A couple of hours later, a doctor entered our rooms shouting, "Wake up, wake up! There's an emergency in the spacecraft! Copy these numbers down quickly."

We came staggering out of bed, trying to get ourselves alert, so that we could copy down the information and respond to the simulated emergency. It reminded me of the old days on air defense alert, where I could be airborne from a dead sleep in five minutes. Each of us passed the test.

John, Ken, and I spent the last few days of quarantine reviewing final corrections in the flight plan and trying to hone our skills. We took our T-38 jets up every day for an hour of acrobatics, which released a lot of tension plus helped us adapt to zero gravity.

A couple of days before lift-off, Dotty brought the boys and our immediate families out to see me. I had to remain behind glass in an environmentally clean area, while the families were in a room on the other side, but it was fun being able to chat with all the family. I was very relaxed and confident and tried to instill this faith in everyone, because I knew they were nervous—especially my mom.

Cocoa Beach returned to its preflight festive, holiday atmosphere. Buses and cars arrived, friends and family took over the motels and restaurants, and everyone greeted one another. Of course I couldn't participate since I was in quarantine, but all that came were having a great time. It was like a high school reunion.

A number of parties were given for Dotty and our guests. One that everyone from my hometown enjoyed was a party hosted by the Henry Pauls. Henry was originally from Lancaster but now was living in Cocoa Beach, an employee of NASA. Since I couldn't be there in person to greet them, I decided I would tape a special message to be played at the party. After welcoming everybody and thanking them for coming, I closed by saying, "We hope we will make Lancaster proud of us when we are on the moon and return. I hope we can do a good job and you will be proud. Thank you and good-bye."

The day before lift-off an incident occurred that created a minor flap among the NASA management. On Saturday afternoon, some of the NASA managers from Washington, D.C., including Rocco Petrone, the head of the Apollo program, were sitting around the pool at the Holiday Inn enjoying the sunshine. Also staying at the Holiday Inn was my identical twin brother, Bill.

As Bill was crossing the pool area, he glanced over at Rocco and his group. About that time Bill realized he had left his wallet in his room, so he turned around and went back the way he had come. Now my brother doesn't know Rocco from Adam's housecat, but when Rocco saw Bill he couldn't believe his eyes.

Rocco, thinking it was me, jumped up and ran to the telephone. He immediately called crew quarters and demanded to know, "Why has Charlie Duke broken quarantine? What are you doing allowing him here at the Holiday Inn?"

Jamye, our bewildered secretary, responded, "But he's here. He's in training. I just saw him five minutes ago."

Rocco was unmoved. So Jamye tracked me down and explained her problem. I immediately knew he must have seen Bill. She passed that on, and Rocco accepted the explanation. Later on Rocco met Bill, and they both enjoyed a big laugh.

This was not the first time that people had gotten us confused, but it's about the most unusual.

We might be twin brothers and alike in many ways, but *neither* of us wanted to swap places that weekend. Bill certainly didn't want to be in my shoes and about to launch on *Apollo 16* to make its rendezvous with the moon—and I wouldn't have missed it for the world!

# *16*

## "NO CIRC"

### April 20, 1972—Lunar Orbit

"This is Apollo Control, Houston, at 91 hours, 24 minutes into the mission. We're standing by now awaiting a wake-up call by CapCom Don Peterson to the crew of *Apollo 16*."

"*Apollo 16,* Houston. *Apollo 16,* Houston."

"How you down there this morning, Houston?" answered Ken.

"Just fine," replied Don. "How are you, *16?*"

"Charging hard." We were already up and working by the time the wake-up call came, on this very special morning. *Today was the day we were to land on the moon!*

On these major event days, we generally tried to start early and get ahead of schedule. There was a lot to do, and if some emergency happened, we wanted to have some cushion, so that we wouldn't fall behind our time line. That was a good thing. We ended up needing every bit of extra time—when we experienced problem after problem later on that morning. Our next instructions from CapCom helped initiate one irritating problem for us.

"Your potassium levels are running a little low, and we'd like to recommend that you drink some orange juice this morning. Also you've got a long day ahead of you, so we'd like to recommend that you eat a bit more food." That specially prepared orange juice was to create minor, but continuous, irritations for us the rest of the day.

We started right into our eat period and waste management necessities. Immediately after that we began preparing for transfer to the lunar module.

"This is Apollo Control at 92 hours, 15 minutes ground-elapsed time. Gerry Griffin's gold team of flight controllers settled in for the day's activities leading up to powered descent and lunar landing." *Apollo 15* astronaut Jim Irwin was assigned to be our CapCom.

When it came time to don my spacesuit, I began to get concerned, remembering the trouble I had experienced with my zipper the day before. First I put on the liquid-cooled garment and urine collection device; then I left off the big diaper, which was the fecal containment system, hoping less padding would help get my zipper closed. I didn't want to be the one to get us behind our time line.

"Hot dog!" The zipper closed without a hitch and I was ready to go.

We opened the hatch to the lunar module and began transferring items over to Orion, including such things as urine bags, scissors, pencils, drink bags, and our flight data file, which contained our checklists and maps.

"This is Apollo Control. *Apollo 16* commander John Young and lunar module pilot Charlie Duke are running almost 40 minutes ahead of the flight plan. They've already donned their pressure suits, and they're in the lunar module, preparing to power it up."

Climbing into the lunar module was like slipping into an old, comfortable chair. I felt right at home. To keep from floating around too much in zero gravity, John and I attached ourselves to the restraint system, which was two cables anchored to the floor, and began to power up.

While we were doing this, Ken was getting his suit on and closing the tunnel. It was an extremely busy time. John and I had about four hours to power up, undock, check out, and activate systems to prepare the lunar module for descent.

For about forty-five minutes, things went well. Then when I began to power up our antenna for the primary communications link with Houston, our problems began. I couldn't get the antenna to rotate left to right in the yaw axis and point toward earth. This resulted in a poor communications lock-on with the tracking network, and therefore they were not able to automatically uplink information to our computer.

"Rats!" This was a *major* problem; there was a potful of data for undocking that needed to be entered into our onboard computer. Now I had to copy down all this information and insert it into the computer *manually*. It was very time consuming and put us under lots of pressure, for it had to be done before we lost radio contact with Houston again. Undocking was to occur on this rev shortly after LOS.

Houston began reading up these 5-digit numbers that I copied and read back to Mission Control to make sure we were entering the right numbers. There were thirty-five 5-digit numbers which had to be entered into the computer, and whenever a mistake was made, it was a complicated procedure to get back into the computer to make the correction. We could hear Houston clearly, but because of our antenna failure, our voice link to Mission Control was scratchy and very weak.

While I was copying feverishly, John began to activate the reaction control system. The RCS was used to control our attitude in space. When he flipped the switch, there was a *double failure* in the pressurization system, and it looked like we were going to overpressurize and blow the relief valve! If that happened we were in deep trouble and would have to *scrub* the flight.

"Darn! What is happening to us? This thing is coming apart at the seams!" I couldn't believe it—we'd been powered up for only an hour and now had *two major malfunctions*!

I was really feeling the tension, so when I saw John open the innerconnect I yelled, "No! Don't do that!" What followed was a big debate with each other and with Mission Control about what to do. It was the only argument I can remember having with John on the flight.

"This is the *worst* jam I was ever in," John exclaimed. *Apollo 16* being his fourth mission, I knew things weren't so good.

We were never able to fix the RCS regulators, but through venting the pressure into the ascent fuel tank, we were able to save the day. It was a difficult procedure, because we had to be careful in the venting that we didn't pump all of our fuel out of the attitude control system.

Now the problems caused by our inoperable, steerable antenna were beginning to compound, and it impacted us terrifically on the checkout and activation of the LM. But we kept pressing on. We were really rushing because we were only thirty minutes from LOS, and only two orbits from our intended landing. We were busier than one-armed paperhangers!

"You got a 331, yet? ENTER? Go ahead, you are cleared to MARK; 33195, go ahead; 33197 . . . 33—wait! Let me recheck that. No, I don't know how you do that," I said, trying to complete the 52 alignments for undocking.

"You got to *ENTER* it, Charlie—33195," instructed John.

We were really strapped and getting more and more anxious. The stress level was beginning to increase exponentially. John and I were getting tense with one another, and things were right at the breaking point.

Mission Control continued having their problems with the noise level on the communications link, and they were getting frustrated. Having been in Mission Control, I knew that the flight director was pacing up and down, and everybody was getting a knot in the pit of their stomachs.

I kept looking at the clock and thinking, *There is no way we're going to get this done on sequence.*

But our training and experience seemed to overcome all of this tenseness and instead of breaking, we settled down and got very methodical and proceeded cautiously point by point. Things began to come back on track.

"Okay, did you get the verb?" John asked me. "Okay, read those numbers to me."

"2933 . . . 28925 . . ."

"Orion, this is Houston," interrupted CapCom. "Assuming you get the P52 [alignment program] complete, you have a GO for undocking. Over."

"Okay." Keep pressing. We can make it.

"Okay. VERB 11, NOUN 10, ENTER, 5 ENTER." I now read off the RCS (reaction control system) checklist to John. "Okay. Commander TTCA, up."

"Okay. TTCA 28." John responded.

"Orion, you are one minute from LOS." The undocking was to occur after LOS on the back side of the moon.

We were getting down to the wire. Like the sprinter lunging over the finish line, we completed all our preparations, and right on schedule we released the latches that held us to the command module.

We had *made* it! John and I had overcome all our problems and achieved undocking. *Look out, moon—here we come!* On our next REV (revolution) we would be heading down for our lunar landing.

After making a small separation burn from the command module, we turned so that we could see Casper out our front windows. It was a beautiful sight. The spacecraft silhouetted against the lunar surface, rushing by beneath it. Soon after that we had AOS.

"Orion, this is Houston. How do you read?" Over the radio came CapCom Jim Irwin's voice. He was coming in loud and clear.

"Roger. Five by, Jim, and we're sailing free," answered John.

"Roger."

"Okay, Jim. It was a little rushed, but we got it done," I reported. "The only thing bad is that I got a packful of orange juice."

Following the morning's request from Houston, John and I had been drinking a lot of orange juice—now I was having trouble with a leaky orange juice bag. NASA had designed a plastic drink bag to fit inside our spacesuits, since we were going to be working on the lunar surface for long periods of time. It was shaped like a hot water bottle and attached to our long underwear. A long plastic straw went from the bag, up through the neck ring of the helmet, right next to our mouths. To drink, we simply grabbed the straw between our teeth and sucked real hard.

Well, right before our separation maneuver, I had donned my helmet and immediately my drink bag began to leak through the straw into my helmet. It seemed like every time I breathed, out would come one or two small drops of orange juice.

I couldn't suck them, I couldn't reach them with my tongue, I could only watch cross-eyed as they floated out in front of my face. Eventually some of the drops would hit me on the tip of the nose and slowly migrate up into my hair, giving me a sticky orange juice shampoo. It was really frustrating not being able to wipe this stuff off, as it touched and tickled my nose.

A little while later I was complaining to John, "This orange juice is beginning to smear up my vision." Of all times to have orange juice floating around in my helmet—the most important day of my life—landing on the moon!

"I'm sick and tired of the stuff," he answered. "It's giving me stomach cramps and gas and . . ." He was really complaining, adding a few choice four-letter words.

Suddenly Houston interrupted, "You men are transmitting over the air." We thought we had been talking to ourselves and didn't realize we had an open mike. We were really embarrassed, and John immediately apologized, but every word had gone over the radio to the world.

The press corps had a field day. Everyone had a big laugh except for the orange growers. I guess they feared *Apollo 16* space gas could kill their business. The governor of Florida even made a statement the following day. "It's not our orange juice that is causing the trouble," he explained. "It's an artificial substitute that doesn't come from Florida." Florida's native son, John, will never live that down.

All systems were go, all flight updates were in; we were in good shape for descent and landing on the next rev. Our lunar module, Orion, continued to drift slowly away from Ken. "Orion, we're coming up on about two minutes to LOS," announced CapCom.

"Roger, two minutes to LOS. See you around for PDI [power descent initiation]," responded John.

"Hey, Jim—I saw the landing site as we passed over it!" I exclaimed. "We're not going to have any trouble recognizing it from the rays. The rays stand out beautifully." I was on ready. The next REV around we would attempt to land. We had overcome all our problems, and now we were going to make it!

On the back side of the moon, it came time for Ken to make an orbit change. He was going to attempt a sixty-mile circular orbit, which would place him in the proper rendezvous path in case we had to abort our descent. We were about a mile behind him now, but could see him clearly. He looked like a little star.

During the burn preparations, suddenly Ken said, "There is something *wrong* with the secondary control system in the engine. When I turn it on, it feels as though it is shaking the spacecraft to pieces!"

*That* really got our attention! That engine and control system were *our ride home*!

John, as the commander of the mission, had to make a quick decision to continue or to abort the burn. "Don't make the burn," he directed. "We will delay that maneuver."

Our hearts *fell* into our boots, as we realized that our landing would have to be postponed and perhaps even abandoned. We knew we had a serious problem. Without that backup control system, we were down to one system and under the mission rules, it meant we were no go for the circulation burn, which also meant we were no GO for landing.

When we regained radio contact with Houston, I reported, "No CIRC, no CIRC!"

"Okay, copy. No CIRC," responded CapCom Jim Irwin. "Anticipate a waive-off for this one. We'll set you up for the next one [revolution]."

We knew in our minds that it was very grim. It looked as if we had two chances to land—slim and none. We were dejected.

After looking over the situation for a while, Houston said, "It looks like we're not going to have a decision on this REV, and we do have the capability of spending about five REVs in this configuration before we have to make that decision. We would like y'all to move into a station-keeping position."

We were really depressed. After the heady exhilaration and excitement of the undocking and getting everything accomplished, now another major problem had surfaced, this time in Ken's spacecraft. This was the worst problem yet. Because of this engine, it looked as though we were going to have to return to earth.

We had trained 2½ years, come 240,000 miles, and were within 8 miles of our landing site—we could look down and see it. We were one hour away from our scheduled landing and now we had this abort. "All of that effort is wasted," we felt.

We rendezvoused with Ken and began to fly in close formation, waiting for the decision. Time was against us. As the moon continued to revolve beneath us, our landing site was gradually moving out from under our orbit. If we didn't attempt to land within a few hours, then the desired landing spot would be out of range, and we would have lost the ball game.

On the next AOS, word from CapCom was, "We still do not have an answer, but people are working feverishly." The NASA team along with contractors and engineers all over the country were frantically studying every possibility available, because this problem had to be solved quickly.

The minutes dragged by as we waited. The only time in the entire mission when I remember praying was during this crisis. *"Lord, let us land,"* I whispered silently.

Another REV, another LOS, and another AOS. Now we were down to only two more revolutions before it would be too late to land, regardless of whether they fixed it or not.

Then after a four-hour wait—four hours after hearing, "No CIRC, no CIRC," came this communication from Houston.

"You do have a GO for another try here at PDI on REV 16."

That was the word we had been hoping for. We had a *GO*! We had been given a *go* for landing on the next REV. Our hearts came alive. Our excitement returned. It was like being called back from the dead!

# *17*

## *"OLD ORION IS FINALLY HERE!"*

John and I were all smiles now. What a relief—*fantastic!* We were going to be able to land after all!

CapCom continued, "I have some words on that problem with the TVC [thrust vector control], whenever y'all are ready to copy."

I was really curious about what had caused the oscillating problem with Ken's spacecraft. "Well, I'm all ears," I answered. "I don't know about Ken."

Ken heard our conversation and quickly added, "I've got my pencil ready."

CapCom proceeded to give us a quick summary of the problem. We apparently had experienced an open circuit in the thrust vector control loop on our backup system. Exhaustive tests at the various contractor facilities on the East Coast and West Coast had found that even though Ken would get some oscillation, it would be controllable. So even if the primary system failed and we had to revert to the backup control mode, everything would be all right.

Because of the change in our flight plan caused by the six-hour delay, we had to reprogram a great deal of our onboard data, and this had to be done before we had LOS. PDI and a try at a lunar landing would begin on the next REV, REV 16, shortly after obtaining AOS. Greatly relieved we began to quickly copy all the information necessary for our descent.

Immediately upon AOS, CapCom gave us our final updates to load the computer for PDI. John and I reconnected our restraint harnesses, which would hold us in place while we descended to the moon. During the first eight minutes of descent, we would fly with our backs parallel to the lunar surface and with our windows facing away from the moon.

"Orion, you're GO for PDI," radioed CapCom. What sweet words to our ears.

"Roger, GO for PDI," recounted John. "Engine start. Descent Engine Command Override is on." The descent engine started right on the second.

"Stand by for throttle up," I announced.

"Twenty-two . . . 23 . . . 24 . . . 25 . . . 26 . . . throttle up!" we shouted together.

"On time!" yelled John. "Feel that beauty come on," I exclaimed.

What a relief it was to get PDI and have that engine start. We were finally on our way down to the moon. *This was it!*

The engine first began on minimum power of about 25 percent thrust, then after twenty-seven seconds throttled automatically to 100 percent. It was like starting an automobile in idle and then at twenty-seven seconds going full power. We could feel the G force build up under our feet, causing us to be planted even more firmly against the floor of the lunar module. We could also feel a high-frequency vibration, as the engine shook the entire vehicle. For the next seven minutes we were at full power.

Although we were relieved, we were also very tense and very attentive to the spacecraft systems and trajectory. The next ten to eleven minutes were going to either result in a landing or in an abort. We didn't have any more chances. If we had to abort for some reason, we'd never get another chance.

We had begun our descent at about 66,000 feet above the lunar surface.

"Hey, we're way high, John. We got to get down. Way high on the H-dot."

"All right. Just a minute, Charlie," John answered. "Down to 45 already." I was concerned because our descent rate was much higher than preplanned. But it turned out that our altitude was higher than projected, so everything was working to get us on nominal trajectory.

"Look good," I said, "passing 1:30" [one minute, thirty seconds into the burn].

*159*

John and I kept up a rapid exchange, as he monitored the flight progress of the lunar module and I made sure we were on the right trajectory. All during the first eight minutes or so of the descent we were high on our profile, but the landing radar was beginning to update our altitude and rate of descent and with each passing cycle of the computer, we were getting closer and closer to the preflight trajectory.

"At five minutes, coming in like gangbusters!" I exclaimed, as I continued to monitor the instruments to make sure all the systems were working correctly. "Six minutes, we should be at 32,000."

"Thirty-five—not back on profile, but almost," said John.

"*Orion,* you're GO at 6." Things were looking good as we kept getting a GO from Mission Control at each of the minute marks. "Throttle down at 7 plus 23. You're GO at 7."

At seven minutes, 23 seconds, we experienced an autopilot throttle down from full thrust and began our final phases of descent.

"Twenty-one thousand, coming up on 8 minutes," I read off the instruments.

"*Orion,* you're go at 8," confirmed CapCom.

"I can see the landing site from here, Charlie." At 8 minutes after PDI, John was able to lean forward and look out his window. Up to this point we had been looking out into space and had no idea where we were in relation to our lunar landing spot. We were depending on our instruments to tell us our altitude and our velocity across the surface of the moon, and had to take it on faith that our instruments were accurate and our tracking from Mission Control was correct.

"Pitchover," John announced. The lunar module had entered the final descent phase, as it made a 40-degree attitude change at 7,000-feet altitude.

"Pitchover. Hey, there it is!" With our windows pointing forward, I could now see our landing area. "Gator! Lonestar! Right on!" I shouted. It was like looking at the landing site model in our training simulator.

"Palmetto and Dot, North Ray. Looks like we're going to be able to make it, John. There's not too many blocks up there." One of our EVAs was to go to North Ray Crater, and we had been concerned that we might have some difficulty driving our rover up there because of rough terrain. But I couldn't see too many big rocks, so it looked good.

Because we recognized the major craters and landmarks we had been studying from our geology training, we knew that our tracking and guidance were almost right on target. The spacecraft had automatically brought us down within range of our landing spot.

We were awed as we looked across this spectacular moonscape. What a contrast—the sun was fifteen degrees above the eastern horizon, so the bottom of the craters were in deep shadow while the rest of the surface was bright gray and bathed in sunlight. The long dark shadows gave the moon an eerie appearance.

The shadows would be helpful in selecting our final landing site, as they gave a feel for the angle of the surface. We had to pick a spot that was less than a fourteen-degree slope—anything greater than that could result in the lunar module tipping over at touchdown.

"*Orion,* you're GO for landing."

John took over the controls. Now it was up to us to find a smooth place to land. We were a little north and a little long of our intended landing spot, so John made the correction.

"Okay. Thirty-nine hundred feet." I read our altitude off the instruments.

"Okay," said John. "Two to the south, Charlie." I checked the computer for confirmation, as John moved the hand controller two clicks to the left.

"Okay. It's in. Okay forty-two—41 LPD [landing point designator], 3,000 on profile." I called out the LPD, so John could make a sighting from the calibrated scale etched on his window. This would show where the spacecraft was headed for landing.

"Okay. We're coming right down," John said.

"Two thousand . . . 1,400 feet, 44 down [descending 44 feet per second]. Looking good. One thousand feet . . . 800 feet, 30 down." I kept up my running commentary to John.

"Okay, Houston. We're going to be just a little long," reported John to CapCom. "We're just now abeam of Double Spot." He picked out a point that was a couple of hundred yards from the crater Double Spot, which had been our intended landing target.

"Some big blocks over here to the left, John. Okay, 300 feet, 15 down. Okay, fuel is good: 10 percent. There comes the shadow. Okay, 200 feet, 11 down."

At a height of about 200 feet, we were practically over our selected touchdown spot. We were moving forward very slowly now, at just a few feet per second, coming in to land almost like a helicopter—with a rate of descent of eleven feet per second.

I glanced out of my window to verify that there were no large boulders on my side of the spacecraft, and the shadow of the lunar module caught my eye. We looked like a big spider poised over the surface.

"Drifting. Okay, looking good. Perfect place over here, John, a couple of big boulders, not too bad; okay, 80 feet, down at 3. Looking super! There's dust!" At eighty feet our engine exhaust hit the lunar surface and

*161*

began creating a small dust storm. The closer we got, the thicker the dust became.

"Okay, down at 3, 50 feet. You're backing up slightly, okay, 2 down." When we were around twenty feet off the surface, John stopped the rate of descent and just hovered. Dust was being blasted everywhere. I could see our shadow through the dust and knew we were close.

"Come on, let her down—you leveled off—let her on down," I urged. I was growing a little panicky even though we were fat on fuel; we still had about sixty seconds of fuel remaining.

John began to slowly descend again, about one foot per second. At five feet above the lunar surface, the lunar module's long landing probes hit the ground. When they did, it closed an electrical circuit that turned on a little blue light inside the spacecraft which said, "Contact."

When that came on, I yelled, *"CONTACT! STOP!"*

John hit the stop button cutting the engine, and *"WHUUMP!"* We dropped the last four feet like a ton of bricks! We didn't want to land with the engine running, in case we happened to come down over a boulder which could plug up the exhaust nozzle and cause the engine to blow up.

"WWWWOW MAN—look at that!" I shouted.

"Well, we don't have to walk far to pick up rocks, Houston," said John. "We're among them."

Both excited and relieved I announced, "Old *Orion* is finally here, Houston. *Fan-tastic!"*

Later we realized just how close we had come to disaster. We had barely missed landing in a big crater. Had we landed on its rim, the lunar module would have tilted and possibly turned over.

I teased John that the landing had jarred my fillings loose, we had hit so hard. For an Air Force pilot it seemed like a crash, but for an old Navy aircraft carrier pilot like John, it was all in a day's work.

We wanted to spend all our time looking out the windows, we were so excited, but touchdown was a very critical period. We had things to do to "safe" the systems and had to be prepared for an abort in case our landing had damaged one of our critical systems, such as ascent propulsion. Conversation went back and forth between checking systems and describing the view.

"Ascent pressures look good. Okay, Ascent Helium Monitor, cycle. Hey, it sure ain't flat, John. Wow!"

"There's a ridge in front of us, one to the side of us, and my guess is that we're in a subdued old crater," added John.

"Say, Jim, about 30 or 40 percent of the surface is covered with boulders that are maybe half a meter in size." I wanted to tell CapCom everything I was seeing. I couldn't contain myself. I was like a little kid with his nose plastered against the candy store window—but what was outside wasn't candy, it was the most fantastic sight of rocks and hills and ridges and craters imaginable.

"On out in front of us and to the right, where we landed. . . ."

"Wait a minute, Charlie," interrupted John. "We gonna stay, Houston?"

"Everything's looking okay up to this point, John. We'll give you a final word here shortly." A minute later CapCom gave us the okay to stay for T-1, a lower level of abort readiness. Over the next thirty-five minutes, Houston gave us a stay of T-2 and then T-3. These were inverse order levels of readiness and allowed us to begin systems power down, as we gained more and more confidence that the integrity of the spacecraft was okay.

With our confidence growing, John and I became more and more exuberant. We were as excited as two little five year olds on Christmas morning with a roomful of toys. Imagine the best Christmas, the best birthday, the best visit to an amusement park—all rolled into one instant of time—that is the feeling we had as we tried to describe what we were seeing. Like little kids, all we could say was "neat place," "fantastic," "super"—we must have said fantastic a hundred times.

*Orion* had landed about two hundred yards to the north and one hundred yards west of our intended landing target, a crater we had named Double Spot. We felt pretty good about that after traveling nearly 240,000 miles. It was probably the most level spot around; everywhere else were rocks and craters. We were literally surrounded by rocks on every side.

"Hey, Jim. Hats off and a case of beer to FIDO (flight dynamics officer). I'll tell you, that targeting was just beautiful. Boy, you guys just burned us right in there. That was superb!" I congratulated our tracking crew, who had been responsible for generating the data our computer used to guide us to the rolling Cayley Plain of the Descartes Highlands.

"Feel that one-sixth gravity, Charlie." John had unlocked his restraint system and began to bounce around in the gravity of the moon. I was having trouble getting free from my harness but finally disconnected and began to experience the wonder of one-sixth gravity, too.

Just by wiggling my toes, I could bounce up off the floor of the LM and with only one hand pick up my 150-pound backpack. I looked forward to getting out on the surface and exploring in that one-sixth gravity. Compared with our training at Kennedy in earth gravity, this was going to be a piece of cake.

Our landing place, Descartes, was in the central highlands. As you look at a full moon, this is almost in the middle—in the left cheek of the "man in the moon." We had landed in a big valley, about ten miles across. Mountains surrounded us; it was like landing in the top of the Rocky Mountains.

To the south about five miles away was a range seven hundred to eight hundred feet high. One of the peaks we had nicknamed Stone Mountain, for Stone Mountain, Georgia, because it was smooth and rounded. We planned to drive the rover there, and we were delighted to see we should have no problem at all climbing its slope.

Five miles to the north was an area we had named the Smoky Mountains, because of their gray color, but due to a ridge that was a few hundred yards from the LM, we couldn't see those mountains, even though they rose nearly one thousand feet above the valley floor.

Off to the southeast we could see the South Ray Crater, which was about seven miles away. It was white in color with distinct black streaks down the side. Then in front of us to the west was the Cayley Plain, not a level expanse, but an area of gently rolling hills.

We were bubbling over with excitement and overwhelmed by the beauty. It was not the beauty of earth, with its cascading waterfalls, majestic Rockies, snow-covered Alps. It wasn't that kind of beauty because there is no life there—not even a blade of grass, or virus, or bacteria—nothing. It is just one great big rock that has been pulverized by meteorites over the centuries and is now covered with a very fine dust. There never had been any life on the moon, because there is no atmosphere.

But the moon has a special beauty of its own. There is almost a purity about it—so still and pristine, unspoiled by any pollution of man. None of the surface looked like the terrain depicted in science fiction movies of jagged peaks or precipitous cliffs. Instead the hills and mountains were all smooth and rolled gently toward the horizon.

The surface was basically gray in color, though some rocks appeared dark gray or even black and a few were white. And everything was covered with this fine, powderlike dust. It was spectacularly beautiful, accented by the sharp contrasts between the dark shadows and gray terrain.

Since there is no atmosphere on the moon, the horizon was sharply defined. We could see a distinct break between the grayness of the moon and the blackness of space. Though the sun was shining brightly, the lunar sky was pitch black; no stars were visible due to the bright reflection off the lunar surface.

We were to be on the moon for three days, and it was always going to be daylight. A day on the moon from sunrise to sunset is fourteen days long. Since we had landed very early on a moonday, the sun was about fifteen degrees above the horizon in the east behind us and caused a very long shadow of the lunar module, which we could see out our windows.

But there wasn't much time for sightseeing. "Okay, Charlie," radioed Jim, "when you get the surface checklist, I have some changes that we want to take care of." We instantly got pulled back to the reality of power down. Because of our landing delay, we had to change all our procedures and go through an extensive rewrite of time lines and checklists for our lunar stay.

"Stand by," I answered. "There probably are a few, aren't there?"

"Yes, there are a few, and we'll have a few more in order to conserve power to give you maximum stay time."

One of the major changes Houston decided was that, due to the extremely long day, we should go right away into our sleep period—instead of our planned moonwalk. We really wanted to get out. After training almost three years and coming 240,000 miles and be told, "wait until tomorrow and go to sleep," seemed crazy, but we knew it was the wise thing to do.

Everyone was tired; John and I, and the Mission Control team. It had been a long, hard day's work. Because of the six-hour delay, we had already been up almost twenty hours.

"Jim, I feel exactly like I thought I would," I confessed. "I really want to get out, but I think that discretion is the better part of valor here."

"Good," answered Jim. "Glad you think that."

John spoke up, "Man, it's really tempting though. It really looks nice out there."

This change in flight plan might have been a fairly easy decision to make, but it was a hard one to implement; it meant we were going to have to copy pages and pages of changes to procedures and checklists.

I began to write, and I wrote and wrote and wrote. It seemed like I was about to run out of pencil lead because of the hundreds of changes—changes in our time line and changes in procedures. This was due to the revised sequence of events and our desire to conserve as much electrical power as possible; we had used up an extra six hours' worth of power by the delayed landing. So for the better part of an hour, we made corrections to the lunar surface checklist.

"This is Apollo Control and *Orion* is safely on the ground at Descartes, having landed at 104:29:36 ground-elapsed time. In local [CST—Central Standard Time] time, that's 8:23 P.M. [April 20]. After the crew has a chance to power-down the lunar module, do some housekeeping, they will have a sleep period which will begin at about 107 hours, with EVA 1 starting tomorrow morning at about 10:30 A.M., Central Standard Time."

There was a change of shift in Mission Control, and Tony England replaced Jim Irwin as CapCom. Tony was a geophysicist astronaut and was to be our CapCom during our lunar surface excursions. We had trained extensively together. He was highly qualified and a good friend and neighbor.

I knew Tony would have given anything to have been in our place, but he seemed perfectly happy and content to be the guy we would work closest with during our explorations, and we were delighted to have him. He had been great to work with during our geology field trips, and he was as excited about this mission as we were.

"Okay, Tony. We've got three of us in here now," I joked; "John's out of his suit." The spacesuits were like another person, they took up so much room.

"And I assume all three are walking around?" Tony asked. "No, not exactly," I answered. "One of them is sort of lying there."

Being in spacesuits for three days would be really uncomfortable, so we had decided while we were inside the lunar module to take off our suits and stand around in our long underwear. After John and I finished stowing the suits, it was time for our first meal on the lunar surface.

"What do you call tomato soup made with cold water, Tony?" I asked.

"Awful!" answered Tony. He was right. I suddenly realized that all of our meals for the next three days on the moon were going to be cold. We didn't have any hot water, and there was no way to heat up the food.

But the one-sixth gravity did make eating effortless. It was the first time in days that we had been able to eat soup without worrying whether we were going to eat it or take a bath in it. Tony suggested we deserved some champagne after our successful landing, but since alcohol was not allowed, we celebrated with the usual—orange juice.

That *orange juice*! "We're definitely not going to get scurvy; we got so much orange drink here. And Tony, I wouldn't give you two cents for that orange juice as a hair tonic," I griped. "It mats it down completely." My orange juice shampoo was a mess, and I was having a dickens of a time trying to get it cleaned up.

When we finished our meal, we got ready to bed down for our first eight-hour rest period. John and I both had nylon hammocks to sleep in while on the moon. Mine attached to the spacecraft from right to left just a few inches off the floor. John's was suspended forward to aft about two feet above me, so that we formed a cross while sleeping. We simulated darkness by placing opaque screens over the windows, just as we had done in the command module during our journey to the moon.

As we were getting ready for bed, little did we know that at this very moment, high-powered meetings were going on at NASA, discussing the strong possibility of canceling our third moonwalk. Because of extra consumption of water and power during the six-hour delay, almost all recommendations pointed toward a scrub. Late into the night, the NASA managers met, reviewing the options and risks.

### Apollo News Center, Houston—Change of Shift Briefing—9:32 P.M.

Terry White, Public Affairs Officer, called the press conference to order and introduced Rocco Petrone, the Apollo Program Manager, and Jim McDivitt, the Apollo Spacecraft Program Manager. Also present were the gold team Flight Director, Gerry Griffin, and CapCom, Jim Irwin.

After briefing the press corps about the problem with the command module's engine, the questions zeroed in on the third EVA. "Has anybody been back into one of the support rooms to see if there is a dogfight going on back there to decide who gets what and when?"

The support rooms being referred to were the geologists and scientists who had helped put our mission together. Since each had a large stake in the scientific knowledge gleaned from our excursions, no one would want to lose out on any of their objectives, and if the third EVA was dropped, something would have to go.

The geologists were anxious to retrieve three different types of specimens—South Ray Crater ejecta and samples from what we called the Cayley formation and the Descartes mountains.

The third EVA was to explore North Ray Crater, a large crater deep in the Cayley formation. It was hoped at North Ray we would find rocks from the deepest depth of the moon of any of the Apollo missions and give the scientists data for discovering the moon's origin. No one wanted to give up the third EVA, but right now it didn't look good. The greatest concern was our consumables.

The meeting ended on the supposition that "a third EVA looks unlikely," but the final decision would be made sometime later in the night or in the morning.

I was glad I was unaware of these meetings and didn't have the additional worry of losing one of our EVAs. My mind was nearly overloaded as it was—thinking about all the things we had to do and filled with all the excitement of being on the moon. One minute I was trying to figure how to fix our broken antenna, the next I was planning where to drill for soil samples during our EVA the next day. It was impossible to get my mind in idle.

I finally told Houston that I was going to take a sleeping pill. The pill helped and I slowly began to drift off for a few hours of fitful sleep. But before getting to sleep, we were warned that during the night we would likely experience two master alarms, alerting us of overpressure in our attitude control system.

I was wearing the COMM cap or headset and barely asleep when the first of those alarms was triggered. It blasted in my ears—"Bong! Bong! Bong!" I almost leaped out of my skivvies and went through the top of the lunar module. My heart was pounding and I was really shook. Then I realized what it was and reset the alarm and tried to go back to sleep.

Besides the two alarms which almost sent me into orbit, I was startled awake from a dead sleep a third time by a big blast of static from our radio, louder even than the master alarm. I was instantly awake, practically jumping out of my skin and thinking I was going to be deaf. Mission Control had improperly changed the communication antenna, causing the static.

Later I asked the docs if during all those disturbances, I had faked out the electrocardiogram. My heart was pounding so rapidly, I felt like I had gone off-scale high.

That first night on the moon wasn't a very restful experience—even so I probably ended up with about six hours of decent sleep and was raring to get going the next morning.

# 18

## MOONWALKER

*April 21, 1972—On the Lunar Surface, Descartes*

"Good morning, Charlie," said Tony. "It's nice to hear your voice."

"Nice to hear you guys. We're up."

Boy, was I excited. The day had finally arrived—today we would *walk on the moon*! The shades were rolled up, and the reflected sunlight was streaming in. It was a beautiful moon day, a perfect day for a moonwalk!

I was eager to go. In fact I had been awake for an hour when the call came from Houston. Their call was a few minutes late, so I even had John awake.

We finished stowing our hammocks and ate a breakfast of peaches, cold scrambled eggs, cinnamon toast cubes, and a lemon food bar. While we ate, Houston reviewed our EVA schedule for the day. "And if you guys are all for it and everything," Tony suddenly said, "we're still trying to crowd in three EVAs."

"What do you mean, are we all for it?" laughed John. "Well, I just thought I'd give you a chance to vote," answered Tony. We thought he was teasing. That was the first we'd heard of any discussion to cancel our last EVA; fortunately the decision had been made to stay.

There were a lot more changes to be made in our time line for this first lunar excursion, and it wasn't long before our eagerness turned to frustration. Trying to get suited up and at the same time making all these fairly complicated changes in our procedures began to undo us. Complicating matters, our signal was coming across garbled, noisy, and scratchy, therefore Mission Control was having a difficult time hearing.

"Can you hear me?" I asked Tony. "We're just not reading you well enough to understand what you're saying there," he answered.

"Do I sound pretty bad too, Tony?" asked John. "Say again, John?" responded CapCom. John shrugged, "I must." I became concerned that once we were in our life support systems, we were going to be in a condition where nobody could talk to anybody.

Along with the COMM problem, John and I were having a terrible time getting into our pressure suits. It's tight in the lunar module anyway, and with our backpacks, boots, everything, we began missing a step or two.

"You're out of sync," I said to John. "Yes, we're out of sync," responded John, frustrated, "but you're supposed to be going back up there." We were on the verge of becoming unglued, as we hastily tried to get out on time.

"My what?" I questioned. "Plug it into this thing?"

"Charlie!" John shouted. "You got hold of a foot some way—in your gear."

We looked like the Keystone Cops falling all over each other, as we tried to get our spacesuits and backpacks on. Finally we stopped, took a deep breath, and began to methodically proceed step by step. We started making up time.

Before long I realized what was part of the problem with my communication—my microphones were full of orange juice! Once I cleaned them out, my COMM was better, but our voices were still coming across weak.

We got the suits and backpacks on, connected all the oxygen and communications lines, then the last thing to put on were our gloves. "Okay, my gloves are on and locked, Charlie," John reported happily.

But I was having trouble finding mine. "You don't see one of those white gloves down there anywhere, do you?" I asked John. "No," groaned John. "I sure don't, Charlie."

"On the floor anywhere?" I was getting worried. "No, I don't see one," he replied, exasperated.

"Ah, here it is," I sighed greatly relieved, finding it in one of the stowage areas.

The whole operation of getting suited up took over two hours. The last hurdle was a suit pressure check. When both suits passed, Houston gave us a go for depressurization of the lunar module.

We began to crank open the valve on the back of the hatch and heard a big whoosh, as the valve popped open and air was dumped out of the module. The pressure decreased from 5 pounds per square inch to 0.2 pounds, low enough for John to attempt opening the hatch.

"Here she comes—she's coming open!" I exclaimed. "There it is. Hatch is open, Houston."

The last thing to do before climbing out was to get our cooling water turned on. Neither one of us could reach our own switches, so as we helped each other we looked like two bulls in a china shop, grunting and scraping against one another and the instrument panel.

"Turn around, Charlie." "I'm just trying to turn around. You're in front of me. Okay, there we go."

"Okay, Houston," I announced. "We're ready to get out. Hey, why don't you go out, John?" I tried to hurry him up. John was to be first out, and I almost kicked him out of the hatch, eager for my turn. "You've got your PLSS [portable life support system] hung up," I told him. "Throw your rear end. There you go. You got it."

The only way out was kneeling down and backing out on hands and knees, through the hatch and onto the porch. It was like backing a ten-foot-wide truck out a ten-foot, two-inch door.

"Okay, Houston," reported John. "I'm standing out on the porch—my golly, what a view!"

"Hey, John, hurry up," I yelled. He seemed to be taking his time climbing down the ten-foot ladder.

"I'm hurrying," he answered. And as he stepped onto the surface for the first time, his opening words were, "Our mysterious and unknown Descartes Highland plains, *Apollo 16* is gonna change your image."

As soon as John finished his speech, it was, "Here I come, babe!" I quickly climbed out the hatch and down the ladder and jumped onto the ground.

"Fantastic! That's the first foot on the lunar surface," I announced. "It's super, Tony. We're making little footprints here about one-half inch deep." It wasn't much of a speech, but I was really excited.

*Just imagine,* I thought to myself, *since the beginning of time, no human being has ever walked in this spot before.* But I could have been the ten thousandth on the moon, instead of the tenth, and it wouldn't have mattered to me. I was overjoyed at being there. I didn't go to get my name remembered; I went for the thrill of adventure and the desire to explore.

Out on the moon I experienced no fear whatsoever. In spite of the hostile environment, I felt like we belonged—not like aliens in a foreign land. Everything was familiar to us, and we felt right at home. We recognized our major landmarks and were comfortable in our spacesuits, plus our communication with Houston improved remarkably like they were right there with us instead of 240,000 miles away. And I didn't worry that some strange creature out of *Star Wars* was going to jump from behind the nearest rock and gobble us up!

However it was a very hostile environment. Because there is no atmosphere but total vacuum, we were completely dependent on the integrity of our spacesuits and the oxygen supply in our life-support systems. A hole or tear in the suit only the size of a nickel would be a disaster, resulting in almost instant death.

The lack of atmosphere also allows all solar radiation and heat to reach the lunar surface. When we landed, the sun was fifteen degrees above the eastern horizon, and the temperature was 85 degrees Fahrenheit. The temperature varies with the elevation of the sun above the surface, so three days later when the sun was fifty-five degrees above the horizon, the temperature had risen to almost *235 degrees* Fahrenheit! Fortunately the suit was designed to protect us from this heat and radiation. Only one time did I think about a suit puncture, and never did I worry about the heat or radiation.

We quickly adapted to our new environment—our home away from home for the next three days. In one-sixth gravity John could run like a gazelle, but I found that tiring and a little unstable and adopted a style of my own, sort of like a duck waddle. Even so it wasn't long before I fell down. To get up, I did a couple of push-ups and bounced myself upright. After that I realized falling wasn't such a big deal, but from my experience in the control room I knew that Mission Control felt otherwise and had moments of fear every time I fell.

"Wow, look at that landing!" I shouted to John. "You almost got a *big* rock." We were startled by our landing spot. Much of our landing area was covered with rocks or had a steep slope, and we had just missed a big boulder and a large crater. Where we had landed was about the only level and smooth place around.

*171*

We immediately went to work, opening the MESA (modular equipment stowage assembly) on the side of the LM, and deploying the rover, watching it bounce from the LM and pop into place.

"It's on the ground, Houston," I reported to CapCom. "Let's pick this baby up and turn it around," suggested John. So we *did*!

John got on his side and I got on mine and we just picked it up and carried it away from the lunar module. The rover only weighed eighty pounds in one-sixth gravity. It was the first car I have ever driven that if you didn't like your parking place, you could just pick it up and walk off with it. We felt like Superman. Even though the rover had reverse gear, it didn't have a rearview mirror; therefore we never used reverse, but instead preferred picking the car up to turn it around.

Not only was it easy to pick things up in one-sixth gravity, but we discovered we could throw things great distances. It was fun to do, and every time I could find something we no longer needed, I'd let it fly.

"Man, can you sling things a long way," I said as I hurled a little black bumper guard across the moon. "Look at that. Went into that crater." In one-sixth gravity it looked like it was in slow motion and would sail and sail and finally hit the surface.

While John began to check out and power up the lunar rover, I unstowed our experiments, the flag, rock boxes, and other things necessary for our EVA. Then I retrieved one of the cameras and, while standing in place and rotating, took a panorama shot which was a series of pictures covering 360 degrees. At every stop on our subsequent excursions, Houston would have us take one of these panoramas.

As I was taking these pictures, John got the rover running. "Ah, this is going to be some kind of different ride," he exclaimed. Unfortunately he experienced a problem with the rear steering; it wasn't working, and we couldn't figure out why. This really concerned us because if it wasn't fixed, our EVAs would possibly be curtailed, so we asked Houston to see what they could come up with.

I proceeded to mount the TV and 16-mm cameras on the rover. We'd carry these cameras with us on the rover for all our EVAs, allowing Houston to view everything. To operate the TV, all we had to do was plug it in, turn on the power switch, then point the antenna, which was about the size of an umbrella, toward the earth, directly overhead.

While I was doing this, John started setting up our first experiment. It was a far-UV camera, which operated in the ultraviolet spectrum and would be like a lunar observatory. Things were going clickety-click, moving right along on our time line. It was evident we had practiced these things hundreds of times before.

"Those guys—Covington and all of them," I named off different ones of our training team, "Jerry and Bob Kain and that group were all slave drivers, but it's really paying off, I'll tell you."

The TV camera was now mounted, and I switched it on. "Hey," shouted Houston, "we've got a picture!" "Of the ground, no doubt," said John, noticing the camera was pointed right at the ground.

The TV was operated from Mission Control by a guy named Ed Fendell. Ed could pan the camera side to side, tilt it up and down, zoom in and out, and even change the light setting.

"Hey, you're looking at me with the big eye."

"Right, the big eye's on you, Charlie," said Tony. Nothing could get by with that big eye on you.

"How's the picture, Tony?" I asked. "Very good picture," he replied. "Beautiful. Outstanding color. You're in living color!"

The 16-mm camera worked perfectly, too, which amazed us because it had given all the previous missions a pain in the rear end—never operating properly. We needed the movie camera for our traverses across the lunar surface when the TV wasn't operating. We finally got the rover loaded with all our maps, geological tools, and experiments.

Now it was time to put up the flag. This was a ritual on every Apollo moon flight—setting up an American flag on the lunar surface and having each of the crew's picture taken saluting the flag. Since there was no wind on the moon, the flag was fitted with a rod across the top to hold it out and give the appearance of a strong breeze.

I grabbed the Hasselblad to get John's picture. "Hey, John, this is perfect, with the LM, and the rover, and you, and Stone Mountain, and the old flag. Come on out here and give me a salute—big Navy salute."

"Look at this," John said, and with that he saluted and *jumped* about a foot off the ground. "Okay, off the ground once more," I said. "There we go"—and it was all caught on camera.

Now it was my turn. "I'd like to see an Air Force salute, Charlie," John laughed, "but I don't think they salute in the Air Force."

"Sure we do—and fly high and straight and land soft," I bragged.

After our picture taking, Tony announced, "This looks like a good time for some good news here. The House passed the space budget yesterday, 277 to 60, which includes the votes for the shuttle."

John and I were delighted. This meant that the space program was going to continue into the next phase—reusable, multimission spacecraft, more like an airliner. We hoped this would be a step toward having an orbital space station and possibly a moon base in the not so distant future.

"Tony," I replied, "again I'll say it. With that salute I'm proud to be an

American. I'll tell you, what a program and what a place and what an experience." I had always been patriotic, and now I was busting at the seams with love for my country.

"And I'll say it, too," agreed John. "So am I," added Tony.

The next thing we were to deploy was the ALSEP (Apollo lunar surface experiment package), containing all of the major scientific experiments, other than geology, that we were to conduct. ALSEP was to be powered by a little RTG (radioisotope thermoelectric generator). The fuel element for the generator was stowed separately on the lunar module descent stage and had to be removed by a special tool and placed inside the ALSEP. This was a critical maneuver because it had a very high temperature and, if it accidentally touched my suit or gloves, would burn a hole causing a decompression.

Therefore I was very careful as I pulled the fuel element out of its stowage area and walked over to place it into the RTG. I sure didn't want to stumble over any rocks. I was relieved when I was able to tell Houston, "The RTG is fueled."

By this time I'd worked up a good sweat and was tired and thirsty, so I paused for a drink. Since there are no water fountains on the moon, we carried about a gallon of water in our drink bags inside our spacesuits. It really tasted great. We had originally planned on having orange juice, but after my episode in orbit with sticky orange juice floating around inside my helmet, we decided to take only plain water.

It was now necessary to carry the RTG package and experiments package about one hundred yards from the lunar module to where we were going to deploy the experiments. I attached each package to the ends of an aluminum tube, making the whole assembly look like a clumsy dumbbell cradled in my arms, and began to jog out. However I had gone only about twenty yards when the RTG package fell off and bounced on the ground!

My heart sank. "Oh, no, I've destroyed the power source and the experiments," I thought. I didn't tell Houston, hoping they hadn't seen that stupid stunt, but when I looked over my shoulder the big eye was pointed right at me. Fortunately everything was intact, just a little dusty.

I noticed the dust getting deeper and deeper; my footprints now were about two to three inches deep. The dust was sticking to our suits and even though the surface of the moon was gray, my suit began to turn black. "Man, I'm black already from the knees down," I complained to Houston. Our Mr. Clean image didn't last long.

For emplacement of our ALSEP experiments, we had been told by the scientists that we needed a fairly level spot. I found a place over a nearby ridge; it was not as flat as we would have liked, but it was the levelest spot I could find. It was difficult to find any decent place because of the enormous amount of rocks, craters, and ridges.

While I worked on the ALSEP, John drove the rover out to the emplacement site for Houston to watch us do the experiments on TV. To this day we haven't figured out what happened, but when John began driving, the rear steering started working. We were elated. We needed both steering systems to complete our traverses according to mission rules.

John turned on the TV and pointed the antenna toward the earth. "Can you see the earth?" I asked. "No," he answered. "Ah, there it is. Oh, you little rascal, no wonder I couldn't find you."

The earth was directly overhead, and I had to rock my suit back and forth to get enough energy to arch backward and be able to see it. "It's not very big," I remarked.

Though the earth is four times larger than the moon, it really doesn't look four times as large from the surface of the moon. It wasn't a humongous earth hanging over our heads, in fact it was close to what the moon looks like from earth, only blue and white. At this time it was a half-earth; on earth looking at us you would have seen a half moon. The phases of the earth and moon are completely opposite, so during a full moon, we would experience a new earth and vice versa.

Unfortunately in that stiff spacesuit, I couldn't look at the earth long; the suit popped me immediately upright. We could only view the earth a few seconds at a time, unless we fell on our backs.

There were five major experiments on the ALSEP; John was responsible for deploying four of them, and I was responsible for one—the heat-flow experiment. This required drilling two holes ten feet deep into the surface of the moon with a small battery-operated, hand-held drill, then placing an electrical probe inside the holes to measure the heat that was escaping from the deep inner core of the moon.

*Apollo 15* had experienced a terrible time drilling into the lunar surface because of a bad design of the drill stems. We had redesigned the stems, and I hoped to have better luck. We were excited about what we might discover.

"MARK. Look at that beauty go. Look at that beauty stop. Look at that beauty go again." The drill would start out great, then hit a rock or something and come to a complete stop, and then get going again. I kept on, and slowly but surely we got down ten feet. Things looked good for a very successful experiment.

I had drilled the first heat flow hole and had begun on the second one, when I heard John sigh, "Charlie?"

"What?" I asked, hoping it wasn't bad news. "Something happened here," John said, very concerned.

"What happened?" I asked, beginning to get worried. "I don't know," said John. "Here's a line that pulled loose."

"Uh-oh . . . that's the heat flow. You've pulled it off." I couldn't believe it! John had accidently *ripped* the electrical power cord to my heat-flow experiment, making it worthless. The cord had gotten wrapped around his foot, and since it's impossible to look down and see your feet in our bulky spacesuits, he had broken the wire right off at the connector when he walked away.

"I'm sorry," apologized John. "I didn't even know—I didn't even know it."

We were *devastated*! We had trained so hard to make this experiment work, and here before the probe even got turned on, the power had been disrupted. Houston said they would look into a way to fix it, and tried to lift our spirits. I felt really low as I moved on to another task. For the next forty-eight hours they worked on ways to fix it. Later they informed us it could be done, but since it would take two to three hours to fix and was a risky procedure, we all agreed we should not try and sacrifice the time. This was our biggest disappointment of the entire flight; the heat flow had been one of our major experiments, and everyone was sorry to lose it.

John deployed his experiments—a magnetometer for measuring the magnetic field and a spectrometer to sample gases escaping from the lunar surface. I began the task of collecting core samples. This required drilling another hole ten feet deep, but this time the drill bit was hollow, enabling the stem to fill with lunar material. Then with a special tool, much like a large car jack, the stem and core sample were jacked out, disassembled, and the soil brought back for analysis. This would give us a vertical cross section of the subsurface.

After much hard work retrieving the core, Houston asked me to measure the depth of the hole with an instrument we called a *rammer-jammer*. This was a long rod, similar to the rods used to ram powder in Revolutionary War muskets. I was sure that the hole had collapsed when I pulled out the core, but when I dropped the rammer-jammer in, it disappeared, dropping all the way to the bottom. The lunar soil was so compacted, it had not collapsed.

Lunar soil is not like our soil here on earth. It's actually pulverized rock, not dirt, because there has never been life on the moon to create organic matter. The powdered rock has resulted from meteor impact and the extreme temperature variations, which cause the rocks to expand and contract and crumble.

The top layer of dust is very fine grained, like talcum powder, and varies from a fraction of an inch to several feet deep, depending on the location. Despite this, when we walked on the lunar surface, we sank only a few inches; it became very firm underneath. Beneath the dust layer is a coarser, loose-grained material.

The moon's soil was discovered to contain the same minerals we have here on earth, nothing exotic like Superman's krypton. It was very rich in these minerals, and when NASA agronomists cultivated seed under controlled conditions in the moon dust, the plants grew between two to five times faster than in earth soil.

The last experiment in the ALSEP required both of us to deploy. It was a seismic experiment to measure moonquakes and consisted of a series of listening devices called geophones, which were attached to a cable one hundred meters long. After we unwound the long cable and emplanted the geophones in the soil, we were able to test the accuracy of the experiment by firing small explosive charges in a device named *the thumper*.

"Okay Charlie. Hold still," said John. "4—3—2—1—FIRE! Sound doesn't travel too good in a vacuum. I don't hear a thing, but it jumped."

"It's firing Babe. I'll tell you," I exclaimed. "Good," responded John. "Getting me all dirty."

"Great!" laughed Tony. "Not great—it's getting you all dirty—great it's working."

Houston wanted pictures of all the experiments in the ALSEP area, so I ran to get a camera. "Ah, footprints in the moon. Can't believe it!"

"They'll probably erode away in about four billion years," said Tony.

John and I were having a great time talking nonstop and joking back and forth, almost like Laurel and Hardy. It seemed like a regular training session with CapCom Tony England joining in.

We had been out on the surface about four hours and had completed the ALSEP experiments and picture taking, now it was time to configure for our geology. The plan was to sample around the ALSEP area, get a few rocks and soil, and then drive the rover about a mile west to a place called Plum Crater for a more extensive geological survey.

Collecting samples was more difficult than we had thought, plus dust was getting on everything—us, the cameras, the bags, the tools. "Charlie, what are you doing with the dirt?" exclaimed John. "You just threw it all over yourself!"

"I didn't mean to," I answered. "The rock fell out. Okay, Tony. It's a white matrix in this rock with some clasts—it's a one-rock breccia. One of the clasts just fell out. But it really looks like a caliche material, sort of friable, bag 373."

"Okay, 373," responded Tony. Each rock was described and bagged.

"What are you going to do?" I asked John, who was walking toward me with a dust brush. "Clean me off? Or clean off the old camera?"

"Naw, I'm gonna clean up the camera, get that dust out of there."

"Hey, can you get my gloves a minute, John? Just clean them a minute, to get that loose stuff off." This dust, we realized, was going to be a major problem, for we were constantly having to stop and use our dust brush.

Now it was time to mount the rover and head out to Plum Crater. I was really excited to jump in—John had already tried it out but I hadn't. Because of the bulkiness of the suits, we had decided that the best way to get in was to grab hold of the rover next to the instrument panel, bounce a few times, then jump up, and pull ourselves in, hoping to land on the seat.

"Okay, babe. Here I come—the old rover for the first time. Oops! Man, am I sitting up in the air." It worked—I landed right on the seat, but it felt like I was suspended in the air. The stiff suit had me extended straight out, and it took some effort to bend it and wedge myself in enough to buckle the seat belt. The seat belts were absolutely necessary because the rough ride would have bounced us right out of the rover.

I felt like Christopher Columbus as we started out. John was the driver and I was the navigator, picture taker, and travel guide. It was my job to describe and photograph the terrain, while directing John from point A to point B. John had his hands full trying to keep the rover out of craters and away from boulders.

I was the typical tour guide, except my tourists were 240,000 miles away in Mission Control. "At our 11 o'clock position, we're at 089 for 0.4. We have two very bright, small craters that are 2 to 3 meters across, and we see some whitish material down below in the walls of the craters there. They're about 25 meters off. Okay, we're going generally west now. We're in another distinct boulder field."

The area was covered with rocks of all sizes, and John was really having a difficult time avoiding them. About seven miles in the distance, I could see South Ray, a spectacular crater about fifteen hundred feet across, flanked by enormous boulders that were probably 90 feet in diameter. These large boulders had been thrown out of the crater by the force of a meteorite impact.

The meteorite had also ejected a great amount of smaller rocks, which formed white and black rays extending for miles in all directions, emanating like sun rays. These rays contained more rocks than the general terrain, and our drive to Plum took us right across some of them.

We continued on west, passing by Spook and Buster craters. We thought we had seen big craters until we came upon these; they were really biggies! Buster was about one hundred fifty feet in diameter; its entire crater bottom was covered with large rocks, which we estimated to be about ten to fifteen feet across.

As we drove on, we began to get more and more confused. Everything looked the same. The navigation system was a simple gyrocompass and odometer. To get from point A to point B, we steered a certain heading on the compass and went a specified distance according to our maps. All this of course was dependent upon our starting in the right place. We estimated we had landed about two hundred meters from our intended landing, but that was just a guess.

Because we weren't certain of our exact landing spot, we experienced a great deal of frustration. By the second EVA we had figured out where we were and were able to compensate, but trying to find Plum on this first excursion got to be almost a joke.

"There it is over there . . . no, here . . . no, no, that's not it"—and we'd drive a little farther. We even stopped and began to get out at one place, but it didn't seem right, and we went on.

"Man, you can't believe this territory," said John. The area was simply covered with angular rocks thrown from South Ray Crater and was rolling and hilly. Finally we ended up at a crater that was similar to what we were looking for, and I think it was Plum, but there was really no guarantee.

"Okay, Tony," I reported. "We're parking right on the rim of Plum. Dismounting." And we jumped out eager to explore.

"Are you still in the ray material there at Plum?" asked Tony.

"No. The ray material is about fifty meters to the east of us, Tony," I answered. "Good," he said. "We don't want to be."

Our task was to do some geological experiments, a magnetometer experiment, and collect samples on the rim of Plum Crater. I jogged over to the edge to photograph a pan of the area.

"Yeow, is that some crater, Tony! Whew, it's a smooth crater, very subdued, but it's really steep. I can't even see the bottom right where we are."

"That is spectacular!" echoed John.

"Charlie," warned Tony, "don't fall in that thing."

"I'm not gonna fall in it." The crater was so steep that if either one of us accidently fell in, it would have spoiled our whole day! There was no rescue from the bottom of a big crater. We had no ropes to pull the other one out, and it would have been practically impossible to climb out by oneself.

We had wanted to bring a tether along, for this reason and also for use as a harness like a mountain climber to allow us to venture down into a crater, but the idea made the managers too nervous and the tether was scrubbed.

The view from the rim was spectacular. To the south, I could see Stone

Mountain and South Ray Crater. Then to the north was the rolling horizon, with the gray of the lunar surface and above it the blackness of space.

John and I got the rake, tongs, and shovel and began to collect samples. We had these specially designed tools, because the suits were such, it was impossible to bend at the waist and pick up rocks. The shovel was for scooping soil, the rake for sifting through and collecting rocks one-half inch and larger, and the tongs for picking up baseball size rocks.

"Okay, Tony," I said. "This one is a breccia with a white matrix, is glass coated on one side, and then typical glass—lunar surface glass coating." Utilizing all our geology training, we described each rock.

"That's rock bag 352, Houston," reported John as he bagged it. "Okay, 352," said Tony.

"I take it back," said John, "that's rock bag number 2." Tony chuckled, "Okay, number 2."

"Come on," I said. "Stick her in; let's go." John dropped the bagged rock into my backpack and off we went. "Charlie," said John, "you're gonna fall down here with all these rocks." My backpack was almost full.

"No," I laughed. "I'll give you the shovel in just a minute when I fill up, and we'll swap. This shovel is a great tool I'll tell you. Oh, boy. Man, here come the Bobbsey Twins!"

John had great balance and could really run well on the moon. He reminded me of Superman—"Faster than a speeding bullet, stronger than a locomotive, leaps tall buildings with a single bound." If John had had a cape behind him, he would have looked exactly like the Man of Steel.

"You guys look like you're having a ball." "We are," replied John. "It really is fun."

"Boy, my kids don't get as dirty as you are," remarked Tony.

Our suits were really getting filthy. We were dropping bags and having to scrounge around in the soil to recover them. It was like rolling around in a coal bin. Plus the lunar regolith was very loose and unconsolidated and with every step, we sprayed dust all over us.

"Now, John, look—look at the footprint. Look underneath that regolith. When you kicked that up a centimeter or so, under it is white, absolutely white." The top layer of soil was gray, but surprising to us about an inch below it was pure white—a unique feature of this part of the lunar surface.

Houston directed us to a big boulder, and John brought out his trusty hammer. Pounding on rocks was one of John's favorite activities during training. He started whamming away and was able to break off a little piece.

We collected a few more samples and then Tony announced, "Okay, it's time to go back and pack up, and as you come around there, there is a rock on this rim that has some white on the top of it. We'd like you to pick it up as a grab sample."

"That's a football size rock. Are you sure you want a rock that big, Houston?" asked John.

"Yeah, let's go ahead and get it," replied Tony. "That's twenty pounds of rock right there," said John.

Because I had to put my back to the crater to retrieve it, I was a little concerned about falling in. "If I fall into Plum Crater getting this rock, Muelhberger has had it." Bill Muelhberger was our geology team leader, and I knew he was calling the shots from the back room. But it was a beautiful rock. Since it was too big to go into any of our bags, we just put it on the floor of the rover. It was the largest rock we brought back and we named it *Big Muley* after Bill.

Our next stop was Buster, a crater we had passed on our way to Plum. Since my cooling water supply was getting low, Houston cut short our station time there.

Buster was a lot bigger than Plum. We parked the rover on a ridge near the south rim, so Mission Control could monitor our activities on TV. While we were unloading, I looked back to the east and about a mile away, I could see the lunar module, Orion, glistening in the sun. The orange reflective material of the descent stage stood out in sharp contrast to the dull gray of the lunar surface.

John was to do another magnetics experiment, and I was to use a 500-mm lens and take pictures of South Ray Crater, Stone Mountain, and make a pan of the area. "Okay, I'm finished my pan and the 500," I announced. "I'm gonna run over to Buster and do some sampling. Man, is this gonna be a steep ridge to climb." Not only were the walls really steep, but there were blocks all over it.

"Yeow whee! Man, John! I tell you, this is some sight up here. Looking down into that beauty, the bottom is covered with blocks—the largest five meters across—90 percent of the bottom is covered with blocks." The general opinion was that this was a secondary crater, made by a big boulder that had been blasted out of another larger crater.

As I collected samples around that steep rim, I was really careful to watch my step. I sure didn't want to fall in. Houston was rushing us up, so I ran around grabbing rocks as fast as I could; sort of like a kid at an Easter egg hunt who was running out of time and wanted to get as many eggs as he could.

We loaded up and headed back to our landing site. John cut loose, and we made about ten kilometers an hour in our rover. We'd hit small craters and bounce right through them and then the back end would break loose and fishtail.

"Yahoo!" I shouted. "Look at that thing dig in."

"Boy, we just missed a—" John began. "Are you steering on all four wheels?" Tony interrupted, getting concerned. It was like driving on an ice-covered road.

Once we got back to the lunar module, our flight plan called for me to take 16 mm pictures of John driving the rover. The previous mission had not taken any movies of the rover underway, so this would be a first.

I dismounted and gave John the high sign, "Okay, let her go," and off he drove. Boy, what a sight it was seeing that rover bounce across the surface. Most of the time one wheel was off the ground. And as the rover dug into the soil, the wheels threw up big rooster tails of dust. These were some of the best pictures we brought back because they were unique.

Our first moonwalk had come to an end. We had been out a little over seven hours and Mission Control was getting antsy about getting us back inside the LM. My normal cooling water was gone, and I was on reserve, caused by all the energy I had expended; it had been a big workout.

Back in the LM we couldn't believe how filthy we were. John laughed. "The only place you haven't got dirt is on your neck ring." That was only because it had been protected by my helmet. All that falling down had covered everything with dust. We had some washrags to wipe off our suits, but that just seemed to rearrange the dirt. The dust was so fine it pressed right into the suit fabric.

I was surprised at the odor of the dust. For some strange reason, it smelled like gunpowder. I could never figure out why. Another puzzle was the dust had a very greasy or oily, slick feeling to it, yet the moon contains no moisture. We suspected that this dry dust was absorbing moisture from our cabin atmosphere.

We were really tired, and when CapCom Ed Mitchell joked that after an eight-minute break, we could start on EVA 2, we said, "No way—you better send a couple more guys up here."

Our fingers were badly bruised. Working in that spacesuit, squeezing those gloves and pressing the tips of our fingers against the ends, caused our fingers to seem like bloody stumps.

After undressing and preparing our equipment for the next day's EVA, we weighed our rocks and soil samples. The total came to 44 pounds, not counting the Big Muley and some other large ones we'd left in the rover. We were allowed to bring back 215 pounds, so we had plenty more collecting to do.

There was time for a thirty-minute briefing with the geologists and scientists in the back rooms of Mission Control; they had lots of questions about the various rocks we had picked up. We figured we had sampled both the Cayley Plain material and South Ray material on this first EVA.

Following the briefing Tony said, "I think you did an outstanding job. The back room was elated. I went back there after the EVA and talked to them, and they were really excited, really pleased with it." We were glad to hear that, because we were still feeling low over the loss of the heat-flow experiment.

"Let me say," I responded, "that all our geology training has really paid off. Our sampling has been real teamwork, and we appreciate everybody's hard work on our sampling training." For the past three years we had worked with these guys—Bill Muelhberger, Lee Silver, Dale Jackson, and others—and they were now in Mission Control, coordinating our moon excursions right along with us.

John and I strung up our hammocks and got ready for bed. Deke Slayton got on the COMM and chatted awhile, "Well we got a nice casual schedule from here, so you might as well power down and get a good eight hours of snoozing. You'll really feel like it in the morning."

"Couldn't ever believe we'd go to sleep, Deke," I said, "but man, this guy John sleeps like a baby up here. I've never seen it."

"It sounds like the best place in the world to sleep," replied Deke. "I wish I was with you."

"We do too, boss," answered John.

I was physically tired, but because I was still so wound up I had a tough time calming down. Racing through my mind were thoughts of all the activities of our first day on the moon and our plans for tomorrow.

I knew I'd never get to sleep with my mind racing like that, so I decided to take another sleeping pill. I popped one down and within minutes was drifting off to sleep. John didn't have any trouble at all. Even before I took my pill, he was dead to the world.

# 19

# SURVIVAL

Dotty, Charles, Tom . . . how were they coping while I was bouncing around on the moon? Houston was a long way away—240,000 miles, plus or minus a few.

Although this might be the greatest distance I'd traveled, separation was nothing new to them. They had certainly gotten used to my being gone. I figured during training I had been out of town about 75 percent of the time. I was constantly packing a bag and saying good-bye to the family.

"Where are you going now, Charlie?" Dotty would sigh as she reluctantly helped me organize my things for another trip. Every trip was necessary for the good of the program, we rationalized. Nothing seemed unimportant. There were our geology trips, trips to oversee Apollo design and development, public relations trips, and survival trips.

One of my most interesting adventures was a survival trip to the jungles of Panama. Why survival training? Suppose our trajectory was not quite right when we reentered the earth's atmosphere, or we had a malfunction in the control system. We needed to be able to survive out in the middle of the ocean a thousand miles from our intended splashdown point—or in the desert or in the jungle. It would be senseless to return safely from the moon, a quarter of a million miles away, and then die waiting to be rescued simply because we didn't know how to survive in adverse conditions.

So in late 1967, we flew down to the Panama Canal Zone where the Air Force operated their jungle survival school. The program began with several days of classes where we were taught how to catch and cook exotic jungle creatures and other delicacies. We ate palm hearts, sampled boa constrictors, iguana lizards, and a creature that looked like a giant rat! I was surprised how tasty everything was. The rats tasted much like pork, and the snake was very good, like chewy chicken.

When our teachers felt we were sufficiently trained as gourmet jungle chefs, they took us by helicopter to the middle of the jungle. In addition to an instructor, we were arranged into groups of three to simulate an Apollo crew. I was with Stu Roosa, Jack Swigert, and our instructor, who was a local Panamanian Indian.

First we hiked for a number of miles, learning how to traverse the jungle; the hills in Panama are not terribly high but they are remarkably steep. And they are covered with brush and foliage, which makes the going extremely difficult. We then began to look for a good place to camp. After descending a steep hill, we discovered this little six-foot-wide creek in the valley—perfect for our water needs.

"Okay, you can camp here if you like," said our instructor, "but be sure to get at least forty feet up the side of the hill above the creek." I didn't see the point of setting camp that high up above our water supply, but before the trip was over I was to discover why.

We picked a spot that seemed suitable and immediately began to construct a lean-to. The jungle floor is very damp and unsuitable for sleeping, so we tied hammocks between trees and covered them with mosquito netting. The next thing we needed was a fire, not only for boiling our water, but as a signal for search aircraft. We gathered a little wood from the jungle floor and shaved it into fine pieces that would ignite easily.

To light the fire, all we had were the items that were contained in our Apollo survival kit. This didn't include matches because of the fire hazard aboard the spacecraft. Instead we had a ball of cotton and a piece of flint. It seemed like such a simple procedure—to strike the flint so that it sent a spark flying onto the cotton and then to blow the spark into a flame.

We created our spark all right, but it just sat there smoldering in the cotton. We huffed and we puffed, but nothing happened. It was like the story of the wolf after the three little pigs, who huffed and puffed until he blew the house down. Only our huffing and puffing wasn't achieving anything.

We worked at least three hours blowing on the spark in our piece of cotton, while our instructor just sat there watching us. We were hyperventilating and practically turning blue. Jack was exhausted—Stu was exhausted—and I was exhausted!

At this point the guide stood up and announced, "Let me show you how it's done in the jungle." He reached into his pocket and pulled out a small object about the size of a package of chewing gum. On it was written U.S. AIR FORCE FIRE-STARTER. He jerked the top off this thing and had an instant flamethrower in his hand. It burned like a blowtorch! He stuffed it into the pile of wood and within seconds we had a roaring fire.

We couldn't believe it. He had sat there for over three hours watching us turn blue, saying nothing, all the while knowing that we weren't about to get that fire started. We almost strangled him! The only value that came out of that experience is that I can vouch for the fact that a cotton ball and a piece of flint don't work in the jungles of Panama.

Our next task was to clear an area of jungle so that we could set up signals for search aircraft. Monstrous trees, 3 or 4 feet in diameter at least 150 feet tall surrounded us, so we started cutting. To accomplish this, we had machetes—which to my surprise cut easily through the soft wood. The trees fell in such a manner as to span the valley, forming a bridge across to the other embankment, about 30 feet over the stream.

The next day it started to rain. It wasn't a light drizzle, but one of those torrential downpours that come with a tropical rainstorm. Within two hours that little creek—that had been only six feet wide and six inches deep—was now a raging torrent nearly forty feet deep!

I could hardly believe what I was seeing. The water rose like a bathtub filling, and for the first time I saw the power of a flash flood. This quiet stream, now turned into a raging river, carried away those huge trees like toothpicks. And the water came to within a few feet of our camp!

We didn't have much luck with our food. Since we had limited rations in our Apollo survival kit, we needed to supplement our rations with food from the jungle. I discovered that it's not as easy to catch animals in the jungle as I had imagined. To learn how to catch and cook in the comfort of the classroom is one thing, but to actually capture your prey is another.

We encountered very few animals—one poisonous snake, a number of scorpions, and in the distance we heard a single roar from one lone jaguar. All we netted in the few days we were there were a few little fish out of the creek. We did gather palm hearts from the tops of palm trees, but that and the fish were all we had to supplement our rations.

After several days we broke camp and hiked a few miles down the creek toward the main river. Here we inflated our survival raft and floated downstream toward an Indian village that was expecting us and had prepared a delicious meal. Thankfully they were much better at catching jungle creatures than we were. We were really rank amateurs.

Our next survival trip took us to the desert. Not many people would think of Washington State as a desert, but this is where we went. It was in the southeastern part of the state, south of Spokane. The land there is not all sand like the Sahara, but it's extremely arid and very much desert.

We spent four boring days out there. Our basic instructions were, "Don't move around; stay in the shade; try to get up off the ground"— because the temperature is about twenty degrees cooler a foot off the ground than it is directly on the surface. So we rested on inflated life rafts and draped our parachutes over the brush for shade.

We did attempt to collect water in a primitive solar watercollector that we had built. As the sun heated up the atmosphere, the moisture in the air was supposed to condense on a piece of plastic that we had suspended over a hole in the desert floor. When the water collected on the plastic, it was to drip down into a tin can placed beneath the plastic, providing about a can of fresh water a day.

Fortunately we had sufficient water in our survival kits to last the four days, because our collector never worked properly and produced only a couple of drops of water the whole time we were there.

In addition to these survival trips, we continued our geology field training. During 1967 and 1968 I looked at rocks on at least twelve different trips from Arizona to California to Hawaii. But of all the places we went, the closest in appearance to the moon was the interior of Iceland.

Iceland is an island that lies between Greenland and Denmark. It is really a series of large volcanoes; around the shore there is vegetation, but a few miles inland it is barren, very nearly resembling the lunar surface.

Upon arriving in Keflavík, we boarded a bus and headed for the interior. Our driver, Gudmunder Johanssen, seemed nonplussed when after a few miles the road ran out and we took off over the trackless wasteland. There was not so much as a blade of grass, but Gudmunder had years of experience and seemed to know where he was going.

We drove for several hours, then Gudmunder announced, "We're here." I looked out the window to see where we were. It looked like everywhere else to me, but we were told this was a spot that the geologists wanted us to study. All around us was volcanic ash and cinders, like you see on railroad tracks. A few thousand feet away was an active volcano.

For several days we moved from spot to spot in this barren interior, driving for hours without seeing a sign of life. Then occasionally we'd suddenly top a ridge and before us was an oasis formed from geysers. In places water would have seeped down through the cinders, collected, become superheated from the geothermal activity of the volcano, and spurted out as geysers. These geysers formed hot springs throughout the island, then from the bubbling springs would flow a stream, and along its banks would be a meadow. One such spot we shared with a group of British hikers on holiday. I couldn't ever imagine spending my holiday trekking across Iceland.

Since there were no roads or bridges, we had to ford the rivers. Gudmunder would don hip boots, wade into the water, and with a long steel pole test the bottom. If he found it safe, he would drive us across the river. The bus was equipped with a special engine and exhaust system, so that we could drive through even when the water was deep enough to come up inside the bus.

Just in case our bus broke down, an organization similar to the U.S. Coast Guard kept track of our location through a radio check-in system. Gudmunder would call in frequently and report our position, just as pilots do when flying an airplane. Fortunately we didn't have any mechanical difficulties.

We had heard that the fishing in Iceland was great and looked forward to trying our luck. One particular day we had been out all morning without seeing a soul when we came to a spot where there was a beautiful lake. Some of the guys jumped off the bus and headed for the water. I was about to follow, but before they had cast twice, a man appeared out of nowhere and tapped Bill Anders on the shoulder. "Let me see your fishing license," he demanded.

*187*

"I don't have one," Bill answered, totally flabbergasted. Of course none of us had one. Who would have thought you needed a fishing license out in the middle of the boondocks?

"Well, it just so happens I can sell you one," he replied. We found out he had been hired by the owner of the lake to collect the fees. So in the middle of Iceland, miles from nowhere, they paid their money and received fishing licenses. Watching from the bus, I decided to pass.

I think the worst trip I ever took was a two-day water survival exercise in the Gulf of Mexico. "Never volunteer," we used to say at the Naval Academy. Why I never learned that lesson, I don't know. But when Jim Lovell approached me to volunteer for a checkout of the flotation capabilities of the Apollo command module, I agreed.

NASA was extremely thorough and covered all the squares. They needed three guinea pigs to sit inside the command module for forty-eight hours as it bobbed around the Gulf of Mexico. Everything had to be checked out—its flotation capability, environmental systems—and so Jim, Stu Roosa, and I insanely volunteered to be the guinea pigs.

I suppose Jim had been able to talk me into this exploit because I saw it as a good opportunity to spend time in the command module to do some further training. We were helicoptered out to a ship where we jumped excitedly aboard the spacecraft. When I got inside, I realized I had been taken—it was practically an empty shell! It contained none of the instrumentation that we would use in flight.

A ship's crane then lifted the command module and dropped us overboard someplace in the gulf, where we spent the next couple of days bobbing up and down on the waves. It was the most miserable two days I have ever spent!

The module spun clockwise, counterclockwise, and every way imaginable! I couldn't *believe* what I had done! I had chosen the Air Force instead of the Navy because I suffered from seasickness, and now I found myself swallowing Dramamine pills every few hours to avoid getting sick.

Also the ventilation system brought in moist sea air that caked the entire interior with salt. It became really uncomfortable, and we were very bored. The experiment was successful; we did demonstrate the module's seaworthiness. Fortunately all the Apollo flights came within a few miles of their intended splashdown spots, so that we were the only astronauts who had to endure being locked in a command module for any length of time. What a *relief* it was when they finally opened the hatch and a helicopter took us ashore.

These official training trips were not the only trips I took. As an astronaut, I had the opportunity of meeting many people who invited me on some terrific vacations. I hunted elk in Oregon, quail in Oklahoma, deer in Florida, played golf at great spots like Palm Springs and went to the Super Bowl a number of times. Almost every weekend it was hunting, fishing, or golf.

Unfortunately this had caused some tension at home because the wives were not included on most of these trips. They didn't have access to T-33s and T-38s and had to stay home with the kids. Since I was gone most of the week working, Dotty couldn't understand why I wanted to be gone over the weekends, too. She thought if I loved her I would want to be home with her. But these trips had been hard to pass up, so off I went.

She had come to me and asked, "Why do you have to do this? You're gone all the time. Why do you have to go hunt? Why can't you stay with us?"

I could tell she had become very unhappy and hadn't appreciated my leaving, especially on these fun trips. My answer had been to brush it aside and say, "Well, in a few years it'll get better. After Apollo, I'll have more time." So she had tried to adjust herself to my schedule and looked forward to a more normal family life after Apollo.

Because of these demands on my time, I had felt pulled in many directions. I had to do a good job to get a crack at a spaceflight and that took time, plus I wanted to do the things I enjoyed doing—like hunting, fishing, and golf. Added to this I had felt pulled by the boys, knowing I had a responsibility to them. But most of all had been this pressure from Dotty wanting more time with me. It had been tough work balancing my time and trying to satisfy everyone, and I had failed miserably at home.

I grew to resent Dotty's demands, but I didn't resent the demands from work—I was having a ball. It was the greatest job I had ever had. I loved being involved in a lot of different things—working hard on one area for a few days and then changing my attention to another area. I loved all these different facets of spaceflight and training. This was my personality and I doubted it would ever change, even after Apollo. Dotty would have to learn to take a backseat.

# 20

# *MOONWALK II*

"Houston, Orion," radioed John to CapCom. "What time are we supposed to get up? What time is wake-up time?" We were excited and anxious to get going on our second day out on the lunar surface.

"You're about 3½ minutes from normal wake-up now," answered Cap-Com.

"How did the system look last night?" inquired John.

"Everything looked real good, John," responded Tony.

I turned on my comm. "Hello, Houston, *15*. I guess it is *16*, Houston. I guess we're *16*."

"How do you feel this morning?" asked Tony. "I feel great," I answered. "Why don't you have the docs tell me how much they think I slept?"

"Charlie," replied Tony, "they say they think you've slept six hours."

"Fine. I was going to say seven. Of course, I don't know exactly when we got started, but once we got started, it was just like a baby, except for one time. I woke up when I got cold and had to put on my sleeping bag.

"Okay," I continued, "here we go with the crew status report. I'd like to say that we stuffed and gorged ourselves, really, and still couldn't eat everything. I tell you one of those meals would fill the whole Roman army on maneuvers for two days." With only two meals a day—they made sure we had plenty to eat.

We continued chatting and completing our housekeeping chores. Tony began describing the EVA plan for the day when all of a sudden everything went blank and we lost communication. Then surprisingly, an Australian accent came over the line, "This is Honeysuckle. We have a comm outage with Houston at this time. Stand by 1, please."

"Okay, Honeysuckle," responded John. "Nice to talk to you. How are ya'll doing there?"

We struck up a conversation with our station in Australia, thanking them for their help. "We'd sure like to come down there and see you folks," commented John.

"You've got a permanent invite," Honeysuckle answered. "Anytime you like. We'll keep the beer cool."

"That's the best idea I've heard all day," I piped in. "A 48-pack, the way I feel. I'd really love one." What great guys, those Australians. When we got back to Houston, there were a couple of cases of Australian Swan beer waiting in our garages.

Comm with Houston returned and we finished reviewing our second EVA. Since we had been finding different type rocks than we had expected, the geology science team decided they would modify our procedures. The destinations were to be the same, but the procedures at each stop were to be different.

We had expected to find volcanic rock on our excursions—viscous basalt in the mountainous area which we called Descartes and less viscous material on the Cayley Plain. The other Apollo flights had collected mostly volcanic samples, so we expected to find the same and were surprised when on the first EVA we found very little volcanic material.

Most of the rocks we had collected were breccias—fragments of rock encased in a fine-grained matrix. A majority had a whitish gray matrix with black inclusions. Some were glass covered; the glass probably forming from rocks that had melted during meteorite impact, and these were black. Others were almost pure white and very friable or crumbly.

Had the highlands been formed by aeons of cosmic bombardment, instead of volcanic activity? Our trip to the highlands would be the only Apollo excursion to this type of terrain, and the geologists were hopeful it would help solve the mystery of the early formation of the moon.

Our major objective was to go south to Stone Mountain, climbing the mountain almost to the summit to a place called Cinco Craters. Ken had noticed from orbit several benches or levels on the mountain that ran east-west, and we were to stop and collect samples on three of these benches. It was believed that the rocks on Stone Mountain would be different from those at Cayley Plain.

Once we had finished sampling on Stone, we would drive westward toward South Ray Crater along a place called Survey Ridge, getting as close to South Ray as they would allow us, since South Ray itself was about eight miles away and out of our range. We were to try to find some of the dark ray material that had come out of the crater. Then we would return to the lunar module, sampling as we drove, bringing us back about seven hours after we started.

After a quicker suit donning, we loaded up and headed out. It was easier driving today—going cross sun rather than heading into it, as on our first EVA return. John was really driving fast—about 10 kilometers (6.5 miles) per hour and we were bucking, and rocking, and bouncing as we crossed the lunar surface. The soil was loosely compacted and looked like a freshly plowed field that had been raked smooth and rained on, although there's no rain on the moon.

## Mission Control Viewing Room, Houston

Dotty settled into her seat, ears strained to hear every word transmitted from the moon. The TV stations had decided not to give live coverage of all the moonwalks, so Dotty had brought her mother and dad and my parents, who had quickly flown to Houston from South Carolina, over to Mission Control in order to view our second EVA.

Of course for all critical phases of flight, like lift-off and landing, these were covered by the major networks; but for TV coverage of the moonwalks, it was necessary to go to the nearby space center and watch in the Mission Control viewing room. Therefore for each moonwalk Dotty spent the entire time period sitting in the NASA facility so she wouldn't miss out on any of our adventures.

Tom and Charles would come for an hour or two at a time—they couldn't sit still for the whole almost-eight-hour EVAs. Also in the viewing area were Werner von Braun and many other vital NASA personnel. The huge ten-foot-high screen gave everyone a great picture of us bouncing around on the lunar surface.

At other times Dotty could listen to the squawk box, a radio that gave live air-to-ground communication between the spacecraft and Houston, which NASA had installed at each of the crew homes.

On the third day my brother, Bill, and the rest of our family joined the large Duke contingency. A special moment for Bill and Dr. Claiborne came when they were invited into the Mission Control console area to observe the medical data being transmitted from our sensors.

Dotty was being kept plenty busy during our flight. The house was full of relatives who had come to keep her company. Then there were the regular interviews by reporters getting their daily stories and pictures for newspaper coverage of the mission, plus friends were constantly streaming in and out, bringing food and watching the important maneuvers which were covered live on TV.

I had visited other wives' homes during the first Apollo flights and knew what Dotty was going through. The atmosphere at a crewman's house during flight fluctuates between a wake and a wedding. During critical maneuvers, everyone is quiet or whispering, hoping for a safe and not tragic conclusion. The rest of the time is joyous—greeting visitors, tables of food, kids running around, telephones ringing—a real celebration.

I did find out later about an unexpected emergency that happened at our home the day of lift-off from the moon. Dr. Claiborne was pulling some things out of a high closet shelf, and a sheet of glass fell and shattered, making a deep gash across his nose. Mrs. Claiborne panicked, and Dr. Claiborne almost passed out; blood was gushing from his wound.

Dotty rushed him to the NASA clinic as he held a handkerchief now well bloodied over the wound. Not wanting to miss any of the flight proceedings, the doctors brought in a radio so that Dotty and her parents could follow our final preparations for lift-off, while they stitched up his nose. Dr. Claiborne was still sporting a bandage when I returned to Houston several days later.

## Back on the Moon in the Rover

Initially it was a smoother terrain than the day before, but as we got farther away, the surface got rougher and rougher; there were more rocks and more craters. Driving along the eastern end of Survey Ridge on the way to Stone, we were pointed almost directly at South Ray Crater and into ray material. The dark material was all around us.

"Boy, you just can't believe the blocks, Houston," exclaimed John. It was difficult driving; the rover would take the six-inch rocks, but the large ones we had to navigate around. Some were as large as six feet—it was impressive! We were afraid we'd be stuck there all day, so we looked for a way out of the ray.

"Houston," said John, "the best idea I can give you of what this looks like, is it looks like about halfway up to that crater that we went to out at the Nevada test site. Man, I tell you. I've never seen so many blocks in my life."

"Sounds like that was a good exercise then," suggested CapCom.

"Good exercise in driving," I answered.

"Oh!" cried John. "That was a baddy!"

"That hit on the floorboard," I informed Houston. "Even getting dust on my helmet. Boy, this is neat, *really* neat." I was having a ball, but we were concerned about hitting a big rock and smashing our radio and TV control. They were situated right on the front bumper.

"Hey, that was *super*! That wheel just left the ground," I shouted. "This is the wildest ride I was ever on," declared John.

"I love it!" I yelled. "This is great. Eight clicks [kilometers per hour], Tony. We got up to twelve there, once."

"Sounds like you're really making money there," said Tony. We were pushing, so as not to get behind schedule. It was up and down slopes, hitting bumps, and dust flying everywhere.

We finally arrived at the base of Stone Mountain and began climbing. From the slope we had a tremendous view of South Ray Crater. It was just spectacular—almost pure white, glistening, with white rays emanating from the center.

"And there's Baby Ray, John," I exclaimed. On the flank of South Ray was a crater called Baby Ray. It was unique because it had black sides instead of white, like a little black dollop on the flank of this tremendous crater.

"Man, we're really going up a hill, I'll tell you," I said. It was a steep climb now, as we pointed toward the Cinco Craters.

The five craters came into view, and we started looking for a good place to park. Can you imagine being the only vehicle on the lunar surface and not finding a satisfactory parking place? But the terrain was rough and steep, and we didn't want to go rolling down the hill if the brakes failed.

As we were settling in to park, Houston called, "Hey fellows, Ken was just flying over and he saw a flash on the side of Descartes. He probably got a glint off you." We figured he must have caught the sun gleaming off our battery mirrors. Ken was sixty nautical miles above, and this was the only time he saw us during our lunar stay. CapCom kept him informed of our whereabouts and our comments of the terrain in order to coordinate both efforts.

Ken had requested a full schedule in order to reap as much scientific harvest as possible. He was really keeping busy with his on-orbit science experiments and picture taking. He had planned so many projects to work on that occasionally he had to be reminded to eat.

The view from up on this mountain was almost unbelievable—the sharp contrast of the gray lunar surface and the blackness of space. And out in the middle of the valley was the lunar module, an oasis of color on the gray terrain.

"We can see the lunar module!" I shouted. "Look at that, John." I was excited. The view all around us was spectacular. South Ray, North Ray, our landing spot . . . but most spectacular of all was the slope we had just climbed—about twenty degrees. Talk about Jack and Jill—we could go tumbling down the mountain, all the way to the bottom without stopping.

"Wow, what a place. What a view! You should really come up, Tony," I said. "All I can say is spectacular, and I know ya'll are sick of that word, but my vocabulary is so limited. Can you guys see how really spectacular the view is?" I had the TV turned on now.

"We sure can," replied Tony. "We're darn near speechless down here."

We began taking pictures and gathering samples, and I measured the compactness of the soil with a penetrometer. Walking around on this slope was like climbing a steep sand dune—the soil was very loose and as we'd climb, we'd slide backward in the soft dust. The best way to go up was to hop like a jackrabbit

My mind was filled with the thrill of being there and the awesome beauty. I knew it was a hostile environment, that we were a long five kilometers from the lunar module, and that I could roll down the mountain and split open my suit. Yet I didn't think about those things at all. It was like a Sunday afternoon hike rather than a dangerous adventure that could be fatal with one breakdown of the equipment.

John and I collected a variety of samples. Dust covered everything, making it difficult to describe what we were finding. We had spent years on our geology training learning to describe and identify rocks; now we were getting frustrated with all the dust and seeming lack of variety. Really all we had to do was pick up one of each color—gray, black, and white.

I was scheduled to take a core, and the first twenty inches went in easily. The soil was so loose, all I had to do was push it in. Then as I hammered the next twenty inches, to pass the time I sang, "I've been hammering on the railroad."

I must have looked like a two-year-old, whacking the handle of that core. The hammer kept bouncing around and twisting in my hand; I even dropped it a few times—the hammer just didn't fit in my glove too well. And when the hammer flipped out and dropped, I'd have to go back and get another tool to retrieve it; I couldn't bend over well enough to pick it up.

This station probably had the most difficult working conditions for our entire stay. The slope was very steep and I got pooped, climbing up and down, gathering rocks and doing the experiments. Plus we had to avoid falling into the craters or down the hill. I must have fallen down five times. We really earned our pay at this first stop.

"Okay. We're headed 354." And we were on our way to the next location. "Downslope is easy," I said.

"As long as the brakes hold out," John interjected.

"Have you got the brakes on?" I asked. "Partially—have to," said John. All the way down the slope we had to use the brakes. It was that steep.

"We're going back down our tracks, Tony," I remarked.

"Ya-ho-ho-ho-ho! Look at this baby!" shouted John. "I'm really getting confidence in it now. It's really humming like a kitten—we're making ten kilometers an hour."

For our next stop on the slope of Stone Mountain, we looked for a primary crater—a crater made by a direct hit from a meteorite. We wanted to find some samples of the Descartes rock of which Stone Mountain was made. The rock from the earlier stop, we felt, had all been thrown there from South Ray Crater.

Most everything looked the same to us, but we kept digging and raking and finally John stumbled across a white crystalline rock which Houston believed was from Descartes. "Boy, Charlie, look at this rock. That has got to be plage—look at these little crystals in it. That's the first one I've seen here that I really believe is a crystal rock, Houston."

"Outstanding," remarked Tony. He named it the "Great Young." Houston was delighted.

We made a third stop on Stone Mountain, on its lowest terrace near a blocky crater. At each stop I would give Mission Control a status report on the rover and our suits and portable life-support system. The rover was performing superbly and using a lot less energy than had been estimated.

When we jumped out we noticed a real difference in the regolith or surface. "Now this is harder—we're just sort of bouncing here," said John.

"Yeah, the regolith character—it's really changed," I added. We weren't making footprints at all and could feel the hard rock underneath our feet.

I had a hammer in my hand and whacked on a big boulder, breaking off a chunk. "That matrix is pure white, John, with black phenocryst in it. It might be clast. And it's got some lathlike crystals in it. It might be breccia."

This was exciting to us. It turned out to be a very productive area of fine-grained crystalline rock. They were quite hard, unlike the friable samples higher up the mountain. We had only twenty minutes to grab a few and take some pictures.

"It's time to load up right now," announced Tony. We raced around getting finished.

"Boy, is this a neat way to travel," commented John, as he jogged in graceful leaps.

"Isn't it great," I said. "I like to skip along." "Oh, Charlie, you're pure crazy," remarked Tony.

"Well, whatever you call it," I laughed, "I can't get my left leg in front of me. Oh, the docs never knew!"

John got in his side of the rover, and I made ready to jump in and said, "Now watch this big leap. Oh, oh—can't leap. I'm hooked onto something, fell down again, John."

"Yes, I saw that," sighed John. "Can you make it? You want me to get out and help you?"

"No, I'm getting it now," I answered, embarrassed. "I'm next to the rover. My backpack hit the seat and just vaulted me off." John didn't take too kindly when I would fall down like that. He was concerned about my safety, plus the time it took to get up and get all dusted off.

We headed west toward South Ray crater to gather some ray material. About three-quarters of the way through this stop, we realized we needed to reload our large bags that we carried on each side of our backpack. We had collected so many rocks, our shopping bags were full.

Trying to get them unlocked and stored on the floor of the rover and getting new ones out was terribly frustrating and taking a lot of time. We were working behind the lunar rover, and as I walked away my suit got caught in the rear fender and ripped off the whole back half.

"We lost a fender, Tony," I informed Houston. "The pusher-downer fender on the right rear wheel is gone." It had happened so many times in training, we didn't think much of it. Little did we realize it was going to create a much irritating problem. When we drove away, we quickly discovered that without the fender, the lunar dust was thrown up and then literally rained down all over us. We thought we were dusty before, but now with the lunar dust shower, we really got filthy.

On these EVAs we had all sorts of unusual requests from the geologists. They wanted soil samples that were underneath rocks, soil that was between rocks in an east-west orientation, permanently shadowed rock that had never seen the sun, to name just a few. At our next stop it was decided that John would collect a lunar dust sample that was undisturbed and uncontaminated. This meant that John could not kick any dust on the sample as he approached it with his special sampling tool.

We had nicknamed it *The Big Sneak*. We figured the only way to do this was to approach from behind a big rock, then reach over and collect it. In training, John had practiced for hours sneaking up on this simulated sample. So now on the moon, he was sneaking up on this rock that was about three feet high.

Sneaking on the moon isn't easy in one-sixth gravity. It was hilarious. He bounced as much as he sneaked! John got there before the rock even knew he was coming. He looked like a cat stalking a canary. Unfortunately Mission Control missed the whole deal. They had the TV camera pointed the other way. "Gee, the first lunar great rock hunt and we missed it," lamented Tony.

We also had been looking for a rock we could push or turn over, in order to sample the soil underneath. The sample would give us information on the variability of the solar radiation. Mission Control wanted one as big as we thought we could move. We found a big six footer and decided to tackle it, but we huffed and puffed and couldn't budge it. Finally John found a four-footer that he was able to topple over.

"He did it, Houston! He did it!" I exclaimed. "So you can not only sneak up on them," said Tony, "you can flip them over, huh?"

"Yeah," replied John. "That's a biggie. Man, it looks like it's been sitting there for quite a while. Look at that soil underneath it."

"A chip off the bottom and the soil will probably do it," directed Tony. John laughed, "A chip off the bottom."

It was time to head back toward the LM. We had been out six hours and had some work to do at the ALSEP area. Driving back, dust was flying everywhere. "Man, I am covered from head to foot with dust," I sighed. "Boy, those fenders really are useful, Tony. This one we lost in the back has resulted in us being—"

"Pretty dirty," interjected John. "A double pigpen," I added.

We joked and bounced our way back, up and down hills and craters. "I can't believe how hilly this place is," I commented. "There's not a flat place around."

"Right," agreed John, "except where that LM is."

When we got back, we were running a little behind schedule, so Houston asked us to drop some of our chores. We started pleading with them for an extension and sounded like two little kids asking Mama for cookies.

"Hey, how about an extension you guys? We're feeling good." "You said all we was gonna do tonight is sit around and talk."

"Ten minutes and we could get all this done, Tony. How about ten minutes, Tony? Please? Come on, Tony. Pretty please?"

Finally Houston relented, "Okay, we'll give you another ten minutes. How's that? Just show that we love you."

"Atta boy," I exclaimed. "Let's hear it for old flight. 'Atta boy' for flight."

As we unloaded the rover, John remarked, "Look at that, Charlie." "What?" I asked.

"Somebody up there likes us. That's bag number 4. See where it is?" John replied. One of his rock bags had come loose during our bumpy ride and instead of falling off and being left behind, it had miraculously wedged itself between the left rear fender and the frame of the rover. And it was still filled with rocks!

When it was time to get in, we couldn't believe how dirty we were. We had a little dust brush, about the size of a paintbrush—six inches across— but it seemed worthless with all of this dirt.

"This is the best way to get the dust off, John, is kick against the strut. Look at that stuff go." I found that when I banged my hands and feet against the landing gear, like beating a dirty carpet, it jarred a lot of the dust off and I was able to get reasonably clean.

"Okay, you're getting pretty far behind now," said Tony. "We're gonna have to ask you to go on in."

We finished up, climbed in, closed the hatch, and repressurized. "Okay. You guys had a 7-hour, 23-minute EVA," Tony announced.

"That's super, that's a lot of fun. Let's go back out," I teased.

Tony laughed, "Tomorrow, Charlie. Tomorrow."

We were tired. Our arms were achy, especially the forearms and tips of our fingers which were still tender and bluish looking. We looked forward to a good rest because the next day would be very long.

Our last EVA was scheduled to last five hours and immediately following we would load up and lift-off from the moon for rendezvous with Ken. Lift-off was going to be a critical maneuver, but we weren't worried about it as we prepared for our rest period. We went right to sleep and slept like babies for about seven hours.

# 21
# MOONWALK III

Twilight Zone—that place where time stands still and the real world and fantasy meet.

Five months earlier, on our last geology training exercise in Hawaii, when I had been delirious from high fever brought on by the flu, I had an unusual dream. This was really significant to me because I rarely dream, and this was one of the most vivid dreams I'd ever had.

In my dream John and I were on the moon, heading north in the lunar rover. We were going to a point four miles north of our landing spot called North Ray Crater. As we were driving across the lunar surface, we suddenly came across another set of tracks.

We got really excited and told Mission Control, "Houston, we've got this set of tracks up here, and they're going off to the east!" We could tell which direction the vehicle was headed because the herringbone pattern on the tire treads looked similar to those on our lunar rover. "Can we have permission to follow the tracks?" I asked.

"By all means," they answered. They were as thrilled over this discovery as we were.

So we started out and drove east for about two or three miles, then as we topped this small ridge we were astounded. There before us was this car sitting on the lunar surface! It looked very similar to our rover—and in it were two people!

"Houston, we've found this car up here, and it appears to have two men in it. We're going to stop and investigate." Mission Control was speechless! Finally they gave us permission, so we drove over and stopped our rover. We were fearful, yet excited.

After turning on the TV camera, John and I ran over to the car, which was almost a copy of our lunar rover, but there was no movement from the two astronauts, and we couldn't see their faces because their sun visors were down. I was really curious to see what they looked like, thinking they might be aliens from a foreign planet who had died on the lunar surface, so I reached over and pulled up the visor of the astronaut in the right seat.

As I did, I looked in—and I was looking at *myself*! Now you would think that was a nightmare, and I should have awakened in a panic, but I didn't. The dream just continued, and I said, "Houston, it looks like me."

Then I ran around to the other side and opened that visor and looked in and it was *John*. "Houston," I reported, "the other one looks like John."

"We can't explain all this," responded CapCom, "but why don't you bring back what you can. We'll do a complete analysis and see if we can get an age date for everything."

We wanted to bring back the bodies, but they wouldn't fit in the lunar module, so we just cut off some pieces of the suits and car. Then we blasted off from the moon and made it back to earth. At the lunar labs, the material was dated and was found to be 100,000 years old! The astronauts had been there 100,000 years! That's when I woke up.

I was so exited! But I didn't tell Dotty that dream; I was concerned that she would be fearful it was a premonition of our dying on the moon. But I never thought of it as that—I always thought we were really going to find that car on the moon.

In fact the dream was so real that when we started down on our actual descent and saw our landing area from an altitude of one mile, the first thing I did was to look up to the north to see if there were any tracks, but there were no tracks.

Now today on our last EVA we would head in our rover to North Ray Crater. Would we find the tracks? The rover? The astronauts? I was really excited at what we might find.

"This is Apollo Control 162, hours and 48 minutes ground-elapsed time. A little over a minute remaining for the rest period. At Descartes landing site aboard lunar module Orion. Standing by for CapCom's call. Peterson's preparing to make his call now."

"Orion, Houston," transmitted Don Peterson. "How are you doing this morning?"

"Super. Is it time to get up?" I asked.

"Yes, sir," said Don.

"Okay. Reveille, reveille," I called to John.

We hustled through our morning meal and suit up. By now on our third try, it was a piece of cake. We knew exactly which way to bend and move to help each other.

North Ray Crater—this was going to be an exciting EVA! We were going to be the farthest away from the lunar module, and we were going to view the largest crater anyone of the Apollo crews had ever seen. North Ray was about four to five miles north of the lunar module and measured about five hundred yards in diameter and two hundred feet deep.

Due to our late landing, this EVA had been cut short to only five hours, therefore we hustled as fast as we could so as not to miss out on any of it. "Incidentally," CapCom reported, "you have about 123 pounds of rocks . . . we can get another 100 pounds."

John and I were elated—we were really anxious to get going and see this enormous crater and gather samples. From the photographs, it appeared there were some large boulders on the rim. They wanted us to collect some of this ejecta, hoping to get the deepest lunar material possible.

By the end of our prep time, we were thirty minutes ahead of schedule and got permission to begin depressurization. While we watched the cabin pressure come down, John commented, "Charlie, it's going to be hot out there today. Can't believe that shadow."

The shadows had shortened considerably; on the moon the sun moves at a rate of about one degree every two hours. The sun angle had moved from about 15 degrees to almost 55 degrees, and the surface temperature had risen from about 85 degrees Fahrenheit when we landed, to over 200 degrees on this last day. But the higher temperature was only a minor irritant; our pressure suits kept us relatively cool.

We began our drive to North Ray and had a comparatively easy time. The small boulders and stones that were on the surface when we went south were absent from this north traverse. I believe that when North Ray Crater was formed, so much lunar soil was ejected that it just covered up the smaller craters and stones. What we saw were more subdued, shallow-bottomed craters.

Thinking of my dream, I kept looking for some other tracks, but so far none were to be found.

As we topped the rim of nearby Palmetto Crater, John spotted Dot, a small crater I had named after Dotty. "Hey, Charlie. There's Dot!"

"Yes," I said. "I see Dot. Great—hanging right in there." I wondered how Dotty and the boys were hanging in there, what with all the news media camped on the doorstep plus a house full of relatives. I knew she'd be glad when this was all over.

If she had known I was looking for another rover and astronauts that looked like John and me, she would have been beside herself. Aliens in space intrigued me; she knew of my desire to be taken aboard a UFO even if I never came home again. That thought upset her a lot, mostly because she couldn't understand why I would chose them over her.

But there were no tracks, no other rover, no other astronauts, and I came to realize it had been just a dream, an adventure of the mind.

The closer we got to North Ray, the more excited we became. We began to see more and more rocks, and they were larger than any we'd seen before. As we passed these boulders, we noticed they seemed to have fractures in them, probably because of the tremendous force of the meteorite explosion.

"Okay. We're definitely on the ejecta blanket here," as I continued in my travelogue with Houston, "and within one hundred meters or so I think is the rim." It turned out I was wrong; it was more like five hundred meters.

We were overjoyed—we were seeing white rocks, black rocks, unusual looking rocks. "That is that—that big—I can't believe the size of that big rock over there," I stammered, as we passed a boulder ten feet tall. "And I don't think that's a breccia, John. But although it might be a . . . I see some large white glass."

Off to the right facing the crater and downslope were some large angular black rocks, one so enormous it stood out from the rest. To the left the rocks were white and fairly smooth, appearing to have been there awhile, some were as high as six or seven feet.

"Oh, spectacular! Just spectacular!" John exclaimed.

"Super! Can't wait to get off!" I shouted. "Gotta get off!" CapCom informed us we were thirteen minutes ahead of schedule.

We parked about one hundred yards from the actual rim of the crater. There seemed to be an outer rim and inner rim; the outer rim was flat but as we jogged downslope to the inner rim, it got extremely steep. In fact the crater walls were so steep we couldn't get close enough to see the bottom.

Everybody began talking at once. Houston was telling us in real time what to do since our planned checklist had been changed, and with John and me running around taking pictures and describing rocks, it was pandemonium for a while.

First we jogged over to sample the white rocks, which were about fifty yards from the rover. These white rocks were unusual—friable breccia with black clasts in them and a bluish tint. They reminded us of some shocked rocks we had seen on our geology trips during training. We had learned that the force of a meteor impact chemically changes rocks, giving them a milky appearance.

John and I tried to operate independently to maximize our stay, but we began to have a terrible time with our sample bags. They were supposed to clip onto our camera mount, allowing us to pull off one at a time, much like pulling sandwich bags out of their box. Well, the brackets wouldn't hold, and the bags kept falling off.

With the bags dropping and having to pick them up, and at the same time carrying our shovels, tongs, and hammer, it was almost impossible to work alone. Therefore we decided to work together to get the most out of the hour we would spend.

After sampling around the white rocks, we came back to the lunar rover, dropped off some of our bags, and headed for a big black rock we had been eyeing all morning. "Look at the size of that biggie," I commented as we began jogging down the hill toward the black rock.

"It is a biggie, isn't it," agreed John. "It might be farther away than we think."

"No," I replied confidently, "it's not very far. It's just right beyond you." Little did I realize that I had made a gross error in judgment—for as we jogged and jogged and jogged, the rock just kept getting bigger and bigger and bigger. We would turn and look back at the rover, which was getting smaller and smaller.

There was nothing to compare sizes to on the moon—no telephone poles or trees, so we really had no idea how large or how far away that rock was. We kept jogging and jogging and the rock got bigger and bigger.

In the back room where the geologists were watching the TV monitor, everyone was on the edge of their seats. This rock was so big it had actually shown up on lunar orbital photos taken by *Apollo 14*.

"Keep going, keep going," Muelhberger yelled at the screen.

The two figures got smaller and smaller and began to disappear behind a ridge. "As our crew sinks slowly in the west," sang out Jack Schmidt, and everyone erupted in laughter.

The scientists watched in amazement as we jogged on and on and began to realize how really big this rock was. Now a tiny figure on the screen, I exclaimed in astonishment, "Look at the size of that rock. The closer I get to it, the bigger it is."

"They're not even there yet," said Muehlberger, flabbergasted.

Once we approached the rock, we realized how really enormous it was.

"Well, Tony," I said, "that's your House Rock right there." It truly was as big as a house, in fact bigger than a house. It was approximately ninety feet long and forty-five feet high, and it just towered over us.

We guessed that it had come right out of the bottom of North Ray Crater, since it was so huge and was sitting right on the crater rim. In fact the rock was so close to the rim, we had to watch our step as we grabbed a few samples. All we had with us was a hammer. It was like trying to dismantle

*203*

the Empire State Building with a crowbar, but I began whacking away at this monstrous rock and finally knocked off a couple of chunks about the size of a grapefruit.

The rock was a giant breccia—veinlets of glass ran through it, plus it contained white matrix rocks with black glass, and black matrix rocks with white glass. Also there were places on the rock that looked like little bullet holes. These were probably the result of micrometeorites that had whizzed in from outer space and impacted into this big boulder.

It had taken us so long to get there, that we didn't have much time at all before we had to start our hike back. We jogged back uphill to the rover, loaded up and headed for our next station, which was to be in a large boulder field about half a kilometer from North Ray, on the way back to our landing site.

"Okay—right down the same way we came. Oh, my goodness," exclaimed John. "This is going to be something going down this hill."

"Look at that slope. Be sure you got the brakes on," I warned John. "Tony, this is at least a fifteen-degree slope we're going down, and that rover came right up it and you never even knew it. Brake, John! Man! Man, that was super. Whoever said this was the Cayley Plain?"

"We just set a new world speed record, Houston," said John. "Seventeen kilometers an hour [eleven miles per hour] on the moon!" Our speedometer was off-scale high.

"Let's not set any more," admonished Tony.

"I'm with you," I agreed. It felt like we were going to launch ourselves into orbit.

We got a scare a few minutes later when the right wheels of the rover ran into a crater, tilting us to the right. As John tried to correct, the thing broke loose and we spun around 180 degrees. *That* got our attention real good! Strangely though, we never felt like the rover was going to turn over.

Our assignment at the next station was to find some permanently shadowed soil that had never seen the sun. John stopped the rover by the ten footer which we had seen on the way up. "Okay, I'm going to get on the sunlit side," I said. "You know, Tony, that might be a permanently shadowed soil right in there. Yes, sir, baby, that is, that is a perfect shadowed soil sample." I had found a hole at least a meter deep way back underneath the rock in the shadow. "John, you couldn't have picked a better rock!"

"O-U-T-standing!" enthused Tony. Houston was thrilled.

"Man, I can't believe I'm going up into that beauty." I got on my hands and knees to try to crawl into the hole. "Well, I don't know how long that rock's been there, but that dirt has been shadowed ever since it's been there." I reached in with the shovel, getting as far back as I could go, and collected one of the most unique samples that we would bring back from the moon. I felt like the college student who just passed his final exam.

"Uh, that there is one of those gopher holes," said John.

"Do that in west Texas and you get a rattlesnake," I joked. "Here you get permanently shadowed soil."

Then I started banging away on the rock with my hammer, and as I looked at it more closely, I saw some very strange holes—larger than the bullet-sized ones in the previous boulder, about an inch wide that disappeared back into the rock. "Tony, this rock here looks like the one on the rim—that great, huge black one—except that one up there didn't have any of these holes in it. I can't really say what these holes are here."

"They look like drill holes is what they look like," I commented. And it sure did look like somebody had been up there with a Black and Decker drill. John guessed they were made from venting gas, and that's probably what they were.

It was time to drive back to the LM and finish up, so we packed all our rocks and let her go. I clicked pictures all the way back and continued describing our location to Houston, "Okay, Tony, between Gator and Palmetto. . . ."

John had mastered the rover after over twenty kilometers of driving. As his confidence grew, he was fearless and even bordered on the reckless at times. In training I had nicknamed him Barney Oldfield after the old time race car driver, and now on the moon he was racing for home, in the lead.

"Uh, oh," alerted John. "Uh, oh," I said as I grabbed hold of my seat. "Ah, we missed it!"

Houston couldn't see what was going on, so Tony pleaded, "Well, we're all holding on to our chairs." I think Mission Control was climbing the wall every time we got in the rover.

I informed them what happened. "Between Gator and Palmetto, we almost hit a great big rock, but old Percy Precision here avoided it."

It's probably good Houston couldn't see, just hearing us describe the near misses was worrying them enough. They were especially anxious that we have no accidents during these few remaining hours before lift-off.

John lightened the mood, "I just finished my two pounds of potassium." We had been drinking out of our juice bags all morning. "I don't know whether I'm driving or sloshing!"

Tony laughed, "Okay, we copy that, and the command module just did their plane change burn and it's a good burn." Ken was readying the command module for our rendezvous, which was to occur in eight hours.

We drove over the top of a ridge, and there she was waiting for us—the lunar module—our ride home. She looked great! "Home again, home again, jiggety jig," I sang. We collected a few more samples and began to unload the rover.

I decided to take this time to place our family picture on the moon, so I walked about thirty feet from the LM and gently laid our autographed picture of the Duke family on the gray dust. As I made a photograph of it lying there, I wondered, "Who will find this picture in the years to come?"

Then I put one of the special Air Force medallions on the lunar surface and said, "Tony, a special salute from me to the U.S. Air Force on their silver anniversary this year. This lunar boy in blue is pretty far out right now." I was so proud that tears of patriotism welled up in my eyes, and my voice almost cracked with emotion.

On previous moon missions the crews had given a little farewell show—Al Shepard hitting a golf ball, Dave Scott proving the theory of gravity by dropping a feather and a hammer. John and I had planned on doing the Moon Olympics to commemorate the 1972 summer games that were to be in Munich. John was going to do the long jump, and I was to do the high jump, but since we were running behind schedule, we didn't think there was enough time.

"We were going to do a bunch of exercises that we had made up as the Lunar Olympics," said John, "to show you what a guy could do on the moon with a backpack on but—" and with that he began to jump up and down.

"For a 380-pound guy, that's pretty good," observed Tony.

"Yeah," said John. "Jump flat-footed straight in the air—three hundred pounds, about four feet."

I decided to join in and made a big push off the moon, getting about four feet high. "Wow!" I exclaimed. But as I straightened up, the weight of my backpack pulled me over backward. Now I was coming down on my back. I tried to correct myself but couldn't, and as my heart filled with fear I fell the four feet, hitting hard—right on my backpack. *Panic!* The thought that I'd die raced across my mind.

It was the only time in our whole lunar stay that I had a real moment of panic and thought I had killed myself. The suit and backpack weren't designed to support a four-foot fall. Had the backpack broken or the suit split open, I would have lost all my air. A rapid decompression, or as one friend calls it, a high-altitude hiss-out, and I would have been dead instantly! Fortunately, everything held together.

"Charlie!" shouted John. "That ain't any fun, is it?"

"That ain't very smart," I replied. John agreed, "That ain't very smart."

"Well, I'm sorry about that," I said. I was really embarrassed at what I had done.

Flat on my back, I couldn't get up, like an upside down turtle, so I asked John for a hand. My heart was still pounding from fear, and I was breathless.

Then I got very quiet and quickly started checking out my suit. The pressure gauge on my wrist read normal, and I could hear the pumps running in the backpack. I could feel the oxygen flow in the suit—everything was normal, thus the panic began to subside and we got back to work. But I was pretty subdued the rest of the EVA.

John drove the rover out about one hundred yards behind the lunar module, to allow Houston to watch lift-off on TV. I went out to help him get everything dusted off, and as I was jogging back, I decided to stop and urinate—I could never go while I was running.

Well, John could always tell and this time he decided to take my picture. "I just got a picture of one of the great moments in history, Houston," he announced.

"How's that?" asked CapCom. John laughed and made up something about my looking down into a crater.

Houston was hustling us; they were getting antsy to get us back in and pressurized, so we could start our activities for lift-off. All our equipment and rocks were now stacked at the foot of the ladder, and we did our final dust off and began carrying our gear up the ladder into the LM. I grabbed one of the rock boxes and climbed in while John began to bring up the other bags of gear.

"This is Apollo Control. Charlie Duke is in the LM behind the hatch trying to make as much room as possible for Young to squeeze through the opening."

As we closed the hatch and repressurized, CapCom informed us, "Okay, you had a five-hour, forty-minute EVA, and the back room sends out a great big outstanding!"

"Thank you very much, Tony," I replied. "They kept us going and thinking, so it was a two-way street." We found out later our total EVA time for the three days was 20 hours, 14 minutes, and 55 seconds—a new lunar record!

The LM was really crowded now with all our rocks and gear—we were squeezed in like sardines. Because of that and because we wanted to lighten our load for lift-off, we planned to leave behind as much gear as possible. Among the things we were to jettison were our backpacks, trash bags, lunar boots, cameras—things we wouldn't need anymore.

Once we repressurized, we decided to take off our helmets and gloves so we could work more efficiently, but our helmets were stuck shut and we couldn't get them loose. Finally I hit John's with the heel of my hand and he did the same to mine and they popped loose.

"Okay, we had one heck of a time getting our helmets off," I reported to Houston. "It turns out that this orange juice is the best cement you'd ever see. It leaked down in between the seals of the helmet and the suit neck ring and we couldn't get the thing unlocked without a great effort. But we managed and we're both out now."

Tony responded, "Well, we may have a new market for orange juice—glue." Who would have imagined orange juice could cause so many problems? It's the little things that can cause the biggest headaches. Fortunately, this was the last of our orange juice related nuisances.

First we weighed our rocks and soil samples, because we needed an exact weight at lift-off for our computer to fine tune our ascent trajectory and burn time. After weighing everything, Houston said we had collected a total of 245 pounds during our three-day stay. When more accurate measurements were taken later on earth, it turned out there were actually 213 pounds. They had a little concern about our weight and for a while we thought we might have to jettison some of our rocks, but Houston decided to go with all we had.

Immediately after jettison we began to stow all the items we had brought back in with us. We didn't want objects floating around and banging into things once we got into orbit, therefore we tied everything down and got it into its proper stowage position.

By now the floor of our crew cabin was covered with lunar dust. On the moon this presented no problem, but we began to worry about lunar orbit. In zero gravity the dust would float everywhere and could pose a problem for our environmental control system, so we tried to clean up as well as we could. All this organization, depressurization, jettisoning, and repressurization took over an hour.

Now it was time to power up the lunar module. Would everything work? All the systems, except our communication and environmental systems, had been dormant now for three days. Our computer had to be powered up, checked out, and loaded; our navigation and guidance and control equipment had to be checked out; our ascent batteries and communications systems and everything that would be needed for lift-off and rendezvous were powered up and checked out. Miraculously, all worked great.

Then there were a lot of changes to be made in our checklist. For this critical portion of our mission, we didn't want to miss a step—one error could be fatal, like forgetting to set flaps on takeoff. So we paid a lot of attention to every detail.

As we continued our preparations, we snatched a quick bite to eat. We had about three hours to get all this completed. Things were proceeding well, as we moved toward lift-off.

"This is Apollo Control, Houston, at 174 hours, 20 minutes ground-elapsed time. Time of ignition—175 hours, 46 minutes, 35 seconds. Duration of the ascent burn—7 minutes, 16 seconds; 60,000 feet in altitude at shutdown. Velocity at 5,525 feet per second at shutdown. Orbit at insertion for Orion—an apolune of 41.1 nautical miles with a perilune of 8.9 nautical miles. We will follow the air-ground conversation live as it occurs."

# 22
# GOOD-BYE, MOON!

"*Orion,* you are GO for lift-off."

At eight minutes before ignition, we were given a go from CapCom. We had checked out all our systems, donned our helmets and gloves, and were watching the computer count down.

I was sad to leave. I had enjoyed it so much and wished we could stay longer and do more exploration. It was like saying last farewells to an old friend, because I knew my chance of returning was very slim.

As the minutes ticked by, we got very quiet in the lunar module; from my experience as CapCom I knew Mission Control was the same. There was little chatter now between John and me. We would occasionally cast a nervous glance over at one another, but our main focus was on the computer as it counted down and on the systems as we checked and rechecked all the switches. The apprehension wasn't because of fear that we would be trapped on the moon, but anxiety that we had made the checklist changes correctly.

During the final few minutes I reviewed a few of the emergency procedures, casting out of my mind any thought that the engine might not light.

About this time I decided to urinate, but unbeknownst to me, my urine collection device condom had slipped off. So when I began to urinate, all of a sudden I felt this warm liquid going down my left leg. I really had to go and wasn't about to stop, therefore I ended up having a squishy left boot at ascent.

"Okay, Houston. Master Arm is coming on," John radioed.

At T minus 2 minutes, we turned on the Master Arm switch. That left us with only one more button to press—the Abort-stage button, which would automatically signal the computer that we were in the proper configuration for lift-off. This would occur at five seconds before lift-off.

"Coming up now on minus one minute. MARK, minus 1 minute," called CapCom. "Minus 30 seconds . . . 20 seconds . . . 10 seconds . . ." Minus 3 . . . 2 . . . 1. Ignition! *Lift-off!* "Houston confirms good ignition start on *Orion*."

Right at ignition a whole series of events occurred. I was surprised at the rapidity of them all and at the noise and movement of the vehicle as we left the descent stage.

The lunar module is held together by three large bolts and at lift-off, the bolts explode, separating the ascent stage from the descent stage. At the same time a guillotine-like affair cuts the electrical, oxygen, and water lines.

When the bolts exploded, instead of being propelled upwards, we dropped. *Oh no, it didn't light and we are dropping!* flashed through my mind.

Then, bang! the engine ignited and instantly there was 3,500 pounds of thrust. A kick hit the bottom of my feet, and off we went—straight up for about 800 feet!

Our lunar module weighed only 1,600 pounds in lunar gravity, and with the engine producing 3,500 pounds of thrust, it was a spiffy acceleration. We were standing up and could feel the force as our feet were pushed against the floor.

"Pitchover 53 degrees, on time."

The lunar module pitched over and we got a quick glimpse of the lunar module descent stage and the rover and could see all of the tracks we had made across the lunar surface.

Our instruments showed we were accelerating correctly downrange, but it felt like we were pitching over in a big arc and going back down to crash onto the lunar surface. The horizon disappeared out the front window, and all I could see now was the moon. I squatted down and looked out the top of the window to catch sight of the horizon and make sure we were okay.

As the sixteen small rocket thrusters of the reaction control system fired away to maintain the correct attitude, the vehicle began to wallow from side to side. "What a ride! What a ride! What a ride!" I shouted. It was one of the most exciting flying machines I had ever been in.

We proceeded through each minute, hearing a go by Mission Control. I don't know what we would have done if they had given us a no go; the only thing we could have done at that point was crash back onto the moon.

By six minutes after lift-off, we were at an altitude of 55,000 feet and traveling about 3,100 miles per hour. Shutdown was to occur at seven minutes, plus fifteen seconds. Right before shutdown, we terminated some interconnects between fuel lines to save the reaction control system for achieving rendezvous and docking later with Ken.

"We have shut down," reported John.

"Houston, copy," responded CapCom. "Shutdown."

Right on schedule the engine shut down and we had our insertion into orbit. Just a minute later, a tweak burn nulled our residual velocities.

We now pitched the spacecraft toward Ken, who was above and in front of us, and got our rendezvous radar locked on. Almost immediately John got a visual of the command module. Casper had a very strong tracking light flashing on board, which we could easily see silhouetted against the blackness of space.

At this point we were 145 miles apart and closing at a rate of 300 miles per hour. Even though we had a lot of work to do and it's easy to miss a rendezvous in space, to have him in sight was a comforting feeling. If the gas holds out, you are going to make it when you can see your target.

As soon as we turned on our tracking light, Ken reported, "Tally ho!" He could see us now and began to track us visually with his onboard equipment, much like a gun sight. "Hey, this stuff is working pretty good today, isn't it," Ken continued. "Man, I can see that light of yours at seventy [nautical] miles on the telescope."

We continued tracking, completing a TPI (Terminal Phase Initiation) burn and two small midcourse correction burns on the back side of the moon. When we regained AOS with earth, we were only three miles from the command module.

"Guess we don't need to tell you that this is a sweet machine," I said to CapCom Jim Irwin, who had flown aboard *Apollo 15*. The lunar module had been flying beautifully—like a fast maneuverable fighter aircraft. We felt like hotshot fighter pilots again.

"Apollo Control, we show a range now of 2½ nautical miles. Range rate of 32 feet per second."

We began to reduce our rate of closure—twenty-seven, ten, now we were a quarter mile apart. We continued to slow down and by the time we arrived seventy yards from Ken, we had reached a relative velocity of one foot per second. As we began to close in, we could see Ken's little reaction control jets firing.

*211*

"Your forward firing thrusters look like little flashlights when they fire," I told Ken. "This looks more like an animated cartoon." We reached station-keeping distance and killed the remaining velocity.

I was surprised when Houston said, "John, looking at the pictures of lift-off, it appeared something might have come loose—skin on the back of the vehicle or that region. We want Ken to take some pictures of the LM, so we'll be asking you to do a yaw 360."

They had seen some panels fly loose at lunar lift-off and were concerned about possible damage to the LM, but we had noticed no abnormalities on board. It turned out pieces of sheet metal covering the back side of the LM had blown loose, but the integrity of the spacecraft and all systems were completely intact.

We did a few more maneuvers to check out the command module, and then got into position for docking. Time kept marching on. We were approaching the terminator, which meant there was only a few minutes to go before sunset. Darkness would make docking difficult, so we were getting a little anxious.

"Okay, I'm approaching," said Ken. "Your attitude looks good." We held our attitude and Ken began to move in very slowly. I couldn't see him, but John observed out the small window overhead on the left side of the spacecraft.

"Okay, about 5 feet. I believe we're there—*Casper*'s captured *Orion*!" shouted Ken. We felt a big jolt. The lightweight lunar module shuddered, as the heavyweight command module made contact.

What a tremendous feeling to be docked with Ken again. We'd made it back. We were docked, and we were secure. The lunar module had performed flawlessly.

Ken was happy to see us, too; however, he hadn't had time to be lonely. Even though he had been orbiting all alone, he had been busy conducting many orbital experiments and taking photographs. And running the command module single-handedly was a full-time job.

Immediately CapCom called. "*Orion*, this is Houston. We're about 28 minutes to LOS, and I have about five pages of time-line changes, whenever you're ready to copy." So while John prepared the lunar module for the transfer of our equipment to the command module, I copied the new schedule.

Our new plan was for John and me to do a partial transfer, power down the lunar module, and then drift over to the command module where we would eat a meal and get some sleep. The next day we would complete the transfer and jettison the LM. I argued for the original plan of doing a complete transfer and immediately jettisoning the LM. I wanted to follow our published procedures which we knew were correct, but Mission Control overruled.

Jim seemed to be trying to set the *Guinness Book of World Records* for "fastest reader of checklist changes read over the air," and I quickly fell behind. "Hey Jim," I implored, "hold a minute. I can't turn the pages that fast."

This was a complicated set of changes, because it required us to do procedures in an order we had never practiced. One procedural error could lead to a whole mess of problems.

Sure enough, the next day when we powered up the lunar module and set it free, instead of holding attitude, the LM began to drift in a random manner. We had hoped to have a controlled impact of the lunar module on the moon to give us some data for our seismic experiment, but we were unable to control it, and it drifted away. I'm convinced that happened either because I incorrectly copied a change or was given a wrong procedure.

The LM eventually crashed due to lunar gravity anomalies. Since Houston didn't know exactly where it landed, it was not useful to calibrate our experiments on the surface. That hurt my ego; I prided myself on never making a mistake. But Mission Control didn't think it was any big deal, although a few scientists were disappointed.

As we readied ourselves for transfer into the command module, our biggest job was cleaning up the dust and trying not to track it into *Casper*. "Sure looks like a dust storm in this cockpit right now," I said. In zero gravity, dust was flying everywhere.

We tried to clean it with a wet towel but didn't do a very good job, so when Ken opened the hatch, dust started floating over into his spacecraft, and he got upset. He grabbed his vacuum cleaner, floated it over to us in the lunar module, and closed the hatch, saying he would open it again when we finished vacuuming. With this little hand-held vacuum, we proceeded to clean up as best we could.

After transferring to the command module and grabbing something to eat, CapCom radioed, "*Apollo 16*, we've got all we need for the night. Just hit the sack. See you in the morning."

"Rog," we replied. "As the sun sinks slowly in the west, we bid a fine farewell to all at MCC [Mission Control Center]."

EVA 3, lift-off, rendezvous, transferring equipment—it had been a long day. Finally after being up almost twenty hours, we were able to put up the window shades and go to sleep.

*213*

**April 24, 1972**

"Apollo Control, Houston; 189 hours, 29 minutes ground-elapsed time. We're standing by now for a wake-up call to the crew of *Apollo 16*."

"*Apollo 16,* Houston."

"That's CapCom Hank Harstfield making the wake-up call on *Apollo 16*'s 59th revolution around the moon."

"Hello, there," responded John sluggishly.

"Good morning," said Hank cheerfully. "Were you still snoozing?"

"You bet ya," answered John.

"How's your writing arm this morning?" asked Hank. I knew he was talking to me and replied, "I don't know."

John came to my rescue, "Wait till he gets the sleep out of his eyes."

After a good night's sleep, first thing the next morning, Houston was waiting for us with a full day's schedule. The decision had been made to cut short our stay in lunar orbit and bring us home a day early. We were disappointed and had argued with Mission Control, but had not prevailed.

Our mission had originally been planned for twelve days' duration, giving us a full day in lunar orbit to conduct further experiments. Because of our earlier problem with the command module control system, management was nervous and asked us to come on home. If the engine didn't work properly, this would give us an extra day to fix it, before getting low in electrical power and other consumables.

Again all our checklists had to be changed. I ended up spending literally hours copying adjustments to our flight plan. It seemed to take as long copying the procedure changes, as it would have taken staying on our original schedule. Making these continuous flight plan corrections was by far the most frustrating part of our flight.

Changes completed, the time came for jettisoning our lunar module. "That *Orion* was a mighty good spacecraft," said John. "Real beautiful flying machine. Had a great lunar base, too. We'll miss her." We were both sad to see her go.

Then five hours later we were ready for our burn to leave lunar orbit and begin our trip home. I was really nervous about this burn. The SPS had to work. If this engine failed, there was no backup. We would be permanent residents of lunar orbit with no hope of rescue.

The burn was to occur while we were behind the moon, out of contact with earth. We received all the data necessary from Mission Control and entered it into our computer. Right before LOS, we received a go from Houston, "*Sixteen,* you're GO for TEI [transearth injection]."

Things got very tense aboard *Casper* as we disappeared behind the moon for the final time. We were super primed to shut down the burn if we noticed any anomaly whatsoever. As the computer counted to ignition, it was quiet as a tomb.

Ignition occurred right on schedule. When that SPS ignited with its 20,000 pounds of thrust, it was a real kick in the pants. I felt like I was being pushed through the back of my seat. Our spacecraft was much lighter now, having burned most of its fuel and the lunar module gone.

The engine thrust vector control worked flawlessly, without even a wiggle in trajectory, and the engine shut down exactly on schedule. The tomb erupted with life, and we all let out a big "Yahoo!" We were on our way *home!*

At AOS John reported to Houston, "Just thought we'd come up like thunder and that's how we're coming. Just going away from it like nothing."

"It's better than an afterburner climb," I exclaimed. Our velocity was now 7,957 feet per second, and we had already traveled over 375 miles from the moon. We climbed away so fast, the moon was visibly shrinking.

I grabbed the TV camera and tried to take some pictures to send back to earth, but I was so excited I couldn't hold the camera steady. "The boys are all at the windows taking pictures," said John. "We got some pictures of earthrise as we were climbing out," I reported to Houston. "I'll bet they're really spectacular."

"I think the general agreement in the cockpit is that morale around here just went up a couple hundred percent," said Ken.

"Rog," answered CapCom. "Morale looks pretty good here, Ken."

"Really a spectacular view. Really get the curvature," relayed John, exhilarated. "The old crescent earth coming up there—the earthrise was just beautiful—just came up like gangbusters. We were looking right out the window, and there you came, and right now you're almost just a crescent earth, just a very thin sliver out there. And I tell you, we can hardly wait. I know we have a couple of things to do before we get there, but we're looking forward to it."

"Looking out the center hatch window," I enthused, "the moon fills the whole window. I can see from horizon to horizon. What a spectacular view. We are really climbing away from the planet. You can see it getting smaller by the second, almost as fast as John was driving that rover yesterday."

We were now over 800 miles from the moon. In only ten more minutes we were 1,600 miles out—really climbing, although our velocity was slowly dropping due to the moon's gravitational pull.

After the excitement of TEI, we settled down for our three-day trip

*215*

home. For us lunar module guys, it was basically an uneventful time, except for a one-hour and fifteen-minute spacewalk that was to occur the following day, on day nine. Ken was busy—he had some more experiments to perform, plus he was the chauffeur. For John and me it was like, "Okay, Ken—home, please."

Meanwhile the geologists back in Houston were in a state of flux over the origin of the highland area we had just explored and were being pushed by the press to give some answers.

At our debriefing conference with Tony, we were told that because of the seeming lack of volcanic samples that were found, the back room had decided to reject their previously held volcanic theory, particularly concerning the formation of the Cayley Plains. The Descartes material was considered still debatable.

Almost everyone had expected the mission to yield samples of relatively simple frozen lava flows. Instead we had found breccias—ancient, puzzling, and complex conglomerate rocks that had been pounded and formed by countless meteorite impact. From these finds and data radioed to earth by instruments aboard Casper, Muelhberger and the others had begun to restore an old theory that had been formally rejected—that the Cayley material was "slosh" or fluid ejecta from Imbrium Basin over five hundred miles away.

John and I didn't agree with that hypothesis, so when Tony asked if we had any questions, John reacted strongly and said, "I think it's premature to be making those kinds of speculations. I'd like to wait until we get all the data in and take a good look at it. It's just too soon to draw conclusions on hearsay and not having the real evidence and not having all the data analyzed."

"I sure agree with you, John," said Tony, "but you know everybody's excited and trying to press with it."

"Boy, I would not press for that sort of thing this early in the game because that's too speculative. In other words, it ain't good science."

"Yeah, John," answered Tony. "I think you're right on, and I hope they heard you in the back room because I think I said the same thing this morning."

Although the reporters continued to push for a statement, our rocks actually brought forth more questions than answers. Scientists would need to spend months and years analyzing the material to come up with some firm answers.

The next day we began preparations for our spacewalk. I was excited, because I was going to participate, too, and be one of only a few astronauts who had gone outside the spacecraft in zero gravity. Ed White had been the first American to walk in space in 1965 during the Gemini program. In Apollo we were to be the second flight with a deep space EVA.

The purpose of our EVA was to retrieve some film canisters from the back of the service module. They contained films Ken had exposed during lunar orbit and would be used for mapping the moon. Ken was to be the retriever, and I was to be the safety observer.

We depressurized the spacecraft and Ken opened the hatch—it was like looking through a picture window, but there was nothing outside except the blackness of space.

Ken went through the hatch first and walked hand over hand to the back of the service module, using some special handholds on the side of the spacecraft. I followed, floating out a body length, and anchored my feet on the hatch sill. My job was to make sure his safety line, plus oxygen and communication lines, didn't get tangled in parts of the spacecraft.

As I floated out, I was again overcome with the awesome beauty of space. The panorama of the universe was spread out before me, and I felt like a spectator in an audience watching the play unfold. Ken was the performer—and the universe was the stage.

To the right was the earth, 198,000 miles away. It was a crescent earth— just a thin sliver of blue and white—yet breathtaking to behold. Over my left shoulder was the moon, only 42,000 miles away and enormous. It was a full moon, and I could see clearly all the major features—Sea of Tranquility where Neil and Buzz landed, Ocean of Storms, even the Descartes highlands. It was spectacular!

Everywhere else I looked it was blackness—the empty blackness of space, so powerful it seemed that I could reach out and touch it. The feeling of detachment I experienced was strange; it was almost euphoric, and I wondered what it would be like to float off into this blackness.

Ken retrieved one of the canisters and brought it back across the spacecraft. It was the biggest roll of film I'd ever seen, weighing eighty pounds and a couple of feet in diameter. It seemed almost as big as Ken and, as he floated it like a big balloon toward the hatch, it bounced off the spacecraft and pulled away. The canister wanted to go one way and Ken another. It was a real battle and the film almost won, but he was able to keep hold and shove it by me into the spacecraft to John.

After retrieving the second canister, Ken floated out onto the end of a ten-foot pole, which was attached to the hatch of the spacecraft, in order to perform a biological experiment. I went back inside to watch him from there. It was beautiful—the sun glistening and sparkling off his spacesuit. I felt like I was looking at a picture on a TV screen—the hatch being the screen and Ken, the picture.

As I was watching Ken, I noticed a flash of gold out of the left corner of my eye. Lo and behold it was Ken's wedding band, floating, tumbling, and going out the hatch. We had been searching for this wedding band ever since Ken lost it on the second day of our flight. Now here it was about to float off into space and be lost forever.

*I'd better get it quick,* I thought and reached out to grab it. But I missed. The ring was just out of my grasp and floated right on out of the hatch. *Well, good-bye wedding band,* I said to myself. *Lost in space.*

The ring continued to tumble, heading in Ken's direction. His back was to me, so he couldn't see it coming, and since he was talking to Houston, I was reluctant to interrupt. The next moment, I saw it hit him on the back of his helmet.

*Man, that's neat,* I thought, expecting the wedding band to ricochet off his helmet and float out into space. Instead it took a miraculous 180-degree bounce and floated right back toward me, along the same path it had gone out. The probability of a round object tumbling through space and rebounding perfectly off another round object is practically zero, but it happened.

Within seconds it floated back in the hatch, and I grabbed it on the rebound—all this while we were traveling about 5,000 miles per hour.

When Ken had finished the EVA and was back in the spacecraft, I held up my glove and said, "Ken, I've got something for you." There was his wedding band on the little finger of my glove.

Ken was overjoyed! As I said earlier, he hadn't been married long, so to lose a brand new wedding ring would have been unfortunate.

After the EVA John and I really didn't have much to do until reentry. I did another light-flash experiment and collected small fragments of moon rocks that seemed to appear out of nowhere. Mostly we just floated around and enjoyed reliving the excitement of our three days on the moon.

When time came for our last rest period, most of the pressure and tension had departed and I was feeling great over the job we had done. I floated under the couch one last time and zipped up my sleeping bag. It was my turn to be on the electrocardiogram monitor, so I attached myself to the BIOMED (bio-medical data) harness and went off to sleep almost instantly.

This last night I slept solidly for eight hours, and they had to holler at me to wake me up. This was unusual for me; every other rest period I had needed a sleeping pill to calm me down.

# 23

# THE RETURN

*April 27, 1972—Aboard Command Module* **Casper**—*Day of Reentry*

"Good morning, *Apollo 16*," radioed CapCom.

"We see on this BIOMED that old Charlie woke up. He was really sawing away there."

"Charlie was sawing away on his BIOMED?" asked John.

"Sure was."

"I wouldn't be surprised that's why it doesn't work," said Ken.

John laughed, "Termites do the same thing." I found out that for the whole eight hours' rest period, my heartbeat averaged around twenty-eight to thirty per minute; I was really in a deep sleep.

"This is Gold Flight," said Flight Director Gerry Griffin. "We're going to be handing it over down here shortly. We wanted to let you know that we really commend you for job well done and will be looking forward to seeing you when you get back to Houston."

"Okay, Gold Flight," answered John. "I tell you we certainly enjoyed you—particularly on that descent. That was something else wasn't it?"

Jerry continued, "Incidentally I talked to Lee [Silver] yesterday, and he sends you all a very well done." We were happy that the geologists were pleased with our performance.

"This is Apollo Control, Houston at 261 hours ground-elapsed time. We now show *Apollo 16* at a distance of 39,820 nautical miles away from earth. The velocity now reads 9,807 feet per second [6,686 miles per hour] and in the Mission Control Center in Houston, we've had a shift changeover. Phil Shaffer is now our flight director. Our CapCom is now Henry Hartsfield."

We ate our last space breakfast and began to prepare for reentry, stowing and strapping everything firmly in place. The next few hours were spent taking care of the updates of our position—our tracking and state vectors and all of the things we needed for a solid reentry.

CapCom sent us up a small midcourse correction burn. The reason for this burn was to target the service module away from an island in the landing footprint and to further fine-tune our entry angle.

"Okay, the burn's complete."

"This is Apollo Control, Houston. You heard John Young report that the midcourse correction seven burn has been completed. We're at 263 hours, 26 minutes ground-elapsed time. We show *Apollo 16* at a distance of 25,048 nautical miles away from earth, traveling at a velocity of 12,316 feet per second [8,397 miles per hour]."

The closer we came to earth, the more we began to accelerate due to the earth's gravitational pull. We didn't feel this acceleration, but our instruments showed a steady increase in velocity.

"*Apollo 16,* our first batch of tracking data shows you right in the groove, and we're going to get another hour's worth of data and then give you your final pad," reported CapCom.

It was critical for the spacecraft to be at a certain angle for reentry. If the angle was too shallow, the spacecraft would bounce out of the atmosphere like a rock skipping across a pond, and we would be slung off into space. If it was too steep, the spacecraft would undergo a tremendous G load, and there was the possibility that we would not survive such a load and the intense heat it would generate.

"This is Apollo Control, Houston, at 265 hours, 14 minutes ground-elapsed time. We now show 1 hour, 9 minutes, 50 seconds till time of entry into the earth's atmosphere. Meanwhile weather around the prime recovery vessel, the aircraft carrier *Ticonderoga,* is good. Our displays here show a cloud cover of 2,000 feet scattered, visibility 10 nautical miles, wind direction coming from 90 degrees at a velocity of 10 miles per hour, wave heights 3 feet.

"And in the area, four helicopters and two HC130 rescue aircraft will be airborne at time of splash. *Apollo 16* now 10,535 nautical miles away from the earth, traveling at a speed of 17,927 feet per second [12,222 miles per hour] and this is Apollo Control, Houston."

We were aiming for a point 1,500 miles south of Hawaii. Velocity was building up quite rapidly now—19,024 feet per second, 20,347 . . . We were anticipating a velocity of 36,276 feet per second (almost 25,000 miles per hour) at time of entry into the earth's atmosphere and a MAX of 7.07 Gs deceleration.

At fifteen minutes before entry interface, we were to jettison the service module and orient the command module with heat shield forward. It was necessary to jettison the service module because it didn't have a heat shield and would burn up when it hit the earth's atmosphere. The service module had been the life of our command module and contained our main engine and oxygen and electrical supply; jettisoning it left us with only an eight-hour oxygen supply and a fifteen-hour supply of electricity.

"Okay, we're a minute and a half to CSM SEP [command and service modules separate]."

"John Young reporting a minute and a half away from service module separation. This is Apollo Control, Houston."

"Separation, Houston."

Separation from the service module went without a hitch; we turned around so we could see it float away. I had a momentary sinking feeling as I recalled one simulation where we did this and then missed the earth's atmosphere. Lost in space. But this was the real thing, and I knew we had made no mistakes.

Just a few more minutes and we'd be home! But these few minutes would be action packed. A thought of disaster flashed across my mind; eleven days of success could end in disaster with one foul-up during re-entry. Things happen fast at 25,000 miles per hour, and we had to be ready.

### Dukes' House in El Lago

The house was packed—Dotty had given an open invitation for friends to view splashdown and many had come, champagne bottles in hand, to celebrate the big event.

All the TVs were on—a special one had been set up in the garage for Charles and Tom and a multitude of cousins and neighbor friends. Picnic benches were lined up movie style, and most faces were glued to the screen. Charles and a few others were releasing excess energy by racing their bikes around the driveway, doing wheelies. The reporters that were waiting outside were invited to join the group in the garage. They were content knowing that Dotty would oblige with an interview later.

In the family room, applause sounded upon spacecraft separation, and then everyone fell silent as *Apollo 16* approached reentry.

Dotty was tired; she had been waking up early during the flight, before dawn every morning. But now the adrenaline from the excitement of the day had her wound up and exuberant, greeting everyone and helping them find a place to sit. Every seat was taken, plus every square inch of the floor in the family room was filled with friends and relatives; some even standing in the hallway and kitchen.

Dotty called for our sons to come in and watch the rest of splashdown with her. They ran in, a little shyly at first as they looked around at all the people; then snuggling beside her, they each grabbed one of her hands to receive some of her strength and confidence.

The week had been difficult for the boys, and their little faces showed some of the fear and confusion they had been feeling, ever since lift-off ten days before. They would be happy when home returned to normal.

Ken now oriented the spacecraft with heat shield forward; this was like riding backward in a car with our windows pointed to the rear. All we could see was the blackness of space, but we knew we were getting close

*221*

as we watched the velocity increasing in our computer—31,000 feet per second, 33,000, 34,000, 35,000.

"One minute, 30 seconds. Apollo now traveling at a velocity of 35,823 feet per second."

"*Apollo 16,* you're still looking good," radioed CapCom.

In less than two minutes, we would experience loss of communication with Houston, because as soon as the spacecraft hit the earth's atmosphere, we would be surrounded by an ionized fireball, causing a total break in communication. Communication blackout should last for 3½ minutes.

"Apollo Control, Houston. MARK. Minus one minute . . . 30 seconds now . . . minus 10 seconds. Velocity 36,173 feet per second. Range to go 1,270 nautical miles. We've seen a dropout in our telemetry data indicating *Apollo 16* now passing through the earth's atmosphere.

"*Apollo 16* going through its maximum heat load. This should be 4,000 to 4,500 degrees Fahrenheit. *Apollo 16* now encountering MAX G, which should be approximately 7 Gs. We're at one minute, 40 seconds since entry. We show the period of ending blackout a little less than two minutes away now."

On reentry we hit the atmosphere at an altitude of about 400,000 feet above the earth and at a velocity of nearly 25,000 miles per hour.

Entry interface was imperceptible at first. Our first indication was a faint glow outside, when the speeding spacecraft began to heat up the atmosphere. We watched as our instruments showed an increase in G level—1 G, 2 Gs. As the G level rose—3 Gs, 4 Gs—we began to feel it on our bodies. The spacecraft was shaking now, and within a minute it had reached over 7 Gs.

When it reached MAX, I felt like there was an elephant sitting on my chest pushing me back into my seat, and it seemed as if the skin was coming off my face. My normal 150-pound weight was now 1,050 pounds. We remained conscious even though it was difficult to breathe. Fortunately all we had to do was monitor our systems, though in an emergency we could still have taken action.

By now the heat shield was white hot and charring away, as it absorbed the tremendous heat of reentry. We could see a huge white fireball encircling the spacecraft, and watched as an occasional piece of tape burned and flew off the spacecraft, and as small sections of the heat shield ablated and disappeared into the fire. I was awed by this fantastic display. It was like the Fourth of July!

At the same time, I was needing to concentrate on the spacecraft and its performance. A lot had to go right for a successful reentry. A normal reentry was to be under computer and autopilot control, but if necessary we could provide a manual backup. This was a very complicated maneuver.

Although the Apollo command module has no wings, and some would say it's like a lead balloon, it does produce a small lift force like the wings of a plane. In the initial phase of reentry, this lift force is pointed up away from the earth to minimize the G forces. Then as the spacecraft plunges into the atmosphere, it wants to skip out due to the lift. If we allowed this to happen, it was adios earth.

So at the proper second, the spacecraft was to roll over 180 degrees to point the lift down, pulling us back into the atmosphere. This was a critical maneuver, and if our computer didn't perform exactly on schedule, we had just a few seconds to take over manually before disaster hit. Mission Control had given us the exact second we should expect rollover.

To monitor reentry, we had our normal computer display and flight instruments, plus a special reentry monitor system. In addition I had two stopwatches, plus the spacecraft timer, and John had his watch. We were taking no chances with a broken watch. When it came time for rollover, I was going to give it two more seconds by counting down "one potato, two potato" and then we'd take over.

Clocks and watches going, we counted off—10 seconds to rollover, 5 . . . 4 . . . 3 . . . 2 . . . 1—right on the *second,* we started rolling over! And as we rolled over inverted through the fireball, we saw the crystal blue Pacific Ocean with little, puffy, white clouds above the water.

*Man!* I thought, *what a beautiful sight. We are definitely coming home. Baring a chute failure, we've got it made!*

We were now securely captured in the atmosphere with no danger of a skipout, for we were falling below orbital velocity. Now the job of our guidance system was to get us to our desired landing point. To do this the autopilot began to roll us back and forth, pointing the lift vector in the proper direction to hit the target. Meanwhile we listened for AOS from Houston.

"Apollo Control, Houston. The ship *Ticonderoga* reports a radar contact. We are 3 minutes, 30 seconds from time of entry. We should be passing out of the period of communications blackout. We'll stand by."

"*Apollo 16,* Houston," called CapCom.

We had acquisition of signal! "Roger. Loud and clear!" we answered, delighted.

As we continued to roll, we sensed the G level beginning to decay. From a little over 7 Gs MAX, the G level dropped to 6 Gs, 5 Gs, 3 Gs and then at about 100,000 feet we began coming almost straight down in a free-fall right over our landing spot.

I braced myself, anticipating the opening of the drogue chutes at 23,000 feet. These small parachutes were to stabilize the spacecraft until deployment of the 83½-foot diameter main chutes at 10,000 feet. But when the two chutes opened, instead of feeling a stabilizing influence, we were whipped back and forth in violent oscillation—like a kite flying on the end of its string.

"Apollo Control, Houston. We have the first visuals of the spacecraft as the drogue chutes are shown deployed. These drogue chutes are 16½ feet in diameter."

Then at 10,000 feet, the drogue chutes were jettisoned and it felt like the bottom had fallen out. Immediately we heard this "poop, bonk," as the mortars fired the three main chutes out of their storage containers. The parachutes deployed first in a reefed or half open condition; this was to prevent any damage happening to them from the opening shock.

At 8,000 feet, the reef lines were cut and the parachutes opened fully. What a *beautiful* sight it was to look out the overhead window and see those three parachutes blossoming and twisting against the blue sky. We were really exhilarated.

I breathed a sigh of relief that the final moments of the mission were going to be nominal. If the parachutes hadn't opened properly, we had only a few seconds before hitting the water at a great rate of speed. Such an impact would probably kill us instantly, and the spacecraft would most likely split open and sink.

We were informed that the *Ticonderoga* had picked us up visually when the drogue chutes began to deploy. For the first time the whole parachute deployment sequence had been covered by TV.

In El Lago the house erupted. "There it is! We can see it! There it is! Isn't it beautiful!"

Everyone was awestruck that the cameras had been able to pick up the spacecraft so soon. And the red and white parachutes did look beautiful as they gently carried the spacecraft toward the sparkling blue Pacific.

Dotty never really had any doubts, but now she knew that *16* was going to make it and her heart rejoiced. The boys laughed and clapped their hands, along with everyone else in the Duke household.

A few people had already begun getting the champagne ready because there would be much toasting after *Casper* was safe in the water.

"Recovery, this is *Apollo 16*." John said, attempting to make contact with one of the four helicopters that had been sent from the aircraft carrier to monitor splashdown.

"*Apollo 16,* this is Recovery, welcome back!" They informed us they had the spacecraft in sight, and that we were only a mile from our intended landing spot.

"Fantastic! How about that, sports fans. The old computer has done it again." I got up on my elbows to look out the right window to search for the helicopters and the *Ticonderoga.*

There they were! The carrier looked like a postage stamp on the water and a helicopter was flying circles around us, while we slowly descended to splashdown.

Ken called out our altitude, "800 feet, 700 feet, 500 feet." At two hundred feet I planned to get back in position and brace myself for impact. "300 feet, 200 feet." I began moving back from the window. "100 feet." And at that moment the spacecraft hit the water.

Our altimeter was one hundred feet in error, so I wasn't in position at splashdown. Like a whiplash, my head snapped back and hit one of the steel supports of the headrest, almost knocking me unconscious. I saw a lot of stars! We hit so hard, splashdown felt more like crashdown!

It was my job to jettison the parachutes on impact, but before I could recover to get that done, the spacecraft flipped over and we were upside down in what is called the stable two position. Fortunately there was no danger because the command module can float either right side up or upside down, but it's very uncomfortable for the crew. It's like being strapped into a chair and having it turned inverted; you are hanging by the straps.

To get the spacecraft righted again, there were three big balloons on top which we inflated by turning on an air pump. Within ten minutes the spacecraft began to bob over; then a wave hit and did the trick! We were upright!

We could hear a helicopter hovering above us and watched as three frogmen jumped out with flotation collar and life raft. The hatch was to be kept closed until the frogmen had put the flotation collar around the spacecraft. Without the collar, there was the danger of a big wave coming along and filling us with water, taking us quickly to the bottom.

It took the frogmen about fifteen minutes to get the collar in place and the raft inflated. Then we heard a rap on the door. This was the all clear to open the hatch. I opened it up and staring back at me was a frogman still in his scuba gear.

"Great job!" he mumbled through his mouthpiece, extending a gloved hand in congratulations. I thought it strange that they were still wearing full scuba gear.

We jumped into the raft and then the helicopter hoisted us aboard one at a time. In true Navy fashion, John, as our captain, was the last to leave ship.

Inside the helicopter we were attended by a NASA flight surgeon, in case of any emergency, and were given fresh flight suits, a change of underwear, and a little deodorant, so we would look presentable for the welcoming ceremony on the deck of the ship.

As we landed, the red carpet was literally rolled out. Charles Hilly, NASA Team Leader, escorted us from the helicopter. The ship's crew were all lined up in their dress uniforms, the honor guard marched out, and the band played. We grinned from ear to ear as we saluted the flag and waved to the crowd.

Admiral Henry Morgan, Commander of the Pacific Recovery Force, and Captain Edward Boyd of the *Ticonderoga* came out to greet us with Larry King, NASA Public Information Officer. "It gives me a great deal of pleasure this morning on this special day," said Captain Boyd, "to welcome the crew of *Apollo 16* to the deck of *Ticonderoga*. The officers and men of *Ticonderoga,* this historic ship, are very proud indeed to be a part of this historic mission. Commander Lex Davis, *Ticonderoga's* senior chaplain will offer our prayer to almighty God."

Chaplain Davis stepped forward. "Let us pray. Almighty God, who alone prescribes the order of the universe, we lift our thanks to You for the safe return of the astronauts Young, Duke, and Mattingly. As the heavens once led wise men to the cradle of Thy Son, so may the knowledge of Thy celestial creation guide us to greater understanding of Thy will for mankind. That Thy goodness may be magnified throughout the world to the honor of Thy holy name. Amen."

Next Admiral Morgan introduced John. John made a tremendously moving talk thanking Ken and me, the people at the NASA Manned Spacecraft Center in Houston, and all the people around the country who helped make the mission go. He acknowledged the American taxpayers, promising that they got their money's worth—that we had brought back some basic knowledge "essential to the survival of humanity on this planet." John closed by thanking the U.S. Navy for picking us up, " 'cause I'll tell you right about now, Charlie, Ken, and myself aren't swimming too good."

Then Ken and I added our appreciation. It was a very moving ceremony, with the music and everyone clapping and waving. The Navy was as happy to see us as we were to see them.

I did notice though that every time someone got close, they had a funny look on their faces. Later on I realized why when, following the ceremony and after enjoying our first shower, we went back to the spacecraft, which was now on board ship. As I began to crawl inside, I found the *odor* almost *overwhelming*! You can imagine what the interior of that command module smelled like—three guys in such a little space for eleven days *without a shower*. It almost knocked me down. And apparently John, Ken, and I had smelled just as bad.

The docs gave us our first physical and, as expected, we checked out very well. No major problems at all, although we were about 20 percent weaker on the stress test than we had been preflight. Also I had lost eight pounds, but this weight loss is normal, due to dehydration, and in a couple of days I was back to normal weight.

President Nixon called to thank us for a great job and for making such a tremendous impact on the exploration of space. We thanked him for his support of the space program and told him we looked forward to coming to the White House and presenting him with a memento of our flight.

Next we were able to place calls to our families. Dotty was bubbling over with excitement. Her voice sounded great, and I told her how I missed her and loved her. Both boys got on the phone and were thrilled they had been able to see the parachutes open; they couldn't wait until I got home.

That night on the carrier we had a huge reception in the officers' wardroom. All the ship's officers, except those on duty, attended. The cooks had baked a big *Apollo 16* cake to welcome us home; compared with our space food, this meal was a gourmet's delight.

By the next day the ship was close enough to Hawaii to launch a plane to fly us to Hickham Field. After a brief ceremony at Hickham—with admirals, generals, the governor of Hawaii, and other well-wishers—we boarded an Air Force 141 and flew nonstop to Houston. Though I was tired from all the shipboard activity and the normal post-flight letdown, I was eager to see the family and say thanks to the welcome home crowd.

It was early evening when the plane landed at Ellington Air Force Base, Houston. As the doors opened, we were greeted by music and the applauding of several hundred people. I was grateful that so many had come to welcome us home.

An area in front of the plane had been roped off in order that our families could be the first to greet us. Immediately Dotty, Charles, and Tom were in my arms. I had a flower lei from Hawaii to put around Dotty's neck and a big kiss to plant on her mouth.

After the rest of the family had come out for hugs and kisses, we were led to a platform so we could speak to the crowd. Charles refused to join

227

us, because he was still too gun shy to be in front of the TV cameras. He stayed below with the grandparents, but Tom didn't want to let me go. I held him while Dotty and I joined John and Susy and Ken and Liz.

Once again John, Ken, and I gave our heartfelt thanks to all those who had worked so hard on the mission. In the crowd I recognized faces of people who had busted their bottoms to make the mission successful—the crew may get all the glory, but nothing is possible without the whole team doing its job.

It was a beautiful night—the moon was full and shining brightly. Looking up at it and pointing out our landing site, I felt proud—proud to be an American and proud to have had the opportunity to walk on the moon. The experience was real to me, not like a dream or something unbelievable. I knew I had been there.

We drove home to be met by another welcoming party. Many friends and neighbors had gathered, and they hollered and cheered and waved little American flags as our car pulled into the driveway.

Over our front porch hung a big WELCOME HOME, CHARLIE poster, and in the front yard was a huge plywood American flag, electrified with red, white, and blue Christmas lights. It had been standing proudly during our entire eleven-day mission. The flag had become a tradition in our neighborhood; it was first built for Bill Anders on *Apollo 8* and since then had made the rounds whenever another neighboring astronaut had flown.

This exuberant crowd of friends then held an impromptu ceremony, presenting me with numerous gag gifts, such as a jar of Tang and fake moon rocks. I was delighted!

After the celebration our friends went home, giving me a chance to be alone with all the family—parents, brothers, sisters, nephews, and nieces. I was bubbling with the thrill of it all and couldn't stop talking; I wanted to share everything with them. Whenever I slowed down, someone would ask another question starting me all over again, and so we talked into the wee hours of the night.

I could tell Dotty was glad to have me home. She was exhausted from all the tension and activity of the past eleven days, plus the many years of separation during training, and so when somebody commented about how much I enjoyed it and I answered, "You bet I enjoyed it! I'm ready to go again tomorrow if they'll launch me!" Dotty almost dropped her teeth. She couldn't believe I was raring to go again so quickly. She was ready to have me home for a while.

Yet after a few hours of sleep, I was up early to report to NASA for our debriefing. It was Sunday, but that didn't matter—they wanted to grab us while everything was still fresh. This began what turned out to be twelve days' worth of debriefing. We were in space only eleven days, however our debriefing lasted *twelve full days*. We talked to all the managers, engineers, and scientists about every area, system, and experiment we had done; each technical detail and fact was gleaned.

This intense work schedule, after just returning, was hard on the families—nevertheless Dotty and I did squeeze in a splashdown party with crew the night after we got back. All the astronauts were invited, along with many NASA employees and contractors. Friends came from as far away as California and Kansas. We had a house and yard full—over two hundred!

It was a *blast* seeing everybody. Many had been at the launch, and now they were here to welcome us home. I even got to serve the case of Swan beer that had arrived from Australia.

I was riding high. What a thrill—what a life! Things couldn't be better!

# 24

# *HOW DO YOU TOP A FLIGHT TO THE MOON?*

When the debriefing was completed, we began a series of postflight appearances. Hometown visits, parades and receptions in cities all over the United States, and most importantly trips to thank NASA employees and Apollo contractors.

One of the significant things about Apollo had been the tremendous teamwork. There were about four hundred thousand people working in the program from janitor to lead engineer, and we knew that it was their commitment and a job well done that had made the mission possible. We were well aware that one error could have stopped the whole thing with disastrous consequences.

So after first thanking all the people at the space facility in Houston, our next stop was Kennedy Space Center in Florida. NASA provided the aircraft to carry us, our wives, and children to a reception in the VAB—the building where our Apollo-Saturn V had been assembled.

I believe every employee at Kennedy came to greet us. There was a tremendous crowd of doctors, engineers, technicians, contractors, and others who had worked so hard on the mission. Saying thank you to them

and shaking their hands was a great thrill, filled with emotion. The grati-
tude we felt towards this group of people for the thousands of hours of
dedicated effort they had put into making *Apollo 16* such a success came
from the bottom of our hearts.

Directly from there we flew to our respective hometowns—John and
Susy to Orlando, Florida; Ken and Liz to Auburn, Alabama; and Dotty,
the boys, and I to Lancaster, South Carolina. Hometowners were probably
the favorite of all appearances; each community went all out for their
hometown boy, and Lancaster was no exception. A committee had been
working on Charlie Duke Day for months, planning all the events, which
would include a parade, luncheon, and formal ball. Many close friends
participated in this project, and they did a great job.

It was late afternoon when we landed at the airport in Charlotte, North
Carolina, to begin a tremendous whirlwind of activities for Charlie Duke
Day. We were greeted by a mob of reporters and TV cameras, plus a welcoming party from Lancaster, headed by my cousin the mayor, Reese Fun-
derburk. Mom and Dad were there, as were my twin brother, Bill, with his
family and my sister, Betsy. I could tell how proud they all were.

Early next morning was a press conference, followed by a reception and
luncheon at the Lancaster Country Club. President Nixon sent his brother,
Edward, to represent the White House. South Carolina Governor and
Mrs. John West were in attendance, along with many state and local
politicians—U.S. Senators Strom Thurmond and Ernest Hollings and
many more.

After the luncheon we left for the parade. The parade was a big deal.
There were bands and floats and military equipment, and they had a special float for Dotty and me and the boys, complete with a bubble-making
machine. It was wild! The bubbles were blowing, and young children were
running alongside the float yelling, "Charlie Duke-y, Charlie Duke-y."
Charles and Tom were a little overwhelmed, but after a while they shyly
began to wave to the crowds.

Lancaster is a small town of only about ten thousand people, but there
must have been twenty thousand men, women, and children lining the
streets. People had come from all around the neighboring communities
and even from out of state. The parade wound through town and then
headed out to the Lancaster High football stadium for the official Welcome Home ceremony.

The stadium was packed with people. The bleachers were decorated
with dozens of Springmaid cotton sheets, which had been silk-screened
with a picture of me in my spacesuit, the *Apollo 16* patch, and the words

WELCOME HOME printed across the top. Everywhere were American and South Carolina flags, waving proudly.

As I stood to speak, I really got choked up; seeing so many friends give all that time and effort really meant a lot to me. After my talk, I was presented with a beautiful oil portrait of me in my spacesuit and a scrapbook of the Charlie Duke Day project. The committee also announced they had commissioned a bronze bust to be placed in the town hall.

Following our hometowner, Dotty and I joined Ken and John and their wives to travel for the next two months all over the United States, thanking companies and contractors and being honored as America's latest heroes.

There were receptions, parades, luncheons, and dinners for over eight weeks—from Bridgeport, Connecticut, to Chicago, Illinois; from New York City to Los Angeles; from Seattle, Washington to Knoxville, Tennessee. We hit the biggies and the not so biggies. We ate more roast beef with mashed potatoes and peas than you can shake a stick at. We cheered when we were served a fruit plate for lunch during our visit to the Palo Alto Science Institute. How a politician stands it I don't know; their stomachs must be made of iron.

It was fun when we ran into family. Dotty's brother, Tom, and his wife, Ruth, were living in Connecticut. We had them jump into our car and ride with us through the crowds and ticker tape in Bridgeport; everybody kept asking if he were an astronaut.

It was an opportunity to make new friends and meet some wonderful and interesting people. The legendary Richard Daley, mayor of Chicago and a great fan of the space program, invited us to the Windy City for a ticker-tape parade. One of my most terrifying moments was when we were taken by police escort through the downtown streets of Chicago, sirens blaring and tires squealing. Landing on the moon was a piece of cake in comparison.

In New York City, Mayor Lindsay was a gracious host, holding a special ceremony on the city hall steps and escorting us to lunch. President George Bush, who was then U.N. ambassador, and his wife, Barbara, entertained us with a private dinner in their apartment. Mrs. Douglas MacArthur was also included, and what a delight it was hearing her relate her experiences with the general.

It was a jam-packed time—press conferences, TV interviews, keys to the cities, signing autographs, and giving a hundred speeches. John, Ken, and I had no idea being an astronaut required being a stand-up speaker, but we always seemed to manage to have the right words to complement each other. Usually one would talk about the flight, one would cover technology and space benefits, and the other the future of space; we tried to cover all the bases.

I especially enjoyed describing our view of earth from space. It was gorgeous—the most spectacular sight I'd ever seen. I told everyone, "In space, I could hold up my hand and cover planet earth, and this view has given me a new perspective. For underneath my hand were four billion people, and it is important that we learn to love one another. If we'd love each other, with that and with man's technology, one day we'll be able to solve all of our problems." This was one of my messages.

I also emphasized the benefits of the space program to the American taxpayer. We were constantly harassed about the amount of money spent on Apollo and on the moon. My response was that no money was spent on the moon, it was all spent in the United States—on jobs, technological advances, and scientific research. The press conferences became especially a battle on this issue. Reading the articles in the newspapers the next day was unbelievable! Quotes were incorrectly given, and the interview was hardly recognizable. I don't know why they never could get it correct, with all the tape recorders and notes they made.

Our most awesome and exciting trip following *Apollo 16* was to Washington, D.C., to attend a state dinner and speak before Congress. I was more fearful and anxious about my few minutes talk to the House of Representatives than I was during my entire flight to the moon.

With much ceremony we were led into the assembly by the sergeant of arms and presented to the Speaker of the House, who ushered us up onto the platform. I felt proud, yet fearful, to be before this distinguished group, and even though they clapped profusely and welcomed us as heroes, I remember stumbling over my words and forgetting what I was about to say. It was a classic case of stage fright. I'd never been so nervous in my life; lift-off wasn't even close.

We then walked over to the Senate to receive their greeting, and I was again impressed by their friendly and enthusiastic applause. We also met with the Space Committee and gave our views of man in space.

From there we proceeded to the White House for a private meeting with President Nixon in the Oval Office. He welcomed us warmly, making us feel right at home. We chatted briefly about our flight and then presented him with a memento—the tongs we had used to collect rocks on the moon. We visited about thirty minutes, talking mostly about the upcoming joint mission with the Soviets; the President had just announced this historic *Apollo/Soyuz* flight to be flown in 1975. He seemed very pleased with the current détente between the United States and Russia.

That evening we enjoyed a White House State dinner in honor of the

President of Mexico, Mr. Echeverría, and his wife. As part of that dinner the *Apollo 16* crew was to be recognized and honored. It was a thrilling experience—driving through the wrought iron gates and being ushered to the formal reception area, being present as the trumpets blared and the President and First Lady descended the spiral staircase, and walking through the receiving line to greet President and Mrs. Nixon and President and Mrs. Echeverría.

The dinner was elegant; each course served with a special wine. After dinner we were directed to the East Room for entertainment by Pete Fountain and his New Orleans jazz group. It was there that President Nixon introduced our *Apollo 16* crew.

We had brought President de Echeverría a special space memento and presented it to him at this time. Mounted side by side were flags of Mexico and the United States, which we had flown to the moon. Then underneath an *Apollo 16* photograph of earth was an inscription in both Spanish and English, which read something like, "You don't see the borders of our countries from space. You just see our lands and the oneness of our people. Thanks for the friendship of the Mexican people and their support. *Apollo 16.*"

At the end of the evening, the six of us were whisked by Presidential helicopter and flown to Camp David for three nights of fun and relaxation. President Nixon gave us free run of the place for the whole weekend, and what a tremendous time we enjoyed.

Camp David is a beautiful place, more rustic than plush. Cabins are scattered all along winding roads and paths which circle through the heavily wooded forest. We biked, shot skeet, went bowling, and thoroughly enjoyed having time away from the frantic pace of speeches and appearances. This was certainly a highlight of our postflight trips for Dotty and me, and we remain thankful to President Nixon for allowing us to use Camp David.

As John, Ken, and I were winding down these public appearances, NASA decided they wanted to put us back to work as backup crew for *Apollo 17*. The *Apollo 15* crew had been serving as backup, but had been removed when the story broke that they had taken some unauthorized items to the moon and had sold these items to a German collector. You can imagine the furor that arose from the press and Congress; it didn't do much for the all-American boy image of the astronaut corps.

Anyway, John and I agreed to be the backup. But Ken wanted to work on something else, so Stu Roosa volunteered to be the third man. The three of us began our training about mid-June, only two months after the return of *Apollo 16*. The launch of *Apollo 17* was scheduled for early December.

*233*

Dotty wasn't too happy with this assignment; she was really counting on a more relaxed schedule following *Apollo 16,* with a chance for us to work on our relationship and have more time together.

But I was excited to get back into training. I loved the routine and the dynamic environment of the Kennedy Space Center. And there was always an outside possibility that I might get a second chance to fly, for if anything happened to the prime crew, we would travel in their place. I think Gene Cernan, commander of *Apollo 17,* was suspicious we were trying to do just that and trip him up—when we played the following practical joke on him.

One afternoon at Kennedy, as Stu and I were finishing up our day's training, John walked into the building white as a sheet and out of breath. He had been jogging on a road in the swamp that we used for practice with the lunar rover.

"What in the world is the matter, John?" we asked.

"It was the biggest rattlesnake I've ever seen in my life!" he gasped. "I threw some rocks at it, but I don't know whether I got him or not."

Curious, we asked John exactly where he'd seen the snake, then jumped in our car and drove to the spot. As we stopped the car and opened the door, we heard this loud rattle—it sounded like a drumbeat! We knew then it was a *humongous* snake.

The noise led us over to the bushes and there it was—a *huge* diamondback! He was the biggest snake I'd ever seen and very much alive. Knowing he could really hurt someone and not wanting to tackle him up close ourselves, we stayed a good distance away and threw some large rocks, finally killing him. Then Stu chopped off his head with a knife and held him up for us to see. He was six feet long, as big around as my lower leg, and had seventeen rattles! He was *enormous!*

We put the snake in the trunk of our car for everyone at the training building to see, and then we got this bright idea. All through training, we had been bugging the prime crew with, "You guys, watch out—we're going to poison you or break your leg or something, so we can fly instead of you." Well, we decided to have a little fun.

Cernan was in the simulator, therefore we were able to sneak the rattlesnake into our office area and coil it under his desk. We made it look very lifelike—as if it was ready to strike. Then we called the secretary on the telephone and told her Gene had a very important telephone call and would she get him out of the simulator; Gene would interrupt anything to take a call. She said, "Right away," and rushed over to the simulator to give him the message.

In a few minutes Cernan came running into the office. While Stu and I watched, he ran over to his desk, sat in his chair, and began to scoot forward. As the chair was rolling under his desk, he happened to look down and *there was the snake!* All we could see were *bug eyes*—and all we could hear was a *bloodcurdling* scream. He pushed back from the desk and got that chair almost airborne! He went flying backward across the room at warp speed, rammed into the wall and hollered, "What's that?"—and then ashen ran out the door.

By this time Stu and I were just cracking up. When he heard us laughing, his initial response was to get mad, but fortunately he didn't know who to blame. After a few minutes his anger subsided and he even had a chuckle. It really did scare him though, and for a minute we were concerned we might have caused a heart attack. As you can imagine, from then on he wouldn't even let us get close.

*Apollo 17* was scheduled to be a night launch—the first nighttime launch of a Saturn V. This created a lot of interest, so because of that plus being the last flight of Apollo, Dotty and I decided to take the boys down for the historic occasion. Our parents joined us and around 10 P.M. on launch day, we drove out to the viewing area. Lift-off was scheduled for midnight.

It was a beautiful December night—warm with the stars twinkling brightly. The boys were all wound up and ran around and around the viewing area, still looking for alligators. Countdown continued smoothly until a problem developed about forty minutes before lift-off, delaying launch nearly three hours. By then Charles and Tom were sound asleep, so we had to shake them to wake them up.

What a spectacular sight! First came a flicker of flame, then smoke and fire belching from the base of the rocket. The enormous fire lit up the sky and the Florida coastline for miles—giving the appearance of daylight.

As the rocket roared away into the blackness of night, I was caught between two feelings—the thrill of flight and the sadness of seeing it all end. *Apollo 17* was the last of Apollo—the last trip to the moon. No one knew when we'd ever travel to the moon again. Apollo was over.

*What am I going to do now?* I wondered. I'd been working sixty to eighty hours a week, making thousands of decisions every day—decisions affecting millions of dollars and hundreds of people. This had been a tremendously dynamic and exciting job, and now it was all over.

I had been too involved in Apollo to give the future any consideration, but with the flight to the moon behind me my thoughts turned increasingly to what I was going to do next.

The crews for the next two programs, Skylab and the *Apollo-Soyuz* joint mission, had already been selected. There was no opening for me there.

The newly announced space shuttle was not scheduled to fly until 1979 or 1980; that was seven years away. I realized I wouldn't get to fly in space again for at least *seven* years.

*What am I gonna do now?* I was still hard charging and ambitious. I was a colonel in the Air Force and hoping one day to be promoted to general. Few active astronauts had made general officer, so the idea crossed my mind to leave NASA and go back to an Air Force job where I could be promoted. But a decent job was hard to find; I really didn't have the experience to manage a wing. And the Air Force had plenty of senior officers and didn't seem very interested in astronauts.

I considered politics—a number of astronauts had taken that route. But I wasn't sure that was for me. Then I heard NASA was looking for a deputy administrator for legislative affairs. This individual would be the one to interface between Congress and the Space Agency. Since Congress was responsible for NASA's budget, it was important to have a good relationship with them.

I was offered the job. It was right down my alley. But there was one snag—it meant moving to Washington. It was a tremendous offer, but Dotty and I decided that we didn't want to move the family to the fast-paced life-style of D.C. Our family was already under enough strain, so I turned the job down.

The space program had been really tough on our marriage and our family. Dotty and I continued having problems, as our lives drifted more and more apart; and I'd really been an absentee Dad. The boys were coming up on six and eight years of age and were beginning to get involved in Little League baseball and youth soccer. I knew that if we went to Washington, I would plunge into twelve-hour days, and they would grow up and never see their dad.

That was the way it had been in Apollo. I remember coming home on weekends to hear them say, "Mama, can you help me with my homework?" "Mama, can you help me with my bike?" I was hurt. *Why don't they ever ask me to help them?* I wondered.

Of course I really knew the answer. Since I was gone so much of the time, Dotty had been forced to fill in both as father and mother. It was always Dotty that they turned to when they were in trouble or needed help. I determined that I would travel as little as possible and stay in Houston.

The space shuttle was on the drawing boards, and NASA seemed interested in utilizing my engineering expertise in a management capacity. I was offered a job working with Owen Morris, who was responsible for part of the space shuttle orbiter.

While I enjoyed the people, the endless engineering meetings left me looking for new horizons. After working with Owen for a year, I was transferred to the operations' office and worked under Don Cheatham. His office was responsible for the operations' budgets and development of shuttle operations, once it got out of the experimental stage.

One of my assignments was looking into on-orbit rescue. If for some reason the shuttle's engines failed to ignite or the payload doors failed to close, the shuttle would be stranded in orbit with no way to get back to earth. It was my responsibility to determine how feasible it was to send up a second shuttle to dock with the disabled craft.

These jobs were challenging for a while, but it was mostly paperwork. We were still five or six years from launch; we didn't have a piece of hardware, not even a mock-up. I began to get more and more frustrated and bored with my duties at NASA. Staff work was tiresome.

I guess the only thing I was really enjoying was flying and being with Charles and Tom. I volunteered to help coach their baseball and soccer teams when I was in town, even though I didn't know beans about soccer. It seemed all you had to know was how to line up the kids on the field, how to kick the ball, and then just let them go. Soccer was a great game. Everybody got a turn to play, and sooner or later the ball was going to come to each one of them.

The kids were hilarious to watch—twenty little six-, seven-, and eight-year-old boys and girls, all bunched together running around in a cloud of dust. Occasionally the ball would pop out. The goalies were the only two not kicking. We ended up winning the championships in soccer and baseball over the three years I helped coach.

Skylab went well, setting records for man days in space. It was now 1975 and *Apollo-Soyuz* was preparing to fly. The frustration with my job had gotten unbearable. There were no challenges—no new goals to hold onto and reach out for. I'd climbed to the top of the mountain. There could be no higher accomplishment for a test pilot, and I was only thirty-seven years old.

*What am I gonna do now? How do I top a flight to the moon?* You can't live forever thinking about a three-day trip to the moon. I still had this tremendous energy within me and was searching for a way to release it.

*What am I gonna do?* I kept asking myself. For the first time I began to consider the possibility of a new career. Many of the senior astronauts had left the program during the past Apollo years of 1972 to 1975.

"If I go into business I'll have a whole new challenge in front of me," I explained to Dotty. "I've already reached the top in the space program. I need new goals." I began to see the possibility of making my mark in the business world and earning a great deal of money, as a means of utilizing my seemingly boundless energy and drive.

In the spring of 1975 I heard a rumor that Coors Beer was expanding their market in Texas; they intended to enter Austin, San Antonio, Houston, and south Texas. At that time Coors was sold only in Dallas, El Paso, and areas north. Coors distributorships were known to be very lucrative, plus I loved drinking their beer. Whenever I stopped in El Paso or Dallas, I'd bring back a case.

"That might be just the challenge I'm looking for. I'll try to get one of these distributorships and start climbing the ladder of success and make my million!" I began to get excited and looked for an investor.

As an astronaut I had met a good many influential and wealthy businessmen, becoming close friends with several of them. One of these was Dick Boushka. Dick was a former all-American basketball player and had played on the 1956 gold-medal U.S. Olympic team. He was now working in the oil business as president of Vickers Energy in Wichita, Kansas.

I approached Dick about forming a partnership and trying to get one of the Coors distributorships. He had a friend in Kansas who was a Coors distributor, and after looking at the numbers we realized it was a gold mine. We decided to try for the one in Austin. The University of Texas is in Austin, and I could picture all forty thousand kids drinking Coors beer.

Beginning in June I started working hard on our application. Still at NASA, I'd work on it in my off time. A lot of research was required in order to draw up a financial and business plan; these distributorships were highly competitive, and it would take a tremendous effort to land one. Our agreement was that Dick would be the primary financial investor, and I would be the operator. With that we would split fifty-fifty.

We submitted our proposal, and after a few months were told that the group had been cut to four or five top finalists for the Austin area, and Dick and I were in the running. In September we flew to Golden, Colorado, for interviews.

I was excited and at the same time a little apprehensive. I knew if we got it, I would have to resign from the military. That was a big decision because I was a colonel with eighteen years' service, only two years away from retirement. Even though I would lose this substantial investment, I reasoned Coors was such a lucrative business that it really didn't matter. I would make a lot more in the beer business than I could from my retirement pay.

Some weeks later I received a call from Colorado. "I'm sorry, we can't give you the Austin distributorship," said Harvey Gorman, the Coors vice president, "but would you be interested in taking San Antonio?"

I didn't know much about San Antonio. I had been there only once when Dotty and I had visited the HemisFair in 1968. "I'll check into it," I told him. When I did so, I discovered San Antonio had about the same kind of market as Austin.

*It is now or never,* I concluded, so in September I took the San Antonio distributorship and made my commitment to leave the Air Force the first of December. Some of my Air Force buddies thought I was crazy, but I replied, "Well, I can finish up my time in the Air Force Reserves in order not to give up the Air Force completely."

Next I told Deke Slayton and Al Shepard, my two immediate bosses. "It looks like I'm going to be leaving. I've got a Coors beer distributorship and I'd like to quit NASA December 1."

"Well congratulations, Charlie, and good luck!" they responded.

It was a pleasant parting. No one in management pleaded, "Oh, please stay." They simply wished me a successful future. I think they were relieved that several of us from the astronaut office were leaving around that time, because they didn't know how they were going to keep us all busy for the next five years until the shuttle was flying.

Immediately I began traveling back and forth to San Antonio, taking the leave I had acquired from the Air Force. It was an exciting and demanding time—buying property, getting the warehouse constructed, ordering trucks, hiring people.

I'm not sure how Dotty felt about this new job. I know she looked forward to leaving the fast way of life of an astronaut. One of her complaints had been the amount of time I had spent away from her. Although I had begun spending more time with the boys, our marriage had continued to deteriorate. I never seemed able to please her and, having no solution, we just muddled along hoping for the best.

Outwardly our marriage looked good—we appeared to be the ideal couple. We always held hands, and when we went somewhere we fit in socially, not letting our problems surface in public. But Dotty was always complaining, "We just aren't close any more, there's no depth to our relationship."

Although our relationship was shallow, I rather liked it that way. I didn't have time to get involved in her troubles. I didn't want to talk about any problems because if we did, it usually ended up in an argument.

"I don't have a problem," I would say to her, "it's your problem." I felt if she'd just change, everything would be okay, so I listened with only one

*239*

ear as she poured out her deepest feelings. I just didn't want to know. I didn't want something else to worry about.

"Can't she understand the pressures I'm under?" I argued. "Why can't she just be happy and not bother me with her problems?" I was enjoying myself the way things were and tried to push her aside by answering, "Well, there's nothing I can do about it."

When we met people at parties and they asked, "How's it going, Charlie?" "Oh, fantastic!" I would answer. "We just got back from skiing, and next weekend we're off to Brownsville to play golf." I put on this facade, "We don't have any problems. Man, life's a bowl of cherries."

But our marriage was heading toward the rocks of divorce like so many other astronaut marriages. The first divorce had hit the office in 1971, another blow to the all-American image. After that a number of marriages had ended, almost like opening up the floodgates. I resigned myself to the possibility that our marriage might not last.

I told myself, *If Dotty decides to leave me, there are lots of other women in the world.* For an astronaut there were plenty of gorgeous women available.

I knew Dotty was unhappy; I could tell she had become very depressed. Then one day she said, "I don't want to live anymore. I want to die." THAT was a *shock*!

# 25

# DOTTY'S STORY

Suicide!

Why would a girl who seems to have everything—famous husband, fancy trips, two healthy boys, big house, two cars—ever think of suicide? But here I was so depressed that ending my life seemed the only answer. Life was too painful.

I had difficulty getting out of bed in the morning and attending to all the things I had to do. It was not easy putting on a smile and pretending that everything was okay.

I didn't tell many people how depressed I had become—only Charlie and my father. I knew that people wouldn't understand and would think I wasn't being appreciative enough of what I had. I didn't want to feel guilty for my depression, too.

My dad's response was deep concern; Charlie's was typical of the way he had been acting toward me for years—*Maybe if I ignore her, she'll stop complaining and the problems will go away and everything will be all right.* I knew he didn't know how to deal with it, but I was hurt that he didn't even seem interested in helping.

One of my pleas had been for us to go to a marriage counselor, because I believed the problems in our marriage were really the major cause for this hopelessness I was feeling. Our marital problems had been going on for a very long time, ever since we were married twelve years ago.

I was so happy when we first began courting in Boston. Charlie was so understanding and compassionate—and romantic. He wanted to be with me all the time, and even nights when he would have to study he would call, and we would talk about our day and how much we missed each other.

Maybe it was because he was five years older, but I felt in him a strong arm that I could lean on, someone to protect me and take care of me. He told me over and over again how much he loved me and how special I was. I had never felt so loved and it was wonderful. I knew I had found the Prince Charming I had been searching for.

All my life, my dream had been the fairy tale "Cinderella." The dream of one day finding my Prince Charming, who would sweep me off my feet and, professing undying love, would fulfill all my needs. We would have a perfect marriage and, as in the fairy tale, live happily ever after.

When Charlie asked me to marry him, knowing how much I needed this special love, I said, "Charlie, I'm going to put you first in my life. Will you put me first in your life?" His answer reassured me that I was truly the most important thing in his life. And so Cinderella and Prince Charming got married.

What had happened? What about happily ever after? Where had Prince Charming gone? My dream bubble had burst. It was no more. The only thing remaining was a wishful memory.

Our honeymoon hadn't been great but was okay. It wasn't quite the "romantic, deserted island with fantastic red glowing sunsets" experience I had dreamed of, but then we had a whole lifetime to look forward to.

However immediately after the honeymoon, when we returned to Boston, I realized things were not okay. I was not first in his life; his job was first.

Charlie had changed. He didn't spend time with me as before. He didn't talk about how much he missed me when he was at school. He didn't linger over our candlelit dinners for two, instead he'd hurriedly eat and rush back to his room to study. Whenever he did take a free moment from studies, he'd often pick up a newspaper or turn on the TV. "I need to relax," he would say, effectively closing me out of his presence. Consequently I felt rejected.

I knew he had to make good grades at MIT in order to graduate. I knew how important the degree was for his career. But I couldn't understand why I had slipped from first place to second or even third place. I was confused and hurt.

I began to think, *Well, as soon as he graduates from MIT, things will be different. He's just worried about school.* With that thought, I looked forward to school ending and going wherever the Air Force would send us next.

When the orders came through that Charlie was accepted at test pilot school, Edwards sounded fine. "Yes, anything will be better than MIT." He was excited and I loved to travel, so California would be a new place to explore and live happily ever after.

Well, Edwards turned out to be not quite so fine. It was like leaving the frying pan and jumping in the fire. Charlie was in school studying just as hard, plus now I had to compete with something new—*airplanes*! He loved flying. The topic of conversation was always flying. The guys were continually sharing one tale after another, and the wives either sat and listened or went to another room.

Also Edwards Air Force Base was in the middle of nowhere—desert, cactus, windstorms, hot and not much to do. I found a job substitute teaching the second grade and joined the Officers' Wives Club and a ceramics class, but mostly I was lonely. Charlie stayed busy at school and at nights studying. I became pregnant and experienced the usual nausea and tiredness, which seemed to compound my loneliness.

Christmas came. It was the first Christmas spent away from my parents, and I missed them. We'd always have a big Christmas dinner with Daddy's relatives and then in the evening, another dinner with Mother's family. Christmas with just the two of us wasn't the same.

Life wasn't working out like I thought it would. Charlie was ecstatic but I was biding my time, hoping the next move would take us to a better place. Maybe then Charlie would start paying more attention to me and loving me the way I wanted to be loved.

Our first son was born and I was delighted. Blond and blue-eyed with an infectious smile; we named him Charles III. Being a mother kept my days busy—washing diapers, making formula, late night feedings.

Charlie was a great dad. I should have been overjoyed at his pleasure and devotion toward this new smiling life in our home, but I couldn't help wishing he would show as much enthusiasm over me. For a while Charles seemed the most important thing in Charlie's life, but then the excitement of school and jets preempted this latest interest.

Upon graduation from test pilot school, Charlie was asked to remain on staff as an instructor. This disappointed me. I didn't know where I wanted to go but felt any place would be better than Edwards. Every opportunity I could, I persuaded Charlie to drive us off for the weekend and explore California. I looked forward to the change in scenery.

Surprisingly, after eighteen months, I began to appreciate somewhat the open spaces, the spring wildflowers, the clear skies of spectacular sunsets and brilliant stars. It was then that Charlie saw a notice in the *Los Angeles Times* announcing NASA was seeking more astronauts and asked me, "Dotty, what do you think about my being an astronaut?"

"An astronaut!?" I had never thought about it. I was proud of Charlie—he had done well in test pilot school and was an excellent pilot. What greater achievement than to become an astronaut?

In my mind I weighed what I knew about the space program. The negative was that he would be gone from home a great deal, traveling about two-thirds of the year. The positive was we'd be living in a real town, Houston, Texas—with trees and lakes and all the things I'd missed. And Houston was at least a thousand miles closer to Atlanta. But most of all, I hoped a new place would improve Charlie's and my relationship.

Our marriage had grown further apart at Edwards and I was ready for a change. I thought *Surely I can get him to love me the way I want to be loved and we can live happily ever after.*

Upon moving to Houston, Charlie was immediately thrown into the hectic pace required of an astronaut. He loved every minute of it and would come home with tremendous excitement of all he had seen and done. I was very happy for him.

In comparison Charles' and my life was the usual—diapers, washing, shopping, cooking. Because Charlie was rarely home, my duties were compounded, and I felt sorry for myself.

Emotionally I was really stretched when a year after moving to Houston, I was responsible for building our new house and having our second child. Charlie was gone constantly and I knew very few people. Our new son, Tom, and two-year-old Charles received minimum attention as I rushed from duty to duty, physically and emotionally drained. Time sped on; I held on as well as I could.

Of course there were the exciting times—the parties, the celebrity status, the thrills of launch and being a part of history. The wives got together once a month for coffee at the AWC (Astronaut Wives' Club) meetings. We had a lot in common and yet possibly because of the competition in the astronaut office and our desire to be individuals, we weren't as close as we could have been. Most of my close friends were wives of NASA engineers and contractors, not astronauts.

There were of course rumors of husbands running around on their wives, but we didn't talk about that. It was understood that divorce would ruin an astronaut's chance to fly, so indiscretions were kept discreet. Every wife had to deal with the knowledge that her husband was a hero and considered prize game by good-looking women wherever he went.

Happiness continued to be elusive—not because Charlie was an astronaut and traveled a great deal, but because I didn't feel the love from him that I wanted. Whether he was gone or at home, I felt alone. His career was the most important thing in his life, and I knew it.

I had put him first in my life when we married, and I continued to look to him for my fulfillment. If he was nice to me, I was happy; if he ignored me, I was sad. He didn't love me the way I wanted to be loved.

When we had gotten married and the Scripture was read, "They shall become one," I thought it meant I was half and he was half and together we would make one. Since we weren't together in so many ways, I felt incomplete. Charlie seemed to be fine without me, but I felt something was missing from my life.

Competing with the space program was impossible, so when Charlie immersed himself in his job, I tried to get involved, too. We could share that. I liked being a part of our country's heroic adventures in space—it was the patriotic thing to do. Fixing our marriage would have to wait. In 1969 Charlie was selected for the crew of *Apollo 13* and following that flight began training for *Apollo 16*. I put my efforts on hold as much as I could—like a war bride, waiting until the war is over to have her husband home again.

My responsibility as wife of a flight crew member was to make sure that my husband was taken care of in such a way that he could do the best job possible. I tried not to bother him with mundane burdens at home. Most wives cut the grass, took out the garbage, and kept the house and kids in order. That was our contribution to the U.S. effort in space.

When time came for Charlie's flight, I was really excited for him. He had worked so hard and now was going to see the fulfillment of that dedication and desire. Although I naturally had some fears, they were rationalized away by the success of previous missions. Why shouldn't his be successful, too?

I had seen Charlie flying now for ten years in many different types of aircraft. I had grown accustomed to the space missions—almost everyone living in our area worked for their success. Their confidence and Charlie's confidence became my confidence that everything would go all right. And I knew everyone in the astronaut office would give their right arm to be going, so I was proud that he had been chosen to make the flight.

My job was to see everything went well with the details of entertaining friends and relatives who came to the launch, taking care of the boys, and running a semiorganized house for the duration of the flight. There were the press interviews, overseeing my wonderful family who had joined me in Houston, welcoming a constant stream of friends and neighbors, plus intently following the space adventures of *Apollo 16*.

There was a tense moment when the mission was almost aborted due to engine problems in the command module in lunar orbit. Even then my greatest concern was not their personal safety, but the possibility they might not get to land on the moon.

Charles and Tom stayed close to me and close to home. They were somewhat overwhelmed by all the commotion. Having their cousins visit was exciting, but all these other people and Daddy in space was difficult for them to handle.

It was a big day when Daddy came home, and we could all give him hugs and kisses. I'd never seen Charlie so filled with joy and enthusiasm. He related adventure after adventure of their space escapades and exclaimed he was ready to go again.

I was ready for something else. *Now,* I thought, *our family life will get back to normal and without the demands of preparing for a space mission, we can focus on each other.*

For a few months we went through the ritual of parades and speaking engagements all over the United States. It was a time to receive the acclaim and recognition of a job well done and to promote future NASA programs. We had a wonderful time, but one thing Charlie said in his speeches hurt. "The best thing that ever happened to me," he exclaimed, "was my flight to the moon. It's the greatest experience of my life."

I wanted marrying me to be the best thing that ever happened to him. I would work on that. Things would be different now.

But they weren't different. Charlie worked as hard as ever as backup on *Apollo 17* and following that committed himself to working on the space shuttle. He did have more time at home, but he spent that coaching the boys, playing golf, or fishing. I'd tag along.

One day Charlie told me, "I am pulled by your demands, by the boys, by work, and pulled by what I want to do. You'll have to take your turn. The boys come before you because they are so young. You are an adult and should understand." I, who had wanted to be all of his life, was instead just an irritating part.

The more I had tried to get his affection, the more he had pulled away. I had tried the sexy approach; I had tried the crying approach, I had tried the angry and nagging approach—even the sensible adult communication had gotten me nowhere. It seemed like all he wanted from me was to cook his meals, take care of the children, and stay out of his way until called upon. My life was to revolve around his needs, but my needs weren't being met.

I had worked ten years to get Charlie to love me the way I had wanted to be loved and hadn't succeeded. When I saw that I wasn't getting the love that I needed and that my life was falling apart, I thought, *I'll divorce him and find someone else. Yes, if Charlie's not my Prince Charming, I'll find the person who is.*

But as I considered all the upheavals of divorce, the awful possibility hit me, *What if there's no one else out there? What if there isn't anyone who will love me the way I want to be loved.* The thought was crushing.

In resignation I reasoned, *Well, maybe this dream of having a perfect marriage is not going to be the answer for me and my life. I'll try to find fulfillment in something else.*

Women's lib was proclaiming that the answer to life for women was finding fulfillment in a career. It seemed to work for Charlie, maybe it would work for me. I got a wonderful job—at a travel agency in downtown Houston. Loving travel, the job was perfect. I liked everything about it, even the detail work of writing airline tickets. My boss and the others in the office were a delight to work with.

One winter I accompanied a tour to England and for my greatest adventure I traveled to Africa on my own, using bonuses I had been awarded as a travel agent. *What could be better?* But it didn't bring me the happiness and fulfillment I was searching for. I was still lonely.

*What is the answer to life?* I asked myself. *Maybe it's experiencing everything—climb every mountain and see what is on the other side.* I tried lots of things.

I experimented with marijuana, but since I wasn't a smoker, inhaling the drug wasn't pleasant to me.

I threw myself into the party circle. *Charlie likes to flirt with the girls, I'll flirt with the boys.* Inwardly I was hoping he would be jealous, but instead he seemed proud that other men found me attractive and encouraged me on. I was lonelier than ever. Experiencing everything didn't seem to be the answer.

*Maybe it's serving the poor,* I thought. In college I had wanted to work in the Peace Corps and help in some third world country. I decided to volunteer at the local Headstart Center and spent many enjoyable hours playing with and teaching disadvantaged kids. I tutored reading to boys at a home for runaways and delinquents.

At Thanksgiving and Christmas I organized a church outreach program of supplying baskets of toys and food to the needy and assisting a local Mexican family—finding them employment and assisting in their other personal needs. Knowing I was helping make a difference in other people's lives gave me great satisfaction, but it didn't fill the emptiness in my own life.

*Maybe the answer to life is church.* So I taught Sunday school, was on our Episcopal church's lay council called the vestry, organized family picnics and retreats, and was involved with every aspect of church life.

I read in *Life* magazine of a movement called the underground church— a group professing to have found a reality outside the traditional organized church. I called one of the movement's preachers in Houston to come speak to our church, but his words were empty, and I felt no warmth or love in him. *Is the answer not even in religion? What is the answer to life?*

Someone suggested I read a book on astrology, which I did, but it seemed too mechanical and nonpersonal and didn't appeal to me. Our church offered a course on positive thinking, and I attended a series of their meetings studying the book *I'm O.K., You're O.K.* That led me to other self-help books, but instead of helping me, they made me feel more and more inadequate.

Positive thinking and self awareness weren't the answer. I knew I couldn't depend on myself to get out of this pit I was in. I wasn't the answer. I wasn't the truth. I wasn't eternal. How could I depend on myself? I needed something to depend on that was constant and faithful and had meaning. Something that was bigger than me.

*Is there no answer to life?* I asked myself. *Is life just a big joke? Do we just live for seventy or eighty years and die and that's it? Is there no purpose to life?*

After trying to find fulfillment in so many different directions and coming to the conclusion that there was no answer, I asked myself, *Why live any more? Life is just one painful, lonely, empty day after day. It always has been; it always will be. Why keep on living in such pain?*

The popular Broadway play title *Stop the World, I Want to Get Off* became my plea. I even imagined the way I would put an end to my life.

It was now the fall of 1975. While Charlie was getting excited about his new career in the beer business, I was in turmoil over what was going to happen to me. I wanted to break free and start a new life, but there didn't seem to be any new life out there worth living. *Divorce? Suicide? Or more of the same? What should it be?*

For the past few months our church had been planning a *Faith Alive!*, a spiritual renewal weekend. I remember the night that our vestry had voted to sponsor this *Faith Alive!* As a vestry member I had argued, "Instead of spiritual renewal we need to do more social work in the community." I didn't even know what spiritual renewal meant, but it certainly didn't sound practical and real-world oriented.

The time came for the weekend and being a faithful church leader, I committed myself to go. Charlie said he would, too. In fact we even offered to host one of the many couples who were traveling to our church in La Porte, as part of the *Faith Alive!* team.

The weekend program consisted of several dinners and luncheons. There was singing, and then we listened as our guests—about thirty laypersons—gave short personal stories of their faith. I had never heard a personal testimony before. It wasn't anything like the sermons I had heard preached in church.

Fascinated, I listened to these people talk about the reality of God in their lives, of prayers being answered, lives being changed. Some were spectacular changes, some fairly simple, but all giving credit to the lordship of Jesus Christ. I had never heard anything like this. *Was it true? Was God real? Was Jesus the Son of God?*

Even though I was a faithful member of my church, I had long ago decided that Jesus was not necessary in a relationship with God. Even though I said the Apostles' Creed, I didn't believe Jesus was the only begotten Son of God. Why, in college I had studied all the major religions and they all seemed the same to me.

I called myself a Christian because I was born in a Christian country and was a member of a Christian church. I could have easily been a Muslim or Hindu. To me Jesus was a good teacher and wonderful example of the way we were supposed to live, like Muhammed and Buddha. They all taught that we should love and help each other—the Golden Rule. Wasn't that all that was important?

These people were telling me that their relationship with God was through Jesus. They actually believed the Scripture that read, "I am the way, the truth and the life. No one comes to the Father except through Me" (John 14:6). They believed that Jesus died for their sins and that trusting in Him they might have eternal life.

I wasn't even sure there was eternal life. Actually I wasn't even sure that God existed. There was a popular book at that time which stated, "God is dead." It said that God is only a figment of our imagination because we need a crutch, something to depend on. Since we are so far advanced and don't need Him anymore, He is dead—the illusion of God has died. Well, I had wondered if that was true, if God indeed is a figment of our imagination.

But these people were telling me that God is alive—that they know He is real—that they talk to Him, hear His voice, and He answers their prayers.

I wasn't sure if God had ever answered my prayers. Yes, I had prayed in church the morning of Charlie's spaceflight and had asked God to take care of him. But I had believed that the expertise of NASA, the excellent hardware built by the contractors, and Charlie, John, and Ken's training were what made it a successful flight.

These people were convinced God had answered their prayers. They said Jesus loved me just the way I was; I didn't have to do anything to deserve it. That He loved me so much He had died for me on the cross. All I had to do was receive it by believing and turning my life over to Him.

*Could I chance it? Could I turn my life over to Someone I wasn't sure existed? Did He really love me that much?*

They said Jesus would give meaning and purpose to my life. *Was it true? Was this the answer I had been looking for?*

It seemed so risky, to take that step of faith. *Wasn't it good enough to just continue in church the way I had been? What if it wasn't true? Everything else had failed me. Would this fail me, too? Would I open the door to the closet where I had kept God and find it empty? Was it better to know He didn't exist than to continue on pretending?*

I looked at these people who had given their time to come be with us for the weekend. They had so much joy, so much love, and so much conviction in their testimonies. *Why not give it a chance? What really did I have to lose, except a last hope in an already hopeless situation.*

That night, alone and kneeling by my bed, I prayed, "God I don't know if You are real. Jesus, I don't know if You are the Son of God. But I have made a mess of my life, and if You are real, You can have my life. If You are not real, I want to die."

With that prayer, I turned over the control of my life. I was now going to look to God for all the answers; I was going to depend on Him for my fulfillment. I had committed myself to finding out if God and Jesus were real.

I didn't tell anyone, not even Charlie, of my decision. The next day the only change I felt was that now I was going to look to only one place for the answers—not to Charlie, not to work, not to books, but to God.

One of the team members had given me a Campus Crusade tract which explained that you were not to depend on your feelings in this new relationship with God, but you were to make the decision on fact and the feelings would follow. I hoped so, because I didn't feel any different.

But I reasoned, *If God is real and loves me, He can and will help me in every part of my life.* Therefore I daily began to ask Him to guide and assist me.

When my first prayer was answered, I thought, *Oh, that's just a coincidence, that isn't God.* Then another prayer was answered and another. *Surely, these are only coincidences.* But after two months of answered prayers, I couldn't put it off as chance any more. I *knew* God had heard me and had lovingly intervened in my life.

About this same time, I had a recurring dream. In the dream I was on a train with other people. I didn't know where the train was going or who was the engineer, but I had a deep peace knowing I was in the right place. After having the dream repeated several nights, I decided to ask God if He had given me the dream, and if He had, what did it mean.

Immediately the following thoughts came to my mind, *Yes, I did send you the dream. You are on a train and Jesus is the engineer. No, you don't know in life where He is taking you, but you can have peace because you can trust Him. He loved you so much that He died for you on the cross, and He will love you always. You can depend on Him. And you are not alone; all the other people on the train have accepted Jesus as Lord, too.*

I was startled! *Was that God speaking to me? It all made sense. Yes, I believe God is speaking to me. He is real! He loves me and I can trust Him!*

Not long afterward God spoke to me again—again in a quiet voice in thoughts which were confirmed by my heart. This time He said, *Dotty, you are born again. All your past sins are forgiven. You are beginning a brand new life. You don't have to look back anymore. Your past is washed away, and you are starting a new life. Now, if you want your marriage to be born again, you must forgive Charlie.*

*Forgive Charlie!* I was convicted and defensive at the same time. I knew, and Charlie knew, that I remembered well all the times he had hurt me— forgetting my birthday, criticizing me in front of my friends, putting me down, flirting with other girls—the list went on and on and was firmly established in my memory. And every now and then I would remind Charlie of them.

Forgive him. Let him off. Why, he hadn't even apologized. He hadn't asked to be forgiven. He didn't even think he was wrong.

"No, God," I answered stubbornly. "He doesn't deserve it. I want to let him suffer for a while. I don't want to forgive him."

This time God spoke with powerful yet loving authority. *You can't call Me Lord, if you don't obey Me. Those that call Me their Lord must do My will.* I was reminded of the Scripture, "Not everyone who says to Me 'Lord, Lord,' shall enter the kingdom of heaven, but he who does the will of My Father in heaven" (Matthew 7:21). At that moment my understanding of lordship became clear—to do what God wanted me to do, not what I wanted to do.

I couldn't argue anymore, but my next question to God was, "But how can I forgive him? You want me to forgive him the same way You have forgiven me. That means wash the slate clean, forgive and forget. There's no way I can do that."

I even reminded the Lord of what I had learned from books on pyschology—that if you've been hurt, you'll never get over it. You'll carry the memories and wounds the rest of your life. All you can do is learn to cope, not forgive and forget. "I can't forgive him the way You've forgiven me, Lord," I said.

The Lord's kind words assured me, *You just agree to forgive him and I'll help you.*

And help me He did. Every time I would be reminded of something Charlie had done in the past, the Lord would say, *You can't think about that. Remember you've forgiven him, so it's been erased. It's not there any more.* And I would remove the thought from my mind.

For two months over and over again, each time I was tempted to remember the past hurts, the Lord encouraged me by repeating these words, and I would cast the thoughts out of my mind. A wonderful healing took place—as the Lord truly removed the resentment and unforgiveness in my heart, along with erasing the memories and hurts that had been there for over twelve years. I experienced a real freedom and understood Jesus' reference to the words of Isaiah, "He has sent me . . . To proclaim liberty to the captives" (Luke 4:18).

The Lord continued freeing me—from my depression, my loneliness, my self-pity. I no longer wanted to commit suicide; I had given my life to Jesus, therefore my death was in His hands. He would determine my time to go, not me. And I no longer wanted to divorce Charlie. God showed me that He had given me Charlie to be my husband; if Charlie wanted to leave me, that was up to him, but I was not to divorce him.

About this time we moved to a small town outside San Antonio, and Charlie began work on his beer distributorship. I was really hopeful that our life would be better now and that Charlie would have more time for me and the children. But instead of things getting better, things got worse. He left before dawn every morning and returned late every evening.

*Faith Alive!* had not changed Charlie. He treated me the same way, plus now he was obsessed with making a lot of money. He had gone to every meeting that weekend, but his mind had been preoccupied with his new business venture.

*251*

When I complained to the Lord, He spoke to my heart saying, *Dotty, I love you, and I want what is best for you. The way Charlie is now is what is best for you.*

I was stunned! *What do you mean, Lord, that the way Charlie is now is what is best for me?* I argued. *I know what is best for me. In fact, I have a long mental list of characteristics that I believe a good husband should have, and Charlie doesn't have them.*

The Lord just continued to repeat the same words over and over in my mind, *Dotty, I love you, and I want what is best for you. The way Charlie is now is what is best for you.* Finally I submitted and asked, "Well then, Lord, what do You want me to do?"

*Love Charlie,* was the firm reply. *Don't try to change him, don't try to save him, I am the Savior. Just love him.* And with those words, I knew the Lord meant for me to love Charlie the way Jesus loves me— unconditionally.

I then realized I had been loving Charlie conditionally—loving him so he would love me back. Maybe I was loving him 75 percent so I could receive 25 percent, but God was calling me to love him the full 100 percent whether he loved me back or not. My prayer began to be, "Lord, help me love Charlie unconditionally and accept him the way he is."

God immediately started revealing to me little things I could do to show my love to Charlie, like bake his favorite pie and not complain when he wanted to play golf. The Lord also began to change my heart and fill me with His love for my husband.

God made clear to me that instead of looking for fulfillment in Charlie and our marriage, I was to let go of that and look for my fulfillment in Jesus. He told me Jesus had enought love to fulfill all me needs and so I was to look only to Him.

Over the months the Lord revealed these truths to me, and my life began to slowly change. I then understood that God's desire—God's best for me—was to teach me unconditional love, and the best way to teach me was to give me someone difficult to love. And I learned that only in God's power through the Holy Spirit could I love someone the way Christ loves me.

How wonderful it was when I realized that everything I had been told about God at the renewal weekend was true! They were right! God did love me and wanted to be my friend and my Lord. He would help me. Life did have meaning. There is a God and Jesus is His only begotten Son.

I wanted to tell someone what I had discovered. I wanted to stand up in church and announce to everyone it's true—everything we say in our worship is true, but they all seemed set in their routine and I didn't think they would understand.

Then a few months after *Faith Alive!* I decided to make my first confession of faith to Charlie. One evening in bed I timidly said, "I can't depend on you anymore, Charlie. I can depend only on God."

He was stunned and answered defensively, "What do you mean you can't depend on me? I pay the bills; I come home at night—that's more than some husbands do!"

I hadn't meant to hurt him and quickly agreed that he did take care of me materially. Then I left it at that. We were on different wavelengths. I couldn't explain, and he wouldn't have understood.

Of course I couldn't depend on him for my fulfillment in life, for my needs of love and purpose. No one is perfect and I never should have tried. By looking to him to fulfill all of my needs, I had put a burden on him that was impossible to carry. Only the Lord Jesus could do that; He is perfect and will gladly fulfill all my needs.

All my life I had been looking for my Prince Charming. I had found someone better than a prince; I had found a King. His name is Jesus, King of kings. "You have changed my sadness into a joyful dance; you have taken away my sorrow and surrounded me with joy. So I will not be silent; I will sing praise to you. LORD, you are my God; I will give you thanks forever" (Psalm 30:11–12 TEV).

# 26

# *TO MAKE MY MILLION*

But *dollars* were before my eyes! I was really looking forward to beginning my new career and becoming a successful businessman. A trip to the moon was no financial bonanza.

Many people have the idea that astronauts are wealthy and that we were paid a million dollars for going to the moon. In spite of published articles so stating, it is not true. Astronauts are paid according to their military rank or their civil service pay grade.

However, we did get a little extra; a trip to the moon was considered TDY (temporary duty). The per diem or daily rate for TDY at that time was $25 per day. To claim credit, we had to fill out an expense report or travel voucher. My itinerary read: Houston to Kennedy Space Center, Kennedy Space Center to moon, moon to Pacific Ocean, Pacific Ocean to Houston.

The moon trip lasted eleven days, so at $25 per day, that equaled $275 extra money. However, government quarters and meals were furnished, and so they deducted that part. I believe we ended up with $1.25 per day for the trip.

I was hoping they would pay mileage. At *five cents a mile,* we would have had it made! Yet no such luck; government transportation was provided. Actually I would have gladly paid them my whole salary for the privilege of going. I did not go for fame or fortune. But now three years later, I decided it was time to take a new challenge and make my million.

In December 1975 I was discharged from the Air Force with eighteen and a half years' service—to become a businessman. The next day I signed up in the reserves, planning to complete my retirement by serving ten more years as a reserve officer. It wouldn't hurt to cover my bases.

We sold our home in El Lago, said good-bye to our neighbors and friends in the space program, and moved to New Braunfels, a community just outside San Antonio. We liked the small-town atmosphere, beautiful Landa Park, the Guadalupe River, and thought it would be a good place to raise the kids. Also New Braunfels was in my market area and wouldn't be far from where I was building my Coors warehouse in northeast San Antonio.

The grand opening was only weeks away. I was really getting excited and proudly named the company the Orbit Corporation. The past few months—building the warehouse, hiring personnel, buying the trucks, taking care of licensing—had been extremely busy and reminded me of the early days of Apollo. There were thousands of things to do, lots of important decisions to be made, and I thrived on all this activity.

But now—instead of a moonflight—my focus was on the millions of dollars in profits to be made. The distributors I had met in north and west Texas and in California were all millionaires. There was lots that money could buy; I could fly around the country in my private jet, play golf in Palm Springs, and hunt in Alaska.

Of course all this work took a lot of time. My hours were longer than in Houston, which didn't please Dotty—but there was money to be made. If she complained, I'd remind her our financial future was at stake. This was different from NASA, it was our *business.* I needed to be there to pay close attention to detail and motivate our employees. I did notice though, that in spite of the long hours, Dotty wasn't nagging as much as she had in Houston. She seemed more at peace with herself.

Opening day finally came. I was down at the warehouse by 4:00 A.M. to watch the trucks being loaded. Coors beer is very difficult to load because the cases are stacked on little sheets of hard plastic, and these have to be picked up with a special forklift. This maneuver takes a lot of practice, so a couple of distributors had sent some of their people to help.

Things were really chaotic this first morning! One of the forklifts brought out a pallet of beer, which is 120 cases, and as I was watching promptly dumped the entire thing all over the warehouse floor. Beer cans went rolling *everywhere*! Fortunately it was cans and not bottles. It took us twenty minutes to clean up the mess! In spite of that the trucks rolled on schedule.

Coors being a new product, sales were fantastic. The first month's profits were outstanding. You can imagine that for a young man who's never been in business before, this was like shooting ducks on water. The next month things did get tougher—the competition didn't lie down—but profits in the business were very good. I was ecstatic!

Once things settled down, I established a routine of getting to work between 6:00 A.M. and 6:30 A.M. and coming home about 8:00 P.M. or 9:00 P.M. I'd arrive before the trucks left on their routes and stay until the last truck came in, always putting down a few beers with the guys before going home. Sometimes I'd go in on Saturdays or Sundays, particularly when we were supplying special events like fiestas, rodeos, and company parties.

Summertime was busy—extra events on the Riverwalk in San Antonio and trying to hustle a spot at the Chilipiad in San Marcos, and then there was the fall Wurstfest in New Braunfels.

Wurstfest is an annual November festival centered on the German heritage of New Braunfels. It is a big event; thousands of kegs of beer are sold in a ten-day period, and I wanted to be part of it. My problem was that the committee allowed only local distributors to participate. At least my home was in New Braunfels, so I vigorously lobbied the Wurstfest Committee. Sure enough, they let us in, and Coors did very well. Our second year, the festival sold six thousand kegs in ten days. It was a river of beer!

Running the distributorship required a great deal of effort. I was as conscientious in business as I had been in the space program. My desire was to give my customers an honest day's work for their dollar—a good quality product, delivered within the Coors Brewery ground rules. No bribing or under the table dealings were allowed by any of my employees.

255

We'd be aboveboard and a company of our word. I was proud of my integrity in running the distributorship. But others weren't so proud of the business I had chosen as my career.

At the time I was serving on the executive board of the Alamo Area Council of Boy Scouts. I noticed that whenever I was introduced at one of their functions, my past astronaut experiences were given, but no mention was made of my beer distributorship. This began to grate on me and hurt my feelings.

Also my twin brother, Bill, was not happy with my being in the beer business. He thought it tragic that an American hero, a man who had walked on the moon, would sell beer and be a negative influence on the young people of the United States. I argued with Bill, "It's an honest business; I'm not doing anything illegal. I'm not forcing anyone to drink. If they don't buy from me, they'll buy from someone else."

His criticism stung, but my greed overcame any problem I might have had with tarnishing my American hero image.

At home I continued in my efforts to be involved with Charles and Tom, especially in sports. Dotty decided to get a soccer league organized in New Braunfels, and I helped as much as my time allowed. The new league generated a great deal of interest and began its first season with over 250 kids participating on twenty teams. I helped coach whenever I could. My career of course came first; that was my top priority, and Dotty and the boys knew it.

Dotty kept busy with soccer and various church activities. Over the months I began noticing a gradual change in her attitude. She had started reading religious books and would mention praying about things. In fact during our first summer in New Braunfels, she decided to attend a Christian retreat at Laity Lodge in Hunt, Texas. I didn't think much about it; I was just glad she had found some activities to keep her busy. She seemed happier and was more understanding with my schedule.

The following summer, we were guests of John and Annie Denver at their home in Aspen, Colorado, and Dotty and John got involved in a deep discussion about God. *Strange behavior,* I thought, but she never bugged me.

During my second year in the beer business, even though things were booming, I began to get bored and frustrated. I had made a lot of money, but the challenge was gone, and there were problems with the other local Coors distributors. I was one of four that Coors had established in San Antonio, and we couldn't agree on marketing strategy. Also I was tired of making the necessary bar rounds, drinking beer with customers. Something was wrong, and I began to question if I was in the right business.

Dotty knew of my frustration and doubts and one day asked, "Charlie, have you ever thought about asking God whether He wants you in the beer business or not?"

"No," I replied. It had *never* occurred to me that God was interested in what business I was in. Surely he had bigger problems than worrying about my job. Dotty insisted that God was interested, and we could ask for His direction.

She then questioned, "Will you be willing to do whatever God wants you to do?" "Sure," I answered.

"Well," she suggested, "let's pray." Not knowing how to pray like that, I said, "Why don't you pray."

Dotty's prayer was very direct and simple. "God, if You want Charlie in the beer business, give him peace; but if You don't want him in the beer business, make it so miserable he sells out."

I promptly forgot about the prayer—however, *God didn't,* because things got worse and worse. My problems with the other distributors got worse, my frustration got worse, and finally in February of 1978 I couldn't stand it anymore and decided to sell out.

I went to my partner and announced, "Dick, I'm selling out. You can do what you want—keep your share and buy me out or whatever, but I'm going to sell."

"Well," said Dick, "I think it's wrong. We've got a super business, and it's going to be worth even more. But if you want to sell, we'll sell." It took only fifteen minutes on the phone to find a buyer for the exact price we were asking.

We made a handsome profit. Dick got his share and I got mine—which was more money than I'd ever imagined possible. I was flush with cash and immediately started dreaming about how I was going to invest this money to make even more. Since I had forgotten about the prayer, God received none of the credit.

A year earlier Kenneth Campbell, a friend from Houston, had asked me to come into business with him. He was a real estate developer and had made a fortune in apartment development; now he was expanding into shopping centers. I had told him then, "Ken, I really don't have time to fool with any kind of real estate development, but if I ever sell the beer business, I'll sure come talk to you."

So I called Ken and began to investigate that possibility, along with some other options. I wasn't in a big hurry. We had plenty to tide us over.

In April of 1978 about a month after I'd sold the distributorship, Dotty and I were leaving church one Sunday morning when Hyl Karbach, a friend and prominent surgeon in town approached us. "There's going to be a Bible study at T BAR M tennis ranch in a couple of weeks. The subject is Bible prophecy and what's happening in the Middle East today; it's called *Walk Through the Bible*. I've taken the course and found it very interesting—I think you would, too. Why don't you consider going?"

He gave us the details and we told him we'd think about it. I knew Dotty was interested in such things so I thought, *She's been so understanding and patient with me, why don't I do this for her.* Also the topic sounded interesting. I enjoyed staying current on world events and how that might relate to the Bible was intriguing. We decided to attend.

I certainly wasn't going because I was looking for God. I thought one hour a week in church every Sunday was all I needed. I was a loyal churchman, even read from the Bible as a lay reader during the service. I went to church because it was the proper thing to do and I enjoyed it. I liked the people and there was a sense of well-being. But I didn't go to church to get close to God; it was a social event.

I had not even felt close to God on the moon. It was not a spiritual experience for me at all—it was a technical experience. One reporter had even told me at the time, "Going to the moon is the best thing to happen since man invented religion." That sounded great and made me feel very important.

If I really thought about it, I believed that man was evolving toward the true consciousness. We can be gods—we can solve all the problems in the world whatever they might be. Look what we had already achieved! I was in charge of my life and things were going well. Who needed God? Only people who couldn't make it needed God. I didn't need God.

Time came for the Bible study, and Dotty and I joined a group of about twenty others at the local tennis ranch to hear about this *Walk Through the Bible*. From Friday night to Sunday evening we were going to cover Genesis through Revelation. I really wondered why it would take a whole weekend; I thought we should be able to complete the material in one or two sessions.

Our instructor began in the Old Testament with Adam and Eve and continued into the stories of Abraham and the covenant, Moses, David, and the prophets. He explained how time and again, the nation of Israel would fall away from God and then later repent and turn back to Him. I was greatly impressed by the love and mercy of God in continually forgiving His people and calling them back to obedience in Him.

Then in the books of Isaiah and Jeremiah, I read prophecies about the Messiah who would bring in a new covenant and who would bear the punishment of many and be put to death for the sins of the people (see Jeremiah 31:33, Isaiah 53). I knew that the New Testament claimed that Jesus was this Messiah—that his death on the cross fulfilled the perfect sacrifice of atonement which had been required for the forgiveness of sins by God (see Hebrews 9).

The question began to come to me, *Charlie, who do you say Jesus is? Who is Jesus Christ?*

Most of the world says Jesus was a nice teacher, a good moral person. Some religions even claim he was a prophet, a holy man of God. But the Bible was saying Jesus is the Messiah, the Son of God.

I read in the Scriptures, "The Lord Himself will give you a sign. Behold, the virgin shall conceive and bear a Son, and shall call His name Immanuel [which is translated 'God with us']" (Isaiah 7:14).

"In the beginning was the Word, and the Word was with God, and the Word was God. . . . And the Word became flesh and dwelt among us, and we beheld His glory, the glory as of the only begotten of the Father, full of grace and truth" (John 1:1,14).

*So, Charlie,* the thought hit me again, *who do you say Jesus is?*

I learned that many during Jesus' life recognized him as the Messiah—Anna, the temple prophetess, John the Baptist. Even the demons recognized him and trembled. And God the Father acknowledged him at the transfiguration, "a bright cloud overshadowed them; and suddenly a voice came out of the cloud, saying 'This is My beloved Son, in whom I am well pleased. Hear Him'" (Matthew 17:5).

Jesus himself claimed He was the Son of God, the Messiah. When the Samaritan woman at the well said to Jesus, "'I know that Messiah is coming' (who is called Christ). 'When He comes, He will tell us all things.' Jesus said to her, ' 'I who speak to you am He'" (John 4:25,26). Then at Jesus' trial, "Again the high priest asked Him, 'Are You the Christ, the Son of the Blessed?' Jesus said, 'I am'" (Mark 14:61–62).

The question, *Who is Jesus?* rang over again and again in my mind and heart. Is the Bible true or not?

I realized God had given me a free choice, and He would not interfere with my decision. I could choose to believe Jesus is the Savior of the world, who died for my sins and is Lord of all, or I could choose to believe He is not and that He is a big liar. I saw there was no other choice. He could not be just a good, moral person—if He is not the Son of God, then He is a liar because He claimed to be the Son of God, and liars are not good, moral people.

I realized I had to make a decision—*Make up your mind, Charlie. Who do you say that I am?*

That weekend on Sunday evening, sitting in the front seat of my car on Highway 46 in New Braunfels, Texas, I looked over at Dotty and said,

"Darling, there's no doubt in my mind that Jesus Christ is the Son of God."

She began to clap and said, "That's just what God has been waiting for you to say." I didn't see any angels or hear any heavenly music, but I knew that I knew—that Jesus is the Son of God—and a peace came into my heart.

Beside the peace, the only change that I could tell was that the next morning I had an insatiable desire to read the Bible. Before this, I never read the Bible. Now I couldn't put it down, and for hours a day I read the Scriptures. I couldn't understand everything I was reading, but the desire was there, and so I consumed every word. Since I didn't have a nine-to-five job, I had plenty of time to read and pray. Over the next few months, I can't say there was a great change in my life, but little seeds were being sown in my heart.

In May I decided to go into business with Kenneth Campbell and we formed a partnership, calling it Campbell-Duke Investments. We joined together for the express purpose of building neighborhood shopping centers, hoping to make millions of dollars. Money still meant an awful lot to me. We began to look for some property.

Later that summer Dotty and I attended a Christian retreat at Laity Lodge, the same place she had gone two years before. Dotty was so happy now to be able to fully share her faith with me. It had been a lonely two and a half years for her since she had put Jesus first in her life. Not only was there no one in our home that was a true believer, there were no other people in our community she had found to talk with about the reality of Jesus. For all that time it had been Dotty and Jesus. Now we began to pray and read the Bible together.

One of the first changes we made in our home was reading Bible stories with our boys. We saw that it was our responsibility as parents to teach our children about God. Before they went to bed at night, we would read and discuss the heroes of the Old and New Testaments—Joseph, Moses, Paul, and David. They loved all the stories, especially the one of David defeating Goliath.

A men's Bible study was formed by those who had attended the *Walk Through the Bible* seminar. Being with other committed Christians was a great encouragement to me. Jim Goodbread offered his store, so early on Wednesday mornings we got together in the basement of Henne's Hardware in downtown New Braunfels. That basement was like being in the catacombs of Rome and reminded me of the early Christians.

Well, the more I read the Bible, the more convicted I became that there were some things in my life that God wasn't too pleased with.

In *The Book of Common Prayer* used in the Episcopal church, there is a prayer called the Confession of Sin that reads, "The remembrance of my sins is grievous unto me, the burden of them is intolerable." For years I had been saying these words with my mouth, while in my heart I was thinking, *This has got to be the biggest joke I've ever heard. The remembrance of my sin isn't grievous unto me; the burden isn't intolerable. In fact I sort of enjoy some of them.* I had never murdered anybody, so I thought I really wasn't a sinner. Of course there were a few things in my life I didn't want Dotty to find out about, but "everybody does that."

However as the Holy Spirit began to speak to my heart about my sins, the burden of them did become intolerable. He said, *Charlie, the problem with your marriage is you. You don't love Dotty the way you should.* I knew this was true. My love for Dotty had been dead for years. Now the Lord was telling me to love her as He loves the church. This was a 100 percent love.

I repented and asked the Lord to forgive me. I went to Dotty and told her I was sorry for all of the troubles and problems and hurts I had brought into her life, and that I was going to try to be the husband God wanted me to be. Then I asked God to help me love her the way He does.

Together Dotty and I dedicated our marriage to the Lord. It wasn't instant, but God has resurrected a marriage and love that was dead. We are not going full speed toward the rocks of divorce anymore, we're going full speed toward the peace and love of God that is in Christ Jesus. We still have arguments, we still have problems, but we know how to solve them by taking them to Jesus and obeying Him.

Next the Lord spoke to me about Charles and Tom and said, *Charlie, the problem with your relationship with your children is you.* He showed me that my criticism and anger had destroyed much of our relationship. I went to my sons and asked for their forgiveness for the way I'd been as a father.

My situation with Tom was especially bad. In Proverbs it says that we have the power of death and life in the tongue (see Proverbs 18:21). I'd spoken curses—not words of profanity, but words of discouragement like, "Tom, you are stupid!" or "Tom, you can't follow instructions. I've told you a hundred times how to kick the soccer ball [brush your teeth, comb your hair]!" He couldn't even brush his teeth or comb his hair to please me.

Tom could never please his father, so he stopped trying and became exactly what I spoke. He was placed in remedial reading; he became very insecure and quiet and would hardly ever open his mouth around me.

When I went to Tom and asked him to forgive me, he said, "That's all right, Dad." My eyes brimming with tears, I grabbed him and gave him a big hug.

From then on I tried to speak words of encouragement and put Tom in the Lord's hands as best I could. "Lord, you give him a sense of well being. You make him into the young man you want him to be."

Again it was not instant, but over the years the Lord has honored that prayer. Tom is now secure in the Lord and with the talents he has been given. He was placed in accelerated English, was elected president of the senior class, and finished high school in the top ten out of three hundred.

I wanted to read and study the Bible all the time. As soon as I came home from work, I sat down with the Scriptures and read for hours, getting upset if I was interrupted. I could tell Dotty was confused—she was happy I was so excited about the Lord, but uncomfortable with the lack of time I was spending with the family. My workaholic tendency was now directed toward being proficient in the Bible. I especially enjoyed reading about Christ's second coming.

Though I had made some major changes in my relationships with Dotty, Charles, and Tom, the truths of Scripture—to love one another as Christ loves us—was not fully rooted in my life. Fortunately God has beautiful ways of teaching us, not only from His Word, but by bringing certain people and circumstances into our path.

One day at Bible study, someone told me about a series of tapes on love called *The Love Command*. I ordered them and then every day, as I drove back and forth to San Antonio, where I had established a small office, I listened to these tapes. There were a total of twelve tapes, which taught not only about God's great sacrificial love for us, but God's command to us as Christians to love one another. As I listened, I realized that what God wants from us is to reflect His love in every area of our lives, in every relationship, and not necessarily be brilliant biblical scholars.

I remember coming home one day after listening to the tapes and saying, "Dotty, I believe what God wants us to do is to love one another unconditionally." That was a real revelation to me and a major step. God does not command us to be theologians and to be intellectual giants in the Bible, but He commands us to put His Word into practice and love one another.

I saw that my excessive scholarly approach to the Bible was a barrier to loving my family the way God wanted me to love them. "And though I have the gift of prophecy, and can understand all mysteries and all knowledge, and though I have all faith, so that I could remove mountains, but have not love, I am nothing" (1 Corinthians 13:2).

I realized God wanted me to read the Scriptures for the purpose of finding out what He wanted in my life. It was to be my training book and would teach me everything I needed to know for living the Christian life. It's like getting in an F-16. Without reading the manual, you won't last long. You're going to crash if you don't know how to operate the thing. I recognized it was the same with my Christian walk. I needed to read the Book, the Bible, and put it into practice to become the person God wanted me to be.

One morning while I was shaving, Tom came into our bathroom and told his mom and me, "Things are different in our family. I like the way we are now." That really blessed us. Later I went to Charles and asked him what he thought of our new life with Jesus. He said, "Daddy, I like it. You talk to me now." That really hit me! Can you imagine? All my boys wanted was for me to talk to them and spend time with them. How I as a father had missed the true meaning of our relationship!

We explained to the boys the difference between a real Christian and a *churchian*—one who goes to church regularly but does not believe in the lordship of Jesus and has not committed his life to Him. One Saturday when Dotty and Charles were out shopping, the Lord touched Charles's heart, and he told his mom he wanted to be a real Christian. They were driving in the car, so she just pulled over to the side of the road and Charles at thirteen and a half years old prayed to ask Jesus into his heart.

That same afternoon Tom, Dotty, and I were out at our hunting lease working on a deer blind to get it ready for the fall season. The three of us were talking about the Lord and, without knowing what Charles had done, Tom said he wanted to make Jesus his Lord and Savior. It was a sweet, joyful time as this eleven-and-a-half-year-old opened his heart and invited Jesus to come into his life. In one day our prayers were answered and *both* boys became believers in the Lord Jesus Christ, with the sure knowledge that they belonged to God. Later as mature adults, they have each recommitted their lives to the Lord.

Our home began to be a home of peace and not a home of discord. There were still arguments and fights and even today not all is perfect harmony; the fruit of the Spirit is not fully ripe. But the discord and tension are fading into the distant past.

Christian life is not trouble free or problem free. We are still human, and we fail and get mad at one another and live for ourselves, and not for God a lot of times. But we know God never deserts us, never leaves us. He's always with us. We reap what we sow, God is not mocked, but He is merciful and always ready to forgive (see Galatians 6:7).

A third area God spoke to me about was money. He said, *Charlie, you love money more than Me. I want to be first in your life.* "No one can serve two masters. . . . You cannot serve God and mammon" (Matthew 6:24).

I saw in Psalms where it says, "Do not be afraid when one becomes rich, when the glory of his house is increased; for when he dies he shall carry nothing away; his glory shall not descend after him [into the grave]" (Psalm 49:16,17).

I didn't want to put money first in my life anymore, and I wanted to be a good steward of the money God had given me. As I prayed and read the Bible about giving unto God, I started seeing the word *tithe* all through the Bible. "Will a man rob God? Yet you have robbed Me! But you say, 'In what way have we robbed You?' In tithes and offerings" (Malachi 3:8).

I believed that God was speaking to me from His Word and that He wanted us to give away 10 percent of the money we had earned the past year. Was I hearing right? I knew it would be a big check, because we had made a lot when we sold the beer distributorship. I wasn't sure, so I asked Dotty, "Would you pray? I think God wants us to give to the church some money from our profits in the beer business. Would you ask Him to give you a figure?"

She said she would, and about a week later she came back and said God had spoken to her heart and had given her a figure. "Well, what is it?" I asked. When she gave me the amount, it was exactly what God had shown to me. The Bible says, "By the mouth of two or three witnesses every word may be established" (Matthew 18:16), so we knew God was speaking to us.

We had a piece of property, and the sales price was the exact amount of our tithe, so I gave the church our property and gave away the love of money. I pray I'll never put money before God again. The Lord was working on my priorities. His desire was for me to place Jesus first, Dotty second, my children third, and myself last.

"Do not lay up for yourselves treasures on earth, where moth and rust destroy and where thieves break in and steal; but lay up for yourselves treasures in heaven, where neither moth nor rust destroys and where thieves do not break in and steal. For where your treasure is, there your heart will be also" (Matthew 6:19–21).

As these changes took place in our lives, we began to see the reality of God. There really is a God and He is interested in our every thought and action. We are to make Him a part of each step of our day. He wants to be our friend and our counselor. A few months later, God began to counsel me about another area in my life—drinking.

When I became a fighter pilot, I learned to enjoy beer. My main purpose was to get high—I wouldn't stop with one or two. At first my partying was limited to weekends and this continued through test pilot school and while I was an astronaut.

Then when I started the beer business, I began drinking almost every day. It became a habit, and now almost a year after selling the business, I was still drinking almost every day and with the express purpose of getting high. I don't believe God was too pleased.

In early 1979 all the family went to Snowmass, Colorado, for a ski vacation. On arrival, I decided to have a beer. I was shocked at what happened—it felt like that one beer was going to blow off the top of my head! I blamed it on the high altitude and the next day had another. But the same thing occurred. *Lord, what is happening?* I asked.

I believe God clearly spoke to my heart saying that I had a drinking problem and my attitude toward alcohol was wrong. God wanted me to stop completely. In obedience I stopped with no desire for another drink whatsoever.

For the next two years I had no alcohol. Then on a trip to Germany, I was invited to lunch by some businessmen who wanted to hear why I believed in God. One of my hosts was the owner of a large brewery, and as we began lunch a large glass of beer was set before me.

I started to refuse, but I remembered the words of Jesus to His disciples when he sent them out in ministry—to eat and drink what is put before you. This I did, and I found that I did not have a craving for alcohol anymore. I had been set free, and six German businessmen prayed to receive Jesus as Lord and Savior, including the brewery owner.

This new life in Christ has delivered me from many areas of bondage—anger, impatience, and prejudice, to name a few. I didn't even know I had a problem, but after receiving Jesus Christ in my heart, I have experienced what Jesus said, "If the Son makes you free, you shall be free indeed" (John 8:36). And God continues to work in my life to perfect me and conform me to the image of His Son, Jesus Christ.

I have come to realize that Christianity is more than a ritual; it is a personal relationship with Jesus, the living God. I know now, that before I gave my life to Jesus, I had been only a churchian—maybe a good churchian, but a churchian nonetheless.

Even though I had been baptized, confirmed, and had done all the things I thought necessary to have good standing with God, I had never made a commitment of faith, accepting Jesus as my personal Lord and Savior.

Now through faith in Jesus, I have been born again and have eternal life. "For God so loved the world that He gave His only begotten Son, that whoever believes in Him should not perish but have everlasting life" (John 3:16).

I will never be alone. I know Jesus is with me every moment to help me in my trials, to comfort me in my hurts, to guide me in my steps, and to fill my heart with His love, joy, and peace.

My daily heartfelt desire is today and was then to know God more.

# 27

# THE LOVE AND POWER OF GOD

"Charlie, look what Lillian gave me at church today—a book on healings and miracles! I can't wait to read it!"

In the fall of 1978, Dotty was given a book called *Power to Heal* written by a Catholic priest, Francis MacNutt. It was about the supernatural healing power of God.

After finishing the book, she gave it to me. I was amazed at what I read. These were stories of miraculous healings happening in people's lives today as individual Christians prayed for the sick. People who had been blind were seeing, ones that were dying of cancer had been healed, deaf people were hearing and more! I couldn't believe it.

*Is this really going on?* I wondered. I had never read about any such stories in the newspaper, and surely it rated front-page news. *And how do you explain it? How could I understand it?* I was an engineer. I had been flying airplanes for twenty years and spacecraft ten years of my life. I could understand systems, hardware, and hands-on types of things. This supernatural stuff was different.

When we heard that Reverend MacNutt was going to be in San Antonio to speak at Saint George Episcopal Church, we got excited and decided to go. We encouraged some friends in Houston to attend; their son was ill with cancer, and we suggested he might receive prayer for healing. With much anticipation and yet a little trepidation, the boys, Dotty, and I, and a special eighty-four-year-old friend from church, Anna Poss, piled into our car and headed for the service. We really didn't know what to expect.

As we walked into the church, an indescribable feeling of liquid love poured all over me, and tears began to well up in my eyes. The music sounded like the melody of angels, and the presence of God was very real.

We were disappointed when our friends from Houston failed to appear, but realized God had a special reason for our being there.

At the end of a stirring sermon on God's desire to heal and how Christians are called to pray for the sick, Francis MacNutt announced that if anyone wanted prayer they could come forward and he and the Episcopal priest, Randy Cooper, would pray for them. He said that since he and Reverend Cooper didn't know what our needs were and God did, they would allow the Holy Spirit to pray through them.

I wasn't sick, but knew I wanted prayer; so taking the boys with me, I joined the lines of people filing forward. My turn came and, with Charles on one side and Tom on the other, I closed my eyes while both priests laid hands on me and prayed.

Suddenly it was like being in zero gravity again. A lightness and a wonderful feeling of joy and love came over me, and I began to sob as waves of love flowed through my body. I knew that something wonderful had happened, and God had touched me!

That night in bed, I had a very vivid dream. I was in space again, but without a spacecraft, and was hurtling rapidly through the blackness; it was so black I couldn't even see my hand in front of my face. But I knew I was moving at a great speed.

All of a sudden, out of the darkness appeared this evil face—the most evil face I had ever seen! His eyes were like fires of hate, and I realized it was the face of the devil. He was very mad . . . with snarling teeth dripping blood and a murderous countenance!

He came right up to my face, but instead of being frightened I had this great sense of peace and knew that Satan couldn't reach me. It was as if I was surrounded by an invisible shield because I belonged to Jesus Christ. We were face to face for what seemed like a few minutes, and then he just faded away into the blackness and I woke up.

I was perplexed and asked the Lord, "What does that dream mean?" The Lord spoke to my heart, *Charlie, you used to be in the kingdom of darkness, but I have taken you out of the kingdom of darkness into the kingdom of light, the kingdom of my dear Son, Jesus Christ.* I knew that these were words from the Bible (see Colossians 1:13) and rejoiced in hearing that reassurance from God.

Then a few nights later, I awakened with a start and sensed a spiritual presence in our bedroom. All of a sudden I felt a touch on my shoulder trying to pull me out of bed. Well, I got very frightened, not knowing what it was, and woke up Dotty.

"Dotty, there is something in this room—I don't know what it is! What should we do?"

Immediately we began to pray, "Lord, we don't know what this is. If it's from You, come back tomorrow night, but if it's not from You, send it away." Peace came, and as I went back to sleep I glanced over at the clock and noticed the time was 1:45 A.M.

The very next night, I again awoke with a start. The first thing I did was look at the clock, and it was exactly the same time as the previous evening. Feeling a touch on my shoulder and sensing the Lord's presence, I quietly got up and went into the living room.

Kneeling down on the floor, I raised my arms above my head in total surrender and began to cry, "Lord, I don't know what's happening, but I give You my life. I surrender all that I am and all that I have to You. Lord, You can do with me what You will in my life." The Lord honored my prayer, and that night I was filled with the Holy Spirit.

Jesus just *exploded* in my life! The reality of Jesus and the reality of the authority of the Bible permeated my every thought. I knew that every word of Scripture was true, and that God wanted me to walk in His fullness and power, like the disciples of old. "You shall receive power when the Holy Spirit has come upon you" (Acts 1:8).

I was overwhelmed by the knowledge of God and His love and power, and the desire to serve Him became a consuming fire in my heart. The same thing happened to Dotty, and we recommitted our marriage and family to the Lord.

Now as we read the Scriptures, we realized God was calling on us to pray for the sick. Ever since we moved to New Braunfels, Charles had been suffering from allergies. The doctor had prescribed shots and medication to control his sneezing and other symptoms, and he had been faithfully taking this treatment for several years.

One night after we had finished reading Bible stories, I said, "Charles, we think if we pray for you, God will heal you and take away your allergies. Would you like us to pray for you?"

"Okay, Dad," he answered. That night and every night following, Dotty and I laid our hands on Charles and prayed that the Lord heal him of his allergies. I prayed, "God, You give us the air to breathe, and You give us our bodies. Lord, we know that they can be in perfect balance. Please give Charles perfect balance and harmony with his environment. In Jesus' name we pray. Amen."

We couldn't see anything happen right away, but we were faithful in prayer and continued for about six months. Then one day Charles said, "Dad, I don't think I need the shots anymore."

He was almost finished with his latest series, so I said, "Why don't you take the rest of the shots, then we'll stop and see what happens?" After the last shot was given, we didn't order anymore and watched Charles closely.

Everything was fine! He didn't have any of his previous symptoms. Since then Charles has not had an allergy shot or needed one. During that period of faithful prayer, God healed our son of his allergies. We were overjoyed! God really does do miracles!

Praying for our son was one thing—but then God began to direct us to pray for others in need. One day our friend, Anna, asked Dotty to go with her to one of the local nursing homes to visit a lady from our church named Cordy. Nursing homes were depressing to us, and Dotty wasn't really looking forward to going. She only went because of her love for Anna, but as soon as she met Cordy, Dotty's attitude changed.

Cordy was a gentle, white-haired lady who had been severely paralyzed by a stroke, leaving her unable to talk or walk. Every day Cordy's husband, John, would come over to sit and hold hands with her; their eyes showed the great devotion they felt toward each other. Dotty was really filled with love toward them and began a two or three times a week visitation to offer encouragement. Many times I would go, too. When John suffered a heart attack and was also placed in the nursing home, I knew I was to pray for their healing, and Dotty agreed.

With great excitement we drove to Colonial Manor, but as we were getting out of the car, I began to have these thoughts. *This is the dumbest thing you have ever done, Charlie Duke. What if nothing happens? What if they laugh at you? What if they die?*

Fear began to creep into my heart, and I almost didn't go in. But then this Scripture came to mind, "For God has not given us a spirit of fear, but of power and of love and of a sound mind" (2 Timothy 1:7). I knew that was God speaking to me, and faith began to rise in my heart.

Dotty and I went into John's room and asked if we could pray for him. He was very touched and pleased, so we prayed for the Lord's healing and the Lord's peace. As soon as we had finished, we heard these sobs coming from the next bed and looked over and John's roommate was pleading, "Pray for me; please pray for me."

"Sure, we'll pray for you," I answered. "What is your name?" His name was Jordan, so we prayed for Jordan, too—he wanted desperately to get well and be able to go home.

Now along with Cordy and John, Dotty began regular visits to Jordan. She discovered Jordan was seventy-eight years old, had lived a very unhappy and bitter life, even showing her scars on his wrists from several suicide attempts. He felt the whole world was against him and had developed a mean disposition.

Through reading the Bible and witnessing to him about the love and

269

forgiveness of the Lord, Dotty shared with him how Jesus had given her peace and taken away her emotional pain. One day she asked, "Do you want to let go of all the pain and unforgiveness and bitterness in your heart and accept Jesus as your Lord and Savior? Think about it and tell me tomorrow."

The next day when Dotty returned, Jordan said, "Yes," and prayed with her to be born again through faith in Jesus. He then forgave all the people who had hurt him and let go of resentment he had been carrying a long time.

He had remembered one time when he was only six years old—he was plowing the field and was having difficulty turning the heavy plow around at the end of the rows. His family was all sitting on the front porch and instead of helping, they had laughed and made fun of him. This experience had filled his heart with bitterness and instilled in him a hate for everyone. He had made a decision that it was him against the world, and he had to be tough.

Dotty continued to minister inner healing to Jordan, and a real change occurred in his heart and mind. The nurses, his wife, and his roommate, John, noticed he wasn't angry and mean anymore but had become kind and gentle.

A couple of weeks later, Jordan experienced a fall and went into a coma; he died the next day. We were deeply grieved but then realized how good God was. God had spared Jordan's life from not only suicide attempts, but from several heart attacks—giving him one more opportunity to hear and receive salvation. Although he was not healed physically, he was healed spiritually and lives now in eternal life with Jesus.

Over the next year Dotty and I were led to pray for many sick people, but I have to admit I began to get frustrated because not many were getting well. It was not like when Jesus prayed and people were instantly healed. The Bible says, "They will lay hands on the sick, and they will recover" (Mark 16:18). But we weren't seeing many recover, and I was very perplexed and questioned the Lord.

The only answer I got was, *Be obedient. Pray for the sick; that's your responsibility. The healing is My responsibility.* I understood obedience. I had served in the military for eighteen and a half years, and I knew obedience to my commanding officer. Jesus was calling me to be submitted to Him in the same way.

Dotty and I continued to be obedient and pray for the sick. Then one beautiful healing took place later that same year.

My personal secretary for Campbell-Duke Investments had been my former receptionist at Coors beer; her name was Sandi Robinson. One morning when I came into the office, Sandi was in tears. "What's wrong?" I asked.

She told me she had been to her doctor for a checkup, that he had found some suspicious signs and was recommending a hysterectomy. This was devastating to Sandi, as she was childless after eight years of marriage and dearly wanted to have a baby. She had even gone through one operation to correct her condition, but it had not been successful.

If I had heard this news a year earlier, my only response would have been one of sympathy, but now the Lord was speaking to my heart saying, *Pray for her*. So I said to Sandi, "Why don't we pray about this situation. Would you like to pray?"

"Yes," she answered. I explained to her that the Bible says to lay hands on the sick and they shall be healed. Then I prayed that the Lord would heal Sandi of this potential cancer, that she would not have to have the hysterectomy, and that the Lord would bless her and her husband, Jimmy, with a child. She thanked me and stopped crying, experiencing a real peace.

A few weeks later, Sandi came bounding into the office all smiles. I asked her, "What are you so happy about?"

"I just came from my doctor," she said, "and he says the cancer indication is gone, and I don't need the hysterectomy!" I was delighted for her, and together we thanked the Lord.

Then a few months later, she came in just *ecstatically* happy, and when I asked the reason for all this joy, she informed me that she was pregnant! How good God is! Even though she did miscarry this pregnancy, we prayed again and soon after she delivered a beautiful baby girl. A couple of years later, she became pregnant again, and now Sandi and Jimmy have two lovely little girls.

Since then I have seen miracles of healing, miracles of deliverance as demons fled at the name of Jesus, and wonderful manifestations of the love and power of God, just like in the Bible.

One such instance was at a military prayer breakfast in San Antonio. Over the years I have spoken for a number of prayer breakfasts—conventions, states, cities, and military. During this particular meeting held at Fort Sam Houston, there was opportunity for ministry following the program. A number of people came up for prayer; one was a young girl and her father.

The father explained, "My daughter's eyesight is failing. She has this disease and is declared legally blind. All she can make out are shadows and shades of light. The doctors say that within a month she will be totally blind."

General Ralph Haines, who had organized the breakfast, and I laid hands on this young girl and asked God to heal her eyes and restore her sight. After the prayer, they thanked us and left. Nothing seemed to have happened—no miracle—so we continued to pray for others who were waiting in line.

A few minutes later, this same girl came running through the back door of the NCO Club, joyously happy! She was screaming at the top of her lungs, "I can *see* . . . I can *see* . . . I can *see!*" Everyone stopped what they were doing while she came running over to us to explain what had happened.

"I was outside in the parking lot," she said very excited, "walking toward our car when all of a sudden I realized I could see the stop sign at the end of the block. *I can see!* I can see everything clearly now!"

We were all thrilled at what God had done for this young lady. Several years later I saw her father, and he confirmed that her sight was still perfect. *Praise God!* How exciting it is, walking with the Lord!

At the dinner table each evening, Dotty and I would share with the boys how God was answering our prayers, and we encouraged them to ask God to help them in all their needs. We told them no need was too small or too big for the Lord.

There were many times the boys saw the Lord answer their prayers. Seeing God meet these small requests not only revealed to them and to us how loving our Lord is, but it also began to build a foundation of faith and trust that would support us in times of greater need. Without the assurance of God's care on our smallest concerns, we would find it difficult to trust Him on our larger needs. Probably the most difficult area to release and turn to Him for help was my business.

Ken Campbell and I had been actively pursuing our real estate ventures in Houston and San Antonio. In San Antonio we had purchased two tracts of land and had made down payments on two adjoining lots, planning to develop a shopping center with Kroger and Walgreens.

But in the summer of 1979, Ken suffered a severe heart attack and wasn't able to work. This left me on my own with many difficult negotiations and problems to overcome. Because I had invested all my profit from the Coors sale and had borrowed a great deal more money to invest in this real estate, I was anxious to make things work.

After a few months, it became apparent that Ken was going to have to considerably restrict his activities, so we decided to split the partnership. He would take the properties in Houston, and I would take over the ones in San Antonio. I told Ken that I was praying for him and for our business deals and spoke with him about my walk with the Lord. We parted good friends.

As 1980 approached, I found myself getting deeper and deeper in trouble. I was about half a million dollars in debt and was committed to another seven hundred thousand dollars in loans to buy the other properties. Quickly running out of money—with no leases signed, I made numerous phone calls trying to negotiate the deal. I was finding it very difficult keeping the peace of God and kept trying to get things to happen, but they wouldn't.

On top of this, Dotty and I were building a new house on a large lot in New Braunfels. We had signed a cost plus contract with our builder and had obtained a mortgage at the bank. At closing we would have to make a large payment, and since we were out of cash, we planned on selling our old home to make this payment.

Dotty and I sought the Lord on what price we should ask for our home, and He gave us a figure. We then signed up with a real estate agent, but because interest rates were high, no buyer was in sight. As the months and weeks went by, we got more and more nervous. Now we were only a few weeks away from zero hour and were highly anxious. All our money was tied up in my business deal, therefore we had no cash for the closing of our new house.

Finally our agent called excitedly to say a buyer had made an offer. But when she told us he wanted a second lien and the offer was less than the figure God had given us, we refused. She couldn't understand and probably thought we were crazy, but we knew God had shown us the figure we were to receive for the house, and we wanted to be obedient to Him. Now time was getting extremely short.

Unbelievably a week later, a call came from our agent saying there was a man from Colorado who wanted to buy our home. He had offered cash and only two thousand dollars less than our asking price. She was really enthusiastic and encouraged us to accept right away. Dotty and I talked and prayed about it. "No," we said, "we feel God has given us this figure and we'll stick with it." She couldn't believe it—but as directed sent in our counteroffer.

Praise God! He accepted, paid cash, and then didn't move into our house for another six months! God had answered every prayer, and we had the funds for closing. Out of this experience, we discovered God might not be early, but He is always on time, and we needed to learn to trust Him more.

In spite of this, I was having trouble trusting God in my business situation. Some areas we can easily turn over to the Lord, but I was finding managing my business not one of them. I knew how to make deals and thought I was a pretty good businessman. I believed I could handle it myself and didn't understand how the Lord wanted me to totally release it all to Him.

Things were getting no better, and payments were looming ahead that I wouldn't be able to meet. I had many sleepless nights over my great debt. Finally I gave up. I can remember sitting in my office in San Antonio praying, "God, something's got to happen very, very quickly. I can't control this situation, and I don't know what to do. I've got myself in a mess and I'm sorry. I give You my business—You can have it and do with it whatever You want. If it's bankruptcy, okay, or deliverance, okay. I'd rather not have bankruptcy, but it's in Your hands. It's Your business now, and I'll do whatever You want."

A few weeks later, a friend of a friend came into my office. Sandy was a total stranger to me, but he was a Christian, and when I related to him the problems I was having and my desire to get out of debt, he said, "Why don't we just pray about it." We joined hands over my desk, and he prayed a powerful prayer asking God to intercede and deliver me from this bondage of debt.

Not long afterwards, I got a phone call from an individual in Houston by the name of Stanley Williams. He was a successful shopping center developer, whom I had spoken to only once before on the telephone—about eight months before. He knew I owned some property in San Antonio and asked what was I going to do with it, mentioning that he might be interested in a partnership. I explained to him my situation and right then over the telephone, he agreed to all my conditions. With only his word and mine, Stanley began taking care of the financial obligations at the bank.

God had answered my prayer. I had been prepared to take whatever happened, even bankruptcy, but praise the Lord, God delivered me from debt through this man who was also a Christian!

Even so I had difficulty believing it was going to work out. We had only a letter of agreement, so I was anxious and kept trying to take things into my own hands and push it along. I was frustrated at every turn—there were problems with leases and property negotiations, and I kept worrying it was all going to fall through.

After six months, even though Stanley had been making payments at the bank every month, we still hadn't closed the deal. Now I had to leave town for a speaking trip and vacation with the family and was going to be gone for seven weeks. "Stanley," I telephoned, "I've got to leave. I don't know what's going to happen with this deal, but I've got to go." He replied, "Go ahead and do what the Lord would have you do."

I wasn't gone ten days before the whole deal closed. God didn't even need me there. I learned that God can cause things to happen, if we'll just leave it to Him. I am to do the work He calls me to do and trust Him to do the rest.

Someone once said, "Everyone needs a Jewish senior partner—Jesus Christ." That's what I have done. I have made Jesus my senior and controlling partner. This requires that I pray to Him for specific direction and guidance and then trust and obey Him. He answers those prayers.

I don't believe in luck or coincidences anymore. Since Dotty and I have given our lives to Jesus, we have seen Him direct our steps and bring situations and people into our lives that are directly God ordained. I realize that what I had previously believed were coincidences are in fact God-incidences. As someone once said, "God's fingerprints are all over it."

I am continually amazed at God's faithful and constant love and His awesome and mighty power. He is interested in every area of our lives and desires for us to be submitted to Him and walk in His fullness and power. Over the years I have repeatedly seen the love and power of God be manifested in situation after situation, for He cares for us.

# 28

# THE CROWNING GLORY

Even my walk on the moon has been used for God's glory. At a Christian meeting in 1979, a prophecy was given that every step I took on the moon would be multiplied many, many times over in my walk with Jesus. This has come true in the miles I have traveled all over the world giving testimony of what God has done in my life.

I have been before kings and prime ministers, junta leaders and dictators, businessmen and beggars, rich and poor, black and white—giving the same message that Jesus is the answer.

One of the most touching times was in the office of one of the cabinet ministers in Israel. An American evangelist had arranged this meeting, and there were about ten of us in this office. After introductions I was asked to share my walk on the moon with the Israeli minister.

"Mr. Minister," I began, "I was able to look back at the earth from the moon and hold up my hand [raising my hand to demonstrate], and underneath this hand was the earth. The thought occurred to me that underneath my hand were four billion people.

"I couldn't see Europe, America, the Middle East. I couldn't see any blacks or whites, Jews or Orientals, just spaceship earth. I realized we needed to learn to love one another, and I believed that with that love and our technical expertise, we could solve all of mankind's problems.

"I came back from the moon and went around sharing this vision, but while I was telling everybody to love one another, I didn't even love my wife. How could I love the people of Israel or Africa?

"I grew up in a small town in South Carolina," I continued, "where there was a lot of prejudice, prejudice against the blacks and the Jews in that order. But Mr. Minister, I don't have any prejudice anymore. Since I opened my heart to Jesus, He's removed all my prejudice and filled me with love—love for my wife, love for the blacks, love for the Jews, and love for everyone.

"Mr. Minister, Jesus sent us here to tell you that we love you and God loves you—and we want to pray for you and your nation."

As soon as I had finished speaking, this Israeli minister began to cry. He wasn't offended but was touched. Then I began to cry, and tears came to the eyes of everyone else in the room. For another ten minutes we shared God's love with this man, who was searching desperately for answers to the many problems he faced in his nation.

At the end of the meeting, we prayed for him and then, with tears in his eyes, he looked over at me and said, "You know, all Israel ought to hear what you just told me."

I'm praying for that, and for the opportunity to share not only with Israel but with everyone who is searching for this peace and love that is found in Christ. No matter the person, the political system, the religious system, or the culture, my message is always the same—Jesus loves you and He can give you peace, love, and joy.

The promises of the Bible are true and I believe speak the truth in every area—whether it be in spiritual matters, nutrition, history, or even science. In 1972 aboard *Apollo 16*, I saw with my own eyes what is written in the Scriptures.

In Isaiah 40:22 it says, "It is He who sits above the circle of the earth." And in Job 26:7 it is written, "He hangs the earth on nothing."

Who told Isaiah that the earth was a circle? Until the fifteenth century, the greatest minds believed it was flat. And how did the writer of Job know that the earth hung upon nothing? The Greeks were sure that it was held up by a giant named Atlas. Others believed that there were five tremendous columns supporting it. We laugh at that now, but this is what the ancients believed.

Not until 1961 did man first view earth from space with his own eyes and prove beyond a shadow of doubt that the earth is round and hung upon nothing. How did Isaiah and the author of Job know?

God inspired these two writers over twenty-eight hundred years ago with the truth. He knew because He was the One who created the earth and the heavens. He was the One who hung the earth, the moon, the sun, and the stars in their places.

The Bible also says that God counts the stars and knows them all by name (see Psalm 147:4). If He knows the stars by name, He certainly knows each one of us by name.

The past few years with our boys now grown, Dotty and I have traveled a great deal together. Wherever we go we pray for the Lord to use us. Traveling by plane through Australia we felt led to pray, "Jesus, whoever You place beside us on the airplane, we will give them a tract of our testimony. You choose the person You want us to share this with and put them in that seat."

A few days later we were flying from Brisbane to Melbourne and seated next to us was a man from the United States. "Why are you here in Australia?" I asked. "What do you do?"

"I'm a chemical engineer," he answered. "I'm in the dairy business and work mainly in New Zealand, but that's not the greatest job I've had. The greatest job I ever had was designing the heat shield for the Apollo spacecraft."

He nearly fainted when I said, "Well, let me tell you something—it worked fantastically. I flew it on *Apollo 16*!"

As we gave him the tract and shared the Lord, he was pensive and said, "I am a Jew, and I have been searching for God. I have gone to synagogues and even churches, looking for Him." God had brought together an Apollo engineer and an Apollo astronaut; a man seeking the Lord and someone with the answer.

A few days later flying from Sydney to Tasmania, we sat next to a young Australian. When he heard our accent, he said, "You're Americans, aren't you?" "Yes," Dotty answered, "we are."

"I know an American," he said. Well, in our travels we've had people say they knew someone from San Antonio, or even a Texan, but we'd never had anyone say they knew *an American*. There are 250,000,000 of us! How could we possibly know this one, but humoring him I asked, "What's his name?"

"Jack Roosa," he said.

This time I was the one that nearly fainted. Jack Roosa is the son of astronaut Stu Roosa, one of my best friends! Dotty and I marveled—another wonderful God-incidence—as we shared Jesus with him.

One of our most memorable trips was to Malaysia. It is an amazing story how God sent us there. It all began one summer when a college girl from Kuala Lumpur, the capital of Malaysia, stayed in our home.

Although Maylasia is a Muslim country, Ching Lo was Chinese and had been brought up in Chinese ancestor worship. Nevertheless she was interested in the Bible and our Christian faith, and by the time of her return to Malaysia, she had met Jesus and become a Christian.

Dotty was concerned about her reception as a Christian and especially what her parents would think, so she said, "Ching, we're going to pray that God will give you favor with friends and family and send us to Malaysia, so that we can see you and meet your parents." But Malaysia seemed light-years away; we had never ever considered going to Southeast Asia and didn't know anyone there.

Lo and behold! Two months later a letter arrived from Malaysia, asking us to come the very next year to speak throughout the country. Unbelievable! We had a wonderful visit with Ching and her family and were able to encourage her in her faith.

During this same trip to Malaysia, while we were visiting a small village where I was scheduled to speak, I received a phone call from the United States and was puzzled when a man identified himself as the editor of *The State* newspaper in Columbia, South Carolina, and asked, "What do you think of the accident?"

"What accident?" I replied.

"You haven't heard?" he said astonished. "Heard what?" I asked.

He continued, "Twelve hours ago the space shuttle *Challenger* blew up and killed all seven astronauts!"

I was stunned and totally speechless. Finally I asked, "Who was on board?" He gave the names and to my grief, one was a good friend named Ron McNair from my home state.

When I hung up, I told Dotty the terrible news and together we prayed for the families.

I had to speak that evening and knew everyone would have heard the news. "Lord," I prayed, "what am I to tell these people?" I had an urge to open my Bible and as I did, it fell open to Ecclesiastes 9:12, which I had highlighted and which jumped off the page at me. It read, "No man knows when his hour will come" (NIV).

That evening at the meeting, I told everyone, "When my friends, the shuttle astronauts, launched the *Challenger,* they didn't know their hour was about to come. Astronauts may be brave, but they aren't crazy and would not fly facing certain disaster."

I continued, "No one knows when his hour will come. Are you ready for your hour when it comes? The Bible speaks comfort to us when it says, 'I write these things to you who believe in the name of the Son of God so that you may know that you have eternal life' (1 John 5:13 NIV). Accept Jesus and be ready," I encouraged.

One person I wasn't sure was ready was my dad, so whenever I visited my parents in South Carolina, I would love to speak to them about the Lord and tell them stories about God's power. They seemed to enjoy listening and Dad would humor me along, yet doubting most every word.

One time I was talking to them about angels and how they watch over us. I said, "Dad, every time some friends of mine get on an airplane, they pray that God will send some angels to protect them. One day as they were flying at thirty-five thousand feet, they looked out of their airplane window and sitting on the wing of the plane was an angel."

Dad just cracked up! He thought that was the funniest story he'd ever heard. He laughed and said, "Well, I'll tell you what, if I ever see an angel, he'd better have on a parachute." "Well, Dad," I said, "I'm praying that you see an angel."

Over the next few years, Dad began to weaken from the result of a slight stroke. He let me pray for him but would never confess Jesus and open his heart to God. Then he developed lung cancer and was put in the hospital. You could tell how much he was fearing death as his time drew nearer and nearer.

One day my brother was visiting him and knowing how fearful he was said, "Dad, can I read from the Bible?" Bill read from 1 John, "Perfect love casts out fear" (4:18), and then added, "Dad, Jesus is perfect love. Do you want to receive Jesus Christ as your Lord and Savior and receive the peace of God?" Dad agreed and my brother led him to the Lord. Peace came to Dad, and everyone noticed how his fear had gone.

A month later I was in California when early in the morning I received an urgent call from my mom, "You'd better get home; Dad doesn't have much longer."

I quickly made a plane reservation and asked Ilie Coroama, a good friend and brother in Christ, to drive me to the airport. As I got on the plane, I asked Ilie, "Please pray for my dad."

When I arrived home in South Carolina, I rushed to the hospital and went into Dad's room—the bed was empty. Dad had died at 5:30 P.M. I had missed seeing him by one hour. I was a little upset with God. "Why didn't you let him last one more hour?" But the peace of the Lord came, and I knew Dad was with God.

I went home to see Mom and the rest of my family, and we had a tearful reunion. There was a message to call Dotty and after telling her about Dad, she said, "Ilie called and he wants you to telephone him. He has a word from the Lord for you."

When Ilie answered the phone, I could tell he was very excited. "Brother Charlie," he said, "I was praying for your dad at 2:30 this afternoon and God gave me a vision!" Now 2:30 California time is 5:30 in South Carolina, when my Dad died. Ilie continued, "God showed me in this vision, two angels who were coming to collect your dad and take him to heaven. The Lord said that your dad would die very soon, but for you not to worry because he's with Jesus."

Almost speechless, I responded, "Praise the Lord! Dad died as you were praying!" Then Ilie added, "But Charlie, there was something very strange about those angels, which I don't understand—they both had on *big parachutes*."

I had forgotten about my conversation with Dad, and I too was perplexed about the parachutes, so Ilie and I asked God to explain their meaning. A few days later, God brought to mind my Dad's comment that if he ever saw an angel he'd better have on a parachute. Can you imagine! God in His love and mercy had given Dad *two*! The Lord's humor, His compassion, and His personal caring for each one of us is shown in this story about my dad.

This is my God—the One who does not forget a single sparrow and tells us that we are each worth more than many sparrows. This is my God—the One who has numbered every hair on our head and the One who lovingly clothes the lilies of the field (see Luke 12:6–7, 28).

This is the Lord I love and serve. This is the Lord who transformed my life. This is the Lord who restored my marriage.

I used to say I could live ten thousand years and never have an experience as thrilling as walking on the moon. But the excitement and satisfaction of that walk doesn't begin to compare with my walk with Jesus, a walk that lasts forever.

I thought *Apollo 16* would be my crowning glory, but the crown that Jesus gives will not tarnish or fade away. His crown will last throughout all eternity (see 1 Corinthians 9:25).

Not everyone has the opportunity to walk on the moon, but everybody has the opportunity to walk with the Son. It cost billions of dollars to send someone to the moon, but walking with Jesus is free—the gift of God. "For by grace you have been saved through faith, and that not of yourselves, it is the gift of God, not of works, lest anyone should boast" (Ephesians 2:8–9).

You don't need to go to the moon to find God. I didn't find God in space, I found Him in the front seat of my car on Highway 46 in New Braunfels, Texas, when I opened my heart to Jesus. And my life hasn't been the same since.

Now I can truly look up at the moon and the stars and with the prophets of old exclaim, "The heavens declare the glory of God; and the firmament shows His handiwork" (Psalm 19:1).

The other day I was listening to the country-western tapes I had carried to the moon. At one point Porter Wagoner began to introduce a song by Dolly Parton and said, "I'm sure during this historic Apollo flight that you'll see many, many beautiful scenes—some that men's eyes have never seen before—which I'm sure as you view them you'll think of God, the Creator of this great universe. And here is one of the most beautiful songs that describes, 'How Great Thou Art.'"

Then Dolly Parton began to sing, "Oh Lord, my God, when I in awesome wonder consider all the worlds Thy hands have made, . . . Then sings my soul, my Savior God, to Thee; How great Thou art, [Oh] how great Thou art!"

Many of the words in this book are *acronyms* (words formed by the initial letters of each word in a phrase) or *jargon* (the technical terminology of a specific group, such as the military or the space program). Following is an alphabetical listing of the acronyms and jargon used in *Moonwalker*.

| | |
|---|---|
| ACRO | acrobatics |
| AERO | aeronautics |
| AFB | Air Force base |
| ALFMED | Apollo light flash medical experiment device |
| ALSEP | Apollo lunar surface experiment package |
| AOS | acquisition of signal |
| ARIA | Apollo range instrumentation aircraft |
| ARPS | Aerospace Research Pilot School |
| ASTRO | astronautics |
| AUTO PILOT | automatic pilot |
| AWC | Astronaut Wives' Club |
| BIOMED | biomedical data; biomedical instrumentation |
| BOQ | bachelor officers' quarters |
| CAPCOM | capsule communicator |
| CIRC | circulation |
| COMM | communications |
| COMM CAP | communications cap |
| COMM LINK | communications linkage |
| CSM | command and service modules |
| CSM SEP | command and service modules separate |
| DELTA-TIG | difference in time of ignition |
| DELTA-VC | velocity change |
| DOI | descent orbit insertion |
| ECS | environmental control system |
| EKG | electrocardiogram |
| EVA | extravehicular activity |
| FCD | fecal collection device |
| FIDO | flight dynamics officer |
| G | gravity |

| | |
|---|---|
| GCI | ground control intercept |
| ILC | International Latex Corporation |
| INFO | information |
| KSC | Kennedy Space Center |
| LCG | liquid cooled garment |
| LM | lunar module |
| LOI | lunar orbit insertion |
| LOS | loss of signal |
| LPD | landing point designator |
| MAX | maximum |
| MAX G | maximum gravity |
| MCC | Mission Control Center |
| MESA | modular equipment stowage assembly |
| MIT | Massachusetts Institute of Technology |
| MOL | manned orbiting laboratory |
| MSFN | Manned Space Flight Network |
| NASA | National Aeronautics and Space Administration |
| NCO | noncommissioned officers |
| PDI | powered descent initiation |
| PLSS | portable life support system |
| PPK | personal-preference kit |
| PRD | personal radiation dosimeter |
| PT | physical training |
| RCS | reaction control system |
| RCS A | reaction control system A |
| REGS | regulations |
| REV | revolution |
| ROG | Roger |
| RTG | radioisotope thermoelectric generator |
| S-IVB | third stage of the Saturn launch vehicle |
| SAC | Strategic Air Command |
| SIM BAY | scientific instrument module bay |
| SIMS | flight simulations |
| SPS | service propulsion system |
| T | time |
| TDY | temporary duty |
| TECHS | technicians |
| TEI | transearth injection |
| TLI | translunar injection |
| TPI | terminal phase initiation |
| TTCA | thrust translation control assembly |
| TVC | thrust vector control |
| UCD | urine collection device |

| USAF | United States Air Force |
| UV | ultraviolet |
| VAB | vehicle assembly building |
| VITALS | vital statistics |